'This is not another "feel good" self-help book th[...]
powerful! It will be as invaluable to young people [...]
will to executives or board members.'
Anne Keating, Chair, Cerebral Palsy Alliance R[...]

'Larry's insights on leadership and communication were transformational to my
own career and my business. In WHY YOU? he shares his philosophy and simple,
yet effective, techniques to make us all better leaders. Anyone who aspires to be their
best should grab a copy.'
Andrew Barnes, Founder Perpetual Guardian & 4 Day Week Global, Auckland

'At 26, I was climbing the ladder at a top Australian law firm when Larry landed
on the scene like a meteorite (only louder). He quickly saw that my future lay
elsewhere and helped me pursue my true calling with zeal. Today, I'm the CEO of
a multinational company that helps governments deliver lifesaving healthcare to
millions of people worldwide. I'm proud to be one of many who is reaching their full
career potential thanks to Larry, the maestro of metamorphosis.'
Jonathan Stambolis, CEO and Founder Zenysis Technologies, San Francisco

'Larry is one of a kind. In WHY YOU? he shares unique, cutting-edge strategies
that can walk anyone to a life-changing outcome.'
Jack Bloomfield, CEO & Founder Disputify, New York

'Larry brings a different lens to what effective leadership is about. His ability to
draw out what works and doesn't is unique and impactful. That said, the journey
with Larry is always eventful and best suited to those who seek to hear the honest
truth, no matter how difficult!'
Peter O'Brien, Partner, Russell Reynolds

'A masterclass on leadership. If you aspire to become a true leader, Larry's insights
and wisdom from his deep experience will help shape your journey.'
Bruce Wolpe, international advisor to government and corporate leaders

'Incredibly detailed and very entertaining. Often funny, absolutely authentic.
Original and deep in its intellectual offering.'
Dieter Kahsnitz, creative director and presenter of television and film

'Larry is a highly effective coach and mentor due to his years of experience, progressive mindset and strong support for diversity including female participation at the top ranks. This book is a must read for those who are looking to take a modern and balanced approach to leadership.'
Liz Cullinan, Partner, EY

'Larry has a fantastic ability to diagnose that is not just addressing the symptoms but the root cause. It's also the way he dragged me completely outside my comfort zone. A key element to my development has been the way he challenged me. This book will do the same for you.'
Vaughn Cotton, Senior Program Manager, Electronic Payment Systems

'Larry shows how you can become the best at communicating with your team, stakeholders and customers. His frameworks, which he shares in this book, have benefitted me over many years across a variety of businesses and executive roles. He has also worked with some of my executives so they could develop their unique leadership style. To the point that we have a new verb ... "to be "Larry'd"!!'
Mike Foster, former CEO Fujitsu Australia & NZ Ltd

'With responsibility for new business within one of the world's largest advertising holding groups, and in what is renowned as an industry whose output relies exclusively on people, Larry's advice resonates at every level. Being the "authentic you" is something I have always placed great importance on, alongside an innate sense of curiosity. It is wonderful to have so many practical tools within this book to ensure these come to life.'
Jodie Stranger, Global Business Development Practice Lead, Publicis Groupe

'Working in a profession where projecting competence is essential (especially as a woman), Larry's methodology is easily grasped and implemented, as readers of WHY YOU? will discover.'
Dr Amely Zaininger, cardiologist

WHY
listen to, work with and follow
YOU?

WHY

listen to, work with and follow

YOU?

The 3 Qualities of
True Leaders

Larry Heugh Robertson

PROFILE
EDITIONS

First published in Great Britain in 2023 by
Profile Editions, an imprint of Profile Books Ltd
29 Cloth Fair
London
EC1A 7JQ
www.profileeditions.com

10 9 8 7 6 5 4 3 2 1

Typeset in Lyon Text by MacGuru Ltd
Printed and bound in Great Britain by
Clays Ltd, Elcograf S.p.A

A CIP catalogue record for this book is available from the British Library.

ISBN 978 1 800817 51 7
eISBN 978 1 800817 52 4

O wad some Pow'r the giftie gie us
To see oursels as others see us!
It wad frae monie a blunder free us
An' foolish notion:
What airs in dress an' gait wad lea'e us,
And ev'n Devotion!

ROBERT BURNS (1759-1796)

I dedicate this book to Mickey, Clementine and Bonnie and to my brothers Nander and Marc and my late sister Marcelle, and to my late parents Ian and Elizabeth, all of whom have given me so much.

And to all those who have survived the 'larrying' over many years and, I hope, continue to benefit from our work together. And to the many others, including you the reader, who may choose to step up, speak out and make a worthwhile difference as you strive to leave people and places better than you find them.

Contents

Note

Thank you for reading this book. I have done my best to refer to my sources where applicable. I deeply regret any unintended errors and omissions.

Many of the examples and stories contained in this book are based on actual events. With the exception of my former employers, the reference to the Firestone Tire & Rubber Company, the Ford Motor Company and the stories in the True Leader's Communication Toolkit, the names of all persons and organisations and, in most cases, the identities of industries and locations and other details have been changed to ensure confidentiality.

Preface

Every leader's situation is unique. For me, it's been my character-forming experiences: a year spent making my way around the world as a student with little more than a backpack; leading an army platoon in sometimes challenging situations; being exposed to heads of state, diplomats and military chiefs; working with some of the world's most creative people; and relocating to the other side of the world where I started and sold my first business.

Add to this building a leadership and communication advisory, before such a concept existed, and helping thousands of people around the world – from corporate chairs, boards and C-Suite executives to professionals, entrepreneurs, politicians, sportsmen and women, families and students – make a measurable difference for themselves and others.

I have led and been led. I have worked with good and bad leaders. I understand what it takes to be a true leader.

People everywhere are craving more meaning, greater connection and better leadership in most aspects of their lives. And those who aspire to lead are searching for straightforward and practical solutions to deliver this in their own unique way.

Increasingly, people feel disengaged from their leaders. In part, this is because many in leadership roles either don't make the effort to connect with their stakeholders or don't know how to ... or both. In turn, stakeholders choose to neither listen nor follow.

The solution is to understand that real leadership is relationship and to look through the twin lenses of clarity and humanity. This often requires those either already in or aspiring to leadership roles to move outside their personal comfort zones.

Within these pages you will discover well-tested advice, examples, pointers, checklists, models and tools to help you to become a true leader and a better you. You will understand how to influence and inspire others to choose to listen to you, work with you, support you, promote you, negotiate with you, solve problems with you, buy from you, follow and come with you on your journey. Put simply, you will learn how to truly lead others and succeed together. Hence my use of the term true leadership.

Context

'Every organisation needs you, Larry. Just as the court jester of centuries ago would address his monarch with a combination of wisdom and humour and live to see another day, you hold up the mirror and say what needs to be said candidly, often cheekily. On occasions, outrageously and without fear ... even to your most senior clients like me. And you are still invited back!'

Thus was I laughingly described by the chairman of a multinational conglomerate.

A start-up founder recently said that I reminded him of an English beer: 'Like a good ale, beneath that welcoming froth, there's real substance flavoured with a crisp wit that gushes out as you pour!'

And a public company chief executive joked that working with me was like being driven over by a friendly bulldozer: 'Thanks for caring ... there's always a big, warm smile on the blade as the full force of being "larry'd" hits!'

It was comments like these that confirmed that I had been right to name my leadership and communication advisory Robertson Burns 30 years ago. Growing up in Scotland, I had been imbued by my father with the words of the poet Robert Burns, the Scottish Bard. Burns was a keen observer of humanity and would often lace his pithy critiques with humour.

You have come across my favourite Burns stanza as the book's epigraph. In so many ways, it sums up my approach to life and what I do. My French mother played her part too, encouraging me to treat everyone the same.

With this in mind and wanting to position my new business as a professional partnership, I decided to add the name Burns to my own. The fictitious Burns became my sleeping partner and alter ego. Clients have often asked to meet Burns!

With everything we do at Robertson Burns, our clients come first. It's the same for you, the reader of this book. Everything included here is for your benefit. While pursuing this aim, one of the hardest challenges I've faced has been to recount the many stories that follow in such a way that I take a back seat. This is why I occasionally involve both Burns and my associate and producer, James Harding, as you will see.

I hope you will enjoy reading *WHY YOU?* as much as I have enjoyed writing it. While there's plenty of substance, my sense of humour is never far away. So it must for every true leader.

As Queen Elizabeth II observed in her 1991 Christmas Address, 'Let us not take ourselves too seriously. None of us has a monopoly on wisdom.'

Larry Robertson

Robert Burns Day 2023

Introduction: Why this Book

Whatever your stage in life, whether you're still a student or setting out on your first job, starting or running your own business, a newly appointed team leader, managing operations with the aspirations of becoming the chief executive, or even already in the role, if you want to be a real leader and a better person, have people want to listen and come with you, this book is for you.

Some Questions to Start

Irrespective of your capability or situation, you might expect those around you to listen to you, to think about what you have said and act upon it. You might assume they are, metaphorically, on your bus and move on.

But what if they're not? Is it their fault? Might you blame them for not listening or getting on with the job?

When it's your turn to listen, do you really? For example, do you automatically listen to your boss? Fully take on board what he or she is saying and wholeheartedly commit yourself to the project in hand every time? What about listening to others in your team? In your workplace? Even at home? And if you don't, whose fault is it?

Leader of Thought

However important or articulate we may be, simply informing or even instructing those around us will not bring them with us. Imparting information is necessary, of course, but insufficient.

Leadership is more about intent than content. It's as much about feelings as facts, about emotion and reason, and about change and outcomes – not just process and task. Irrespective of the situation, leadership starts with oneself; then it's about leading the thinking of others – what I refer to as being a leader of thought.

True leadership is relationship with mutuality at its heart. We'll explore this in the next section. As with every relationship in our lives, if we are to give our all, we choose to whom we give it. Just being in a leadership role is no guarantee we will be chosen, supported or followed.

Leaders Choose ... and Are Chosen

Yes, leaders choose the objective and decide the plan to achieve it. And they choose whom they want to come with them on the journey.

And those who are chosen also choose. They choose whether to give their all and wholeheartedly follow. Or not.

Leaders choose. And they are chosen. As it is for each of us every day. It's our biggest challenge and our biggest opportunity: having others choose us. We will not get far on our own. We are human beings. We socialise and enjoy the company of others. We form tribes and do things together.

Our lives, our well-being, our progress, our achievements and our self-fulfilment depend on others. We choose with whom we wish to connect and engage. Wherever possible, we choose whom we want to befriend, help, live and work with, buy from, invest in; especially, to whom we listen.

So why do we choose her, him or them? And why do they choose us? On what basis does each of us actually choose?

Answering these questions will give us a better chance of having others choose to listen to us, engage and support us, team and come with us. It will also help us be a better person and a true leader.

What's in the Book?

On the following pages, you will discover why people choose people and how you can help others choose and come with you.

My well-proven approach, advice and methodologies explain how to be an inspiring and impactful leader, not only in the workplace but in every aspect of your life. At their heart is the power of mutuality.

I include many stories to bring the concepts to life. At the end of each, you will find a checklist and a '21+90 days' challenge to help adopt them. Why 21+90 days? Because research shows that if we commit to a personal or professional goal for 21 straight days it will become a habit. Once we have established that habit, we need to continue another 90 days for it to stick. Please give these challenges a go!

Parts 3 and 4 form the reference section. Here, you will find the True Leader's Communication Toolkit and Pitching to Win. These provide details of many of the concepts and methodologies to which I refer, as well as instructions explaining how to apply them and make them your own.

This is not a typical 'self-help' book. As well as helping you, I've written it to help you help others.

Managing *and* Leading

I am sometimes asked the difference between management and leadership. You may be familiar with the saying, 'Leaders are expected to do the right thing and managers to do things right.' I add that, to be successful, leaders need followers while managers need doers.

Most of us have had management ingrained in us from a young age: for example, 'tidy your room', 'run faster', 'get top marks', 'obey the rules', 'make your budget', 'cut costs', 'exceed the target' and so on. Management is primarily about 'doing stuff': skills, things, tasks, processes, compliance and measurement. Typically, it is how most of us are still rewarded.

As a result, we have relied on becoming technically efficient, metrics-driven, self-focused managers. While good management will always be required, it is not leadership. True leaders manage well and lead better.

Employing a simple metaphor, I liken the difference to a standard metal coin. Although coins are used less today due to the ease of the digital wallet, I imagine you have a few at home or even a couple in your pocket or purse now. Most of us typically regard a coin for its face or monetary value alone – what it quantifies. A true leader also turns it over to see *intrinsic* value that it represents, such as character, heritage, values, purpose, opportunity, culture, humanity and legacy – the essence of leadership.

My work is about helping people reveal their own intrinsic selves, their inner hero. I'm passionate about creating a world of enthusiastic, engaged and energised leaders at every level. True leaders whom people trust, choose to support and follow. I encourage them to look beyond the metrics and flip the coin.

I am direct and cut through the guff to get to the heart of the matter. I challenge aspiring and current leaders to give their all, truly connect with others and, together, achieve notable, sustainable results.

While I love my job, I am the first to acknowledge I can be an acquired taste. Happily, I'm told that working with me is fun as well as challenging. Clients call it being 'larry'd'! As you read this book, you'll gain an understanding of what this means.

Perhaps there's a coin in your pocket or purse right now. Why not take it out and, after identifying its monetary value, turn it over. What do you see?

Part 1: Setting the Scene

We know what we are, but know not what we may be.

WILLIAM SHAKESPEARE (1564–1616)

The Need for Better Leaders

Just as no one is born knowing how to ride a bicycle, no one is born knowing how to lead. Leadership is learned over time and on the job. It requires awareness, dedication and application. Even proficient riders fall occasionally and experienced leaders don't always get it right. They accept their imperfections, are willing to learn and determined to lift their game. And they are prepared to seek help to do so.

I've been fortunate enough to have experienced leadership up close all my life. From the selfless examples set by my family and teachers to forging my way around the world as a student, from my days in the military and in advertising to my own start-ups, two of which continue to keep me fulfilled today.

People around the world have encouraged, guided and sponsored me. Many have given me opportunities to step up and have a go. They were true leaders. Irrespective of their position in life, they were givers. They saw opportunities and willingly reached out and engaged me and others along their path and enabled our successes. Yes, I let them and myself down on occasion. I learned that, if I was to grow, acknowledging my frailties, accepting disappointment, taking ownership and not giving up were all part of my leadership journey. Fortunately, these people have successors many of whom I see around me today.

There have been others, of course. People who saw themselves as leaders but who were just about themselves. They were the takers. People who never admitted to weakness, showed little generosity of spirit and saw leadership as more about status, about being number one. Sadly, at every level – from national leadership to workplace supervision – there are still plenty of this group around today.

Playing at the Top of Our Game

I am in the help business. Since embarking on my current mission 30 years ago, I've had the privilege of working around the world with a broad range of people. They include business executives, professionals and politicians, entrepreneurs, and highly qualified and smart younger achievers who want to step up, develop their personal presence, propriety, mettle, sensitivity and gravitas, and make their mark as leaders of others.

Even before they work with me, many are already performing well much of the time. Yet, as current and future leaders, each has to be certain of consistently playing at the top of their game, especially when the stakes are high and the pressure is on.

High Stakes

The world faces multiple and growing challenges: the economic power shift from West to East, rising geopolitical tensions, increasing urbanisation, depleting resources, exponential technological impact. The climate is also changing and society's expectations seem to be evolving faster than ever before. Never was the acronym VUCA, first articulated by scholars Warren Bennis and Burton Nanus in 1987, more applicable than to the world we all live in today – it stands for Volatility, Uncertainty, Complexity, Ambiguity.

We are already experiencing the implications. They include increasing wealth disparity, disruption of business models and a clash of ideologies that are reducing global consensus; widespread disease and rising average temperatures and sea levels; and, most critically, declining trust in almost every aspect of our lives.

Organisations face increasing demands to be more proactive regarding environmental and social issues. Employers are seeking innovative ways to achieve greater productivity. And employees are becoming more vocal about the concept of work and more discerning about how and where they wish to share their labour. Added to this is the threat of further pandemics with the unpredictability and uncertainty they create, impacting most aspects of people's lives. All this contributes to the complexity of leadership.

At a macro level, the world is responding to many of these challenges. Vaccines are produced and rolled out in record time. Improving nutrition is now universally recognised as the pathway to better health. Investors raise the bar in terms of environmental, social and governance practices for those who seek their backing. Nations and organisations work together to reduce carbon emissions. Countries impose sanctions on those who refuse to commit to a recognised world order. The United Nations Global Compact is showing the way and business practices are changing, even where some politicians still drag their heels.

True Leadership

On the ground, to respond to these growing challenges effectively, the world needs better leaders. Real leaders who are fully aware of the changing context, appreciate what it means for their nations, organisations and communities and are willing to respond appropriately. Leaders who are humble, keen to learn and resolute in their desire to help others. Leaders who are in touch, know their place and their purpose within it and who are able to identify and realise opportunities.

We need bold leaders who look ahead, think for the long term, identify how best to proceed, engage with those around them, offer hope and act. Selfless leaders who, despite uncertainty, understand the need to provide clarity, generate confidence, serve and make a real difference for those around them. Ethical leaders who strive to do the right thing and do it as best they can. And we need authentic leaders who have the courage to be imperfect and not have all the answers, yet willing to stand up and speak out for what they believe.

These are the true leaders. And they are becoming ever more important in the face of the superficiality of identity politics, the misplaced victimhood of cancel culture, the revisionist attempts to blame and shame current generations for the sins of the past and even to rewrite history, the growth of fake news and political spin and intolerance for opposing views, and the challenge, from some quarters, to our basic human right to think for oneself and share one's thoughts freely and, yes, respectfully.

We need leaders who are anchored in their own reality and accept the reality around them while seeking to understand context. Leaders who are not in denial and are capable of grasping opposing ideas concurrently. Leaders who are prepared to stand up for what they believe and not succumb to bullying or to becoming the bully. And leaders who are also willing to listen, to learn, to identify better ways and, through engagement, perspective and reason, to help us do the same.

A Better Way

For many years, business schools and universities have groaned with leadership courses but not, I suspect, about the fees they earn. Yet, in almost every aspect of life, we are still lacking good leaders. Across the board, we continue to see people in leadership roles who disappoint and let their constituents down. Worse, as I have indicated, we see bad leaders whose attention and intent appear to be almost entirely self-focused.

So, what's causing this? Are we over-complicating things? Are we focusing on the wrong areas? Most of all, are we rewarding the wrong things?

Many years ago, shortly after starting my current role, I received a telephone call from the head of human resources of a large insurance company. He had heard that I had some interesting new ideas on leadership. I told him that my approach to leadership, while interesting, was certainly not new. Its roots went back over 2,000 years, founded on age-old values such as camaraderie, civility, courtesy, decency, dignity, humanity, purpose and valour. I sensed his disappointment and was not surprised that I did not hear from him again. Today, this organisation's share price is a fraction of what it was then.

Am I suggesting a new kind of leadership? No, just better leaders. Leaders who understand the fundamentals of leadership and are willing to put up their hand, step forward and truly lead.

Is there really a better way? Yes. Can we teach leadership in a more realistic, more practical and more simple way, so that leaders at every level can evolve and grow every day? I believe so. While not exhaustive, this book gives some answers.

Leadership is about the who, the why and the where. As already pointed out, none of us can achieve anything on our own. Leaders need to recognise that engaging and communicating with others is 80 per cent of their role. That it's through communicating effectively that they will create teams of followers and supporters who choose them. To be effective, leaders themselves must be team players who want to engage, relate and bring people with them, with purpose, to achieve outcomes that will benefit all in a sustainable way.

Why You?

Returning to the question posed earlier, why should people choose you? Why choose to work with you, or even want to listen to you? Why team with and follow you? Why support and back you? If you think it's because you're smart or deserving, you are likely to be disappointed!

As also indicated, true leadership is never about the leaders themselves. It is not about position but disposition. More art than science, leadership is about the heart more than the head, about character more than capability.

True Leadership Quiz

OK, you're in a leadership role. How are you doing?

Please rate yourself from 1 (not really) through 3 (sometimes) to 5 (yes, always).

1 Are your own, your organisation's and your team's values aligned? And do you consistently live those values, uphold your organisation's purpose and pursue its vision, and set a good example to others?

2 Do you create and foster a collaborative, open, trustful and inspiring environment?

3 Do you explain and break down complex, technical concepts, data and strategies simply, clearly and succinctly – both orally and in writing?

4 Do you meet with your team regularly, plan efficiently, and set and communicate clear direction including goals and outcomes?

5 Do you demonstrate trust in your team members while maintaining accountability by delegating effectively, including setting clear tasks, time frames and measurable targets?

6 Are you a good, active listener, encouraging others to speak out and debate ideas, and willing to acknowledge, consider and even embrace different opinions and perspectives?

7 Do you regularly engage with, care about and respect your people, including providing appropriate informal feedback and coaching, encouraging personal development and excellence at all levels and without favour, and acknowledging and rewarding achievement?

8 Are you confident and decisive, while also accepting responsibility for and willing to own your mistakes, and show flexibility to change direction when required?

9 Are you self-aware and resilient, remaining calm in adversity or uncertainty and maintaining a positive, 'can-do' attitude and demeanour, whatever the circumstance or pressure – and occasionally laughing at yourself?

10 Do you encourage a customer- and society-focused culture, proactively seeking opportunities to maximise existing and prospective relationships and checking that all your stakeholders' expectations are met?

So, how do you rate? If not 50 out of 50, please read on!

Self-Leadership: True Leadership Starts with You

Be yourself. Everyone else is already taken.

OSCAR WILDE (1854-1900)

The primary focus of this book is to help you be a better person and a true leader of others.

First, let's discuss you choosing you: the relationship you have with yourself. It's important to regularly self-reflect, take stock and affirm who you are, what makes you tick, your virtues, your frailties and your purpose. Think about the impact you make, and for whom, what success looks like for you and how you're doing.

It is also the opportunity to check your confidence in yourself, happiness in what you are doing and fulfilment in the difference you are striving to make for yourself and for others. This is not about you as some kind of celebrity. It's about you knowing and being your real you. This is where your true leadership starts.

Who: Your Brand

The biggest conversation we have in our lives is with ourselves. Yet do we actually listen? Listening is hard, even to ourselves! Given the volume of thought that passes through our brains in just one single moment, it is understandable that we rarely do so. We are so busy being busy! It's too easy to take ourselves for granted ... to ignore who we really are, how we are feeling and where we are going.

It starts with mindset: how we see the world around us. This is ours alone; what we do with it is up to us. It is about you and me taking ownership of our lives – designing and living our own story and not one that others may wish for us. It requires developing a greater sense of awareness of ourselves, of those around us, and of our circumstances.

I encourage you to find time to listen to yourself every day. Aim to schedule a period when you can reflect deeply on your human being, not only on your functional doing. Ask questions of yourself and really listen to your answers. Questions such as:

How am I feeling?
Who am I really, what is my unique essence?
What are my values and beliefs?
What matters to me?
What drives me, my purpose?
What do I want in life?
What excites me?
What does success look like for me today, this week, this year, in the future?
How am I pursuing this and what is hindering me?
How am I connecting with people around me?
What difference do I or can I make for them?
What is going well and what could be better?
What do I need to improve or learn?

To enable you to think deeply and creatively about your well-being, goals and performance, identify the optimal time and place for these conversations with yourself. It could be during a few moments of early-morning mindfulness, an hour of meditation, a walk outside to 'smell the roses', or simply sitting with your eyes closed enjoying your favourite music.

If you're unable to access the perfect spot, simply close your eyes and try to imagine something or somewhere of beauty or peace. Even 10 to 15 minutes each day will help you restore balance in your life and refocus on what really matters. The important thing is to make it a daily habit in order for your brain's cognitive function (in the prefrontal cortex) to think at its best.

This is especially so when you're feeling stressed or overwhelmed, had a setback, unsure how to deal with a particular situation or just lost confidence. This is when your amygdala (a component of the brain's limbic system in the primitive brain) generates an unhelpful emotional response that inhibits your ability to think calmly and rationally.

Between stimulus and response there is a space. In that space is our power to choose our response. In our response lies our growth and our freedom.
MAN'S SEARCH FOR MEANING, VIKTOR E. FRANKL (1905-1997)

So, to counter what is often referred to as the 'amygdala hijack', sit still with both feet apart and flat on the floor (legs uncrossed), close your eyes and count to five as you inhale deeply through your nose. Hold your breath and, again, count to five; then breathe out slowly through your mouth, counting to five once more. Now sit still without breathing for five seconds. After doing this exercise three times, open your eyes, stand up and take a 10- to 15-minute walk outside. If this isn't possible, go to a window, stand still and look through it in silence. Repeat the process until you feel more composed and can see beyond the immediate issue. The aim is to shift your thinking from internal to external, from event to opportunity.

Be kind to yourself and accept that uncertainty and even failure are part of life. The important thing is to resolve to move forward. While it can be uncomfortable to ask for help, I am never ashamed to do so. It's not weak to seek the support of others. However, sometimes I do not know whom to approach or the people I need are unavailable.

This is when we can feel alone. As I describe above, we need to go deep into ourselves, draw on our inner strength to find the best way forward. We must try to resist the human negativity bias, the tendency to slip into pessimistic self-talk, to regard our glass as half empty and to let the amygdala-driven 'ball and chain', that I describe on page 212, distract and pull us down.

In the words of Vince Lombardi, the American football coach: 'It's not whether you get knocked down, it's whether you get up.'

To build resilience, stay in the moment and tell yourself you are fundamentally a decent person. Like each of us, you're not perfect, but, when you're giving your most and being your best, it's enough. Remind yourself that you do most things you can control well. Reflect on and be grateful for even your smallest achievements. Acknowledge you're not friendless and tell yourself you have permission to feel worthy. In the words of author and professional speaker Keith Abraham: 'Move from asking yourself "Am I...?" to telling yourself "I Am...!"'

Now think about what you might learn from the current situation. Persevere as you refocus on the road ahead, even if the destination is still unclear, and seek out opportunities beyond the obstacles. Imagine what might be possible and then let go as you ponder how to realise it.

Why: Your Purpose

Despite my promising career with what was then universally recognised as the world's most creative ad agency, Collett Dickenson Pearce (CDP)*, my wife Mickey and I decided on a whim to move to Sydney, Australia. It was risky, of course. We left London with little money and no jobs to go to. However, reflecting on former colleague Grant Duncan's advice to 'look beyond the car in front', I felt the time was right for a change.

Mickey and I made two simple promises to each other. We would no longer work for anyone other than ourselves and the bank manager; and we would not live in another terraced house. Thirty-six years on, we continue to uphold both, especially the bank manager! I started an advertising business and Mickey pursued her interior design career, initially partnering with fellow designer Paul Arrowsmith.

After a few years, at the beginning of the deep 1990s Australian recession, I sold my ad business. I then used a straightforward device to help me decide

---

* I understand that CDP was the model for Puttnam, Powell and Lowe, the British ad agency that acquired Sterling Cooper in the multi-award-winning American TV series *Mad Men* (2007–15).

what to do next. Taking an A4 page, I entitled it 'Who, Why and Where Larry'. In the middle, I drew a solid black line from the top to the bottom. Next, I drew a minus (–) sign at the top of the left column and a plus (+) sign at the top of the right column. Reflecting on my career and life experiences to date, I gave myself one month to answer questions such as:

· What bores me?

· What do I dislike?

· What is not important to me?

· What type of people and situations are uncomfortable for me?

· What do I do that makes others feel uncomfortable?

· What am I not good at?

· What are my shortcomings?

· What causes me to feel inadequate?

· What have been my three biggest disappointments or failures, and why?

· What does a bad experience or day look and feel like for me, and why?

· What are my personal values and beliefs, and why?

· What are my attributes, skills and competencies?

· What are my strengths and points of difference?

· What excites me, and why?

· What do I like and what puts a smile on my face, and why?

· What is important to me, and why?

· What type of people do I enjoy being with, and why?

· What do they enjoy about me?

· What difference do I make for others, and how?

· What have been my three biggest achievements, and why?

· What does a good experience or day look and feel like for me, and why?

After 30 days, and well into my third page, I stopped writing. Over the following week, I read it all through – the negative column first and the positive second. I then closed my eyes and, using the breathing exercise I describe above, paused for a few moments to reflect.

Returning to the positive column, I read out loud what I had written several times. I highlighted the top five words, descriptors or phrases that most identified my passions, strengths and beliefs. Limiting it to five was not easy but it was important to hone my thinking. I also kept an eye on what I had written in the negative column. I needed to acknowledge where I had failed, and to accept what I was not good at and did not enjoy.

Taking a fresh page, I placed those five descriptors together in a box in the centre and, from there, developed a mind map to unpack the Larry whom I had begun to identify: 'Who, really, am I? Who do I want to be? And what do I want to be known for?' I challenged myself to identify meanings, not just features, to answer the 'so what?' questions, the differences I wanted to make and felt I was capable of.

I then considered the bigger picture. I thought long and hard about my current situation. I had been living in Australia for almost five years; I asked myself what I felt was good about it, what was not and what was missing. With this context, I reflected on my background, experience and the words in front of me. Now, mindful of what was within my sphere of influence, I challenged myself on where and how I felt I could best make a worthwhile difference. My core five narrowed to three.

Further mind-mapping, deliberating and tightening enabled me to discover the single phrase that articulated my purpose: my personal offer or value statement: 'I want to make a difference by helping those in leadership roles do the same.'

I wrote down two qualifying statements to support it. Finally, I added a short anecdote to bring each qualifier to life. This exercise, followed by research and study, set me on the path to start Robertson Burns, a bespoke leadership communication advisory, the like of which did not exist in Australia at that time. It continues to keep me busy and fulfilled to this day.

I have encouraged several clients to do a similar exercise when they found themselves at a personal or career crossroads. I hope you will give it a go should you find yourself questioning your own 'who, why and where'.

Where: Your Impact

Having settled on my who and why, I looked ahead to think about my where: my vision. What impact do I aspire to make and what will success look like? The answers now came quickly. You will find them in my charter (page 283).

When pursuing your own vision, you need to check in to see how you're going: your attitude, your progress and the difference you're making for yourself and others.

As I identified in my self-discovery journey, communication is the true leader's most vital trait. Unless you are engaging, listening and sharing your thoughts clearly and meaningfully with yourself and with those around you, you won't move forward and they won't come with you or support you.

This is why the stories in the following sections largely focus on the need for effective leadership communication. Despite the ongoing developments in technology, including artificial intelligence, virtual reality and the metaverse, I am confident that face-to-face communication will remain the most compelling form of human interaction. This means engaging with others in the manner and voice of a leader in both formal and informal situations.

At the end of each day, please think through this short self-examination:

- With whom did I meet today and why?
- Metaphorically speaking, where did I intend to take them – what did I want them to think, feel and do?
- How was my attitude?
- If I needed to introduce myself, did I just say my role (the who and what) or did I give a sense of the difference I strive to make (the who, why and where)?
- Was I really the best of the real me in each interaction and meeting?
- Did I make the effort to be fully present every time?
- Did I get my ideas across clearly, convincingly and appropriately?
- Was I confident, at ease and aware of myself, of them and the circumstance?

- Did I really give 100 per cent in terms of actively engaging, listening, showing genuine interest, curiosity and compassion while seeking to understand their ideas, motivations and concerns?
- How did I respond to any challenges or disagreements?
- Did I remain positive and engaged?
- What feelings did they and I take away and what will we each do now?

Please recognise that, if you so choose, you can make even the smallest difference for yourself and others every day. Irrespective of your and their individual environments, this is what true leaders do.

You: In Summary

Our deepest fear is not that we are inadequate.
Our deepest fear is that we are powerful beyond measure.
It is our light, not our darkness, that most frightens us.
We ask ourselves, "Who am I to be brilliant, gorgeous, talented, fabulous?"
Actually, who are you not to be? You are a child of God.
Your playing small does not serve the world ...
We are all meant to shine ...

A RETURN TO LOVE, MARIANNE WILLIAMSON (1952–)

As I hope is already clear, you will not succeed on your own. Be comfortable engaging with others and have them support you. If you live by the qualities described in this book, there will always be people who will be happy to do so. Do not hesitate to seek them out. This requires accepting that you are not perfect – no one is. Nor is it about needing to prove or being hard on yourself.

But you do need to be accountable to yourself. While vulnerability may cause self-doubt and even invite criticism, they help you discover who you truly are. So, be brave. Find the strength to believe in you and not let yourself down. Lean into yourself and be willing to take risks. Resolve to be the best version of your unique self, by working at being your personal best and by giving your most, your 100 per cent.

Success is when you meet these standards to the best of your abilities every time. That's enough. Then you can really enjoy being you and others will enjoy your true leadership too.

Part 2: The 3 Qualities Of True Leaders

If your actions inspire others to dream more, learn more, do more and become more, you are a leader.

True Leadership Is Relationship

Given the magnitude of uncertainty facing us, and with rising community expectations everywhere, seeing leadership as relationship has to be the bedrock on which every leader can build success. Leading effectively is about the relationships leaders build with those around them, what they achieve together and how.

As with every sustainable relationship, true leadership and followership are founded on the core principles of mutuality – mutual trust, mutual respect and mutual purpose. With reference to Aristotle's rhetorical pillars of persuasion, *ethos*, *pathos* and *logos*, I codify them as the 3 Qs of True Leadership – the Quality of Authenticity, the Quality of Empathy and the Quality of Intent.

The 3 Qs in Practice

Thinking of past leaders I admire, such as Joan of Arc, Abraham Lincoln, Winston Churchill, Mahatma Gandhi, Ruth Bader Ginsburg, Steve Jobs, Martin Luther King, Nelson Mandela, Franklin D. and Eleanor Roosevelt, Lee Kwan Yew, Queen Elizabeth II and many others, I can identify their personal attributes within these three qualities. In their own unique way, each was able to communicate their trust, respect and purpose. They were leaders who did not just want to be seen as leaders. No, they were not perfect but they were real leaders who did their best to behave as true leaders and lead for the greater good.

Among living examples, Volodymyr Zelenskyy, the president of Ukraine, Jacinda Ardern, the former prime minister of New Zealand, Australian businessman Andrew Forrest and Alex Ferguson, the former manager of Manchester United, come to mind. Of the first of these, *The New York Times* summarised his leadership succinctly in April 2022: 'We admire [Zelenskyy] ... because he grasps the power of personal example and physical presence. Because he knows how words can inspire deeds – give shape and purpose to them – so that the deeds may, in turn, vindicate the meaning of words ... because he maintains a sense of human proportion ... impressive without being imposing; confident without being cocksure; intelligent without pretending to be infallible; sincere rather than cynical; courageous not because he is fearless but because he advances with a clear conscience.'*

I suggest it is similar for the truly good leaders we come across in our own lives: for example, a teacher, community or religious leader, sports coach, supervisor, boss or even a family member or friend.

As previously mentioned, we all make choices every day. We like to choose with whom to live and work, where to get our medical, financial, legal and other advice. We choose where to eat, get a coffee, where to shop and so much more. And we choose whom we wish to listen to, support and follow.

Creating Mutual Trust, Respect and Purpose

So, again, on what basis do we choose? When we feel we know and are comfortable with the people we are dealing with: their character, values, candour, confidence, competencies, strengths and frailties. We sense their authenticity, credibility and humanity. We recognise and trust their personal brand. Mutual trust is the first quality of true leadership – *the Quality of Authenticity*.

We also feel these people are genuinely interested in us. They are curious, listen well and seem to really care. They have a concern for us. They appreciate us and laugh with us. They seek to understand what matters to us, and our concerns, and respond appropriately. They identify and relate to what it is we're seeking and enable us to achieve it. We feel their respect for us. Mutual respect is the second quality – *the Quality of Empathy*.

* Bret Stephens, 'Why We Admire Zelenskyy', *The New York Times*, 19 April 2022.

Third, they have a clear concept of what success looks like and how we will achieve it together. As if in partnership, even for those brief moments at our local café or shop, they understand that it's about the experience, not simply the process or event. It is the transformation – the outcome and the journey that gets us there – and not simply the one-off transaction. We are excited by their clarity and strength of purpose. Mutual purpose is the third quality – *the Quality of Intent*.

In workshops, I often start with the sentence 'A true leader is someone who ...'. I then invite participants to complete it by naming the strengths of leaders they admire or with whom they have enjoyed working. Their responses are captured in three columns on a board or a screen. I then ask them to nominate the traits of leaders they do not rate and place these in the same columns in red ink.

Finally, I insert Trust (Who) at the top of the left-hand column, Respect (How) at the top of the middle column and Purpose (What) at the top of the right-hand column. Each time I facilitate this exercise, most descriptors, both positive and negative, are in the Trust (Who) column. The Purpose (What) column has the least. This confirms that true leadership is more about heart, who we are and how we relate to others, than head – what we say and do.

On the following page, the 3 Qs Trivium shows how the core strengths and positive traits of each quality come together. These are explained in more detail at the end of the AQ, EQ and IQ sections that follow.

The Value of Diversity and Inclusion

You may be familiar with the saying, 'Birds of a feather flock together.' It refers to people who share similar backgrounds and interests and naturally tend to spend time with each other. While we can all relate to this, I am conscious how it can undermine the richness of diversity, equity and inclusion, not just in the workplace but in every aspect of our lives.

By celebrating each other and our unique differences and traits, we collectively generate vitality, challenge and creativity. These are the critical ingredients that enable us to succeed. I experienced their strength on joining ad agency CDP.

The 3 Qs Trivium

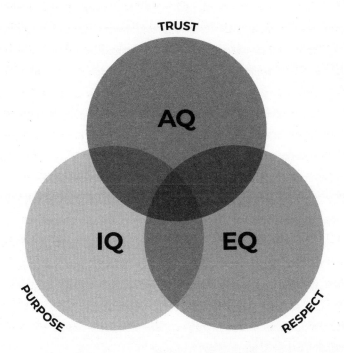

I was just 27 and had left the army as a captain after spending my final two years as the aide-de-camp to the British Chief of the Defence Staff in the Ministry of Defence. It had been an exciting if somewhat rarefied two years, with frequent visits to 10 Downing Street in London, the Pentagon in Washington and NATO Headquarters in Brussels interspersed with official trips to several countries around the world.

As a boy, I had toyed with the idea of becoming a diplomat one day. This role gave a taste of what that life might have been. It also helped me to recognise that the traits of diplomacy, such as being able to see through the eyes of those around us, are fundamental to successful leadership.

Wherever my boss went I went. At my fingertips were executive jets, helicopters, limousines and a large personal staff. Much of this work made me privy to top-secret information of national and international importance.

This prepared me well for the need to observe confidentiality with our clients' information today.

Then I retired from the army and, within a few months, everything changed. Swapping my ceremonial aiguillettes, sword, spurs and frock coat for a leather jacket and jeans was both a shock and exciting. Riding my motorbike or bicycle to work also brought a very different perspective to travel in London, especially in the rain!

But the biggest change was the equity and diversity. I had come from what was, in those days, a largely white, masculine, monocultural and elite environment where tradition, rank and discipline ruled. My ultimate boss was the late Queen, after all.

Don't get me wrong – I loved it! In just a few years, I served in East Asia, the Middle East, Central America, Africa and Europe with wonderful, witty and brave people. Wherever I went and whatever the challenge, I knew all would be well. I belonged to what I regarded as the greatest team on earth, my regiment, my professional family, the Irish Guards. However, for all that, we were not truly diverse. Nor, unsurprisingly given the era, were we particularly inclusive.

Rightly, we hear a lot about the need for diversity and inclusion today. I think noted diversity advocate Vernā Myers explains it best: 'Diversity is being invited to the party; inclusion is being asked to dance.'

I first experienced the value of diversity and inclusion at CDP all those years ago and have never forgotten. Appreciating and upholding this approach is critical if you are to truly lead today.

My first day at the agency was an eye-opener. Jenny was my age, much smarter and, being a marathon runner, fitter. Even from her accent, it was clear she had grown up in different circumstances to me. Jenny was my boss. Hers was Sue, head of client service. After a few months, when Sue asked Jenny how I was getting on, the latter commented that she felt I was fine but perhaps finding that the job was interfering with my social life more than expected. She was right! It did not take me long to discover that advertising is not a nine-to-five career.

Women comprised almost half of the agency's 300 or so employees. They included some of the most recognised art directors and copywriters at that time. While society was growing more accepting of homosexuality, it was still not openly discussed. Yet, gay men and women and those of other orientations were all part of the rich fabric that made up the agency's workforce.

Gender and sexuality were not the only diverse aspects, of course. Mark, the brilliant young head of strategy, had been afflicted with poliomyelitis since childhood. As a result, he was less physically able than most but he still attended and contributed to meetings. From a religious perspective, I am Christian. For the first time, I found myself working alongside colleagues not only of my faith but Buddhists, Jews, Hindus, Muslims and others, as well as non-believers. I am no zealot, nor was anyone with whom I worked, and was curious about these different beliefs, so I naturally and openly engaged with all those who followed them.

Client project teams formed and re-formed daily. These discussions were regularly populated by people of different ages, genders, backgrounds, physical abilities, sexualities, religions, colour and with a variety of accents, skillsets and experience from across the agency. Our differences were welcomed and celebrated. It seemed so natural to do so.

At its heart was diversity of cognitive thinking, which encouraged fresh ideas and constructive challenge. Of equal importance, the diversity championed at CDP was not the result of arbitrary quotas. It was founded on merit and encouraged by the agency's leadership, as should be the case in every organisation.

The Power of Community: 'Ubuntu'*

Everyone was treated as equal. We were expected to make a difference by volunteering our thoughts and contributing to those of others. We were listened to and, more often than not, our ideas were forcefully yet respectfully interrogated and the merits debated. I learned then that diverse teams make better decisions and deliver better outcomes.

This mindset and approach carried throughout the agency. Neither a silo nor fiefdom existed. Irrespective of function or role, the primary focus of each

*Ubuntu is a Nguni Bantu word that means humanity and community; in Zulu it translates to 'I am because we are'.

department and every employee was on producing the most creative and best commercial solutions for our clients. This was the agency's single, overarching purpose. The purpose that took it to number one in the world three years in a row.

It was brilliant! I had found what I had so hoped for ... another community. Here was an enterprise-wide team, passionate about its craft and striving to better its own excellence. I loved each day of my almost six years at CDP before moving to Sydney and am fortunate to have worked there.

Diversity and inclusion continue to be strong themes in my current work.

I work with people across Australasia, Africa, the Americas, East and South Asia, Europe, the Middle East and India: men and women in almost equal ratio with ages spanning from mid-teens to mid-seventies. They hail from widely diverse backgrounds and several have little spoken or written English.

In my army days, just before the 1979 Iranian revolution, I once sat through a formal dinner in Tehran hosted by the late Shah with whom I had stayed when a student. No one seated around me spoke or appeared to understand English. I was not going to give up and my part-French heritage assisted my efforts to communicate. The three or so hours passed remarkably quickly amid a great deal of laughter and enthusiasm.

Later, my boss, the Field Marshal who had been seated with the dignitaries in the middle of the long table, commented that I appeared to have been enjoying a very jolly evening and he was unaware that I could speak Farsi. I couldn't, of course, but I did enjoy leaving him wondering what my fellow guests and I had been talking about! Nor can I speak or write Arabic, Cantonese, Hebrew, Japanese or Mandarin, yet work with people for whom these are their primary and, in some cases, only languages. As always, communication starts with the right attitude and the willingness to have a go.

Unsurprisingly, I support the growing voice for more diversity and inclusion in the professions, business, sport and politics. Nevertheless, given my own career experience that began so many years ago, hearing this call actually saddens me. If more leaders had been true leaders over the past decades, and even today, there would be no need to speak up. There would not be the shocking tales of bullying, exclusion, exploitation, harassment, psychological abuse and worse that continue to emerge. And more organisations would have benefited from the varied thinking and creativity that true diversity brings, as evidenced by the success of CDP.

Similarly, had the business owners of the 19th century, and earlier, been true leaders, I believe there would have been little need for the union movement that began then and that we see today. Naive? I don't think so.

People Every Time

There is an oft-quoted business mantra, 'People are our greatest asset.' I am sure it's familiar to you. Yet survey after survey consistently reveal that the main reasons people leave organisations include the quality of leadership – a toxic culture, feeling unappreciated or uninspired, limited development opportunities, poor communication and unclear or inconsistent purpose, strategy and goals.

To grow, businesses often merge, joint venture with or acquire other businesses. On paper in their advisors' offices, it all makes good sense. The synergies are palpable; the potential cost savings evident; the market growth irresistible; the value accretive. Yet why do many of these unions ultimately come apart? Why is the human aspect often overlooked in the planning?

I am reminded of two of the world's greatest corporations, Bridgestone/Firestone Inc. and the Ford Motor Company. From 1897, through two world wars, the Great Depression and the Vietnam War, Firestone was the principal supplier of tyres for all Ford vehicles. In the midst of a very public dispute about vehicle safety, it all ended in May 2001, where it was reported in *The New York Times*:

'Business relationships, like personal ones, are built upon mutual trust and respect,' Mr. John T. Lampe, Firestone's chairman and chief executive, wrote in the letter addressed to Mr. Jacques A. Nasser, Ford's chief executive and president. 'We have come to the conclusion that we can no longer supply tires to Ford since the basic foundation of our relationship has been seriously eroded.'*

I understand that no new Ford vehicle is fitted with Firestone tyres today.

What had gone wrong? The answer is here in your hands so please read on.

* Keith Bradsher, 'Firestone to Stop Sales to Ford, Saying It Was Used as Scapegoat', *The New York Times*, 22 May 2001.

'If—' (1910)

If you can keep your head when all about you
Are losing theirs and blaming it on you,
If you can trust yourself when all men doubt you,
But make allowance for their doubting too;
If you can wait and not be tired by waiting,
Or being lied about, don't deal in lies,
Or being hated, don't give way to hating,
And yet don't look too good, nor talk too wise;

If you can dream – and not make dreams your master,
If you can think – and not make thoughts your aim;
If you can meet with Triumph and Disaster
And treat those two impostors just the same;
If you can bear to hear the truth you've spoken
Twisted by knaves to make a trap for fools,
Or watch the things you gave your life to, broken,
And stoop and build 'em up with worn-out tools;

If you can make one heap of all your winnings
And risk it on one turn of pitch-and-toss,
And lose, and start again at your beginnings
And never breathe a word about your loss;
If you can force your heart and nerve and sinew
To serve your turn long after they are gone,
And so hold on when there is nothing in you
Except the Will which says to them: 'Hold on!'

If you can talk with crowds and keep your virtue,
Or walk with Kings – nor lose the common touch,
If neither foes nor loving friends can hurt you,
If all men count with you, but none too much;
If you can fill the unforgiving minute
With sixty seconds' worth of distance run,
Yours is the Earth and everything that's in it,
And – which is more – you'll be a Man, my son!

RUDYARD KIPLING (1865–1936), TO HIS SON JOHN*

---

* John Kipling was killed in 1915 at the Battle of Loos while serving in the Irish Guards, the regiment I was privileged to join many years later.

AQ – The Authentic Leader:
Being Your Trustworthy 'Who'

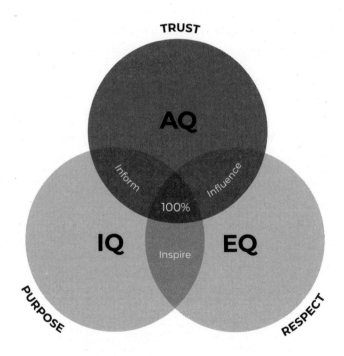

Trust is the bedrock of relationships and of leadership.

As I have pointed out, trust is in decline. What do I mean by trust? Many people get trust and respect muddled up. Leaders need to *be* trusted and to *show* respect. This starts with being trustworthy and ends with earning respect and, ultimately, loyalty.

The core strengths of AQ are character, confidence, competence and consistency (your *ethos*). As a leader, you are constantly being judged. The 'who of you' that shows up each time, the appropriately authentic you, is how you give, build and maintain that trust.

Character

By character we are asking, who are you really? We are certainly not seeking perfection. We just want to know your unique truth – your authenticity, your values and beliefs, and what drives you. To understand where you find your strength, your resolve and your will. To witness how you reveal your humanity, your sincerity, your humour, your humility and your vulnerability. It's how you come across, how you behave, how you're perceived and what you're known for. It's the rock on which your leadership is built.

Confidence

We want to believe in you. We want to feel your confidence and to have confidence in you. This starts with your self-belief and self-awareness, supported by personal fortitude and optimism. We want to hear your clarity of thought and to experience your passion, energy and enthusiasm. This is not about massaging your ego but it does mean telling yourself you are OK. You must find your voice and share your ideas because we want to hear them, even if we may not agree. And we expect you to treat our own thoughts in confidence when we need you to.

Competence

Competence derives from your knowledge, skills, experience and acumen. All too often, these factors alone are regarded as the qualifications for leadership. Too many people are appointed to leadership positions on the basis of their capabilities. This can be a big mistake! As important as it is, capability is but one factor in the mix. Indeed, many of the best past and present leaders throughout the world were not and are not the most technically competent in their field. Their real skill is to surround themselves with a team of people who have the necessary capabilities and experience.

Consistency

Consistency is about openness, congruence and reliability. It is having the courage to face up to challenge. It's about meeting expectations by accepting personal accountability. Doing what you say you will do and striving to do the right thing as best you can. It is walking the talk, being the role model that, as the true leader, you must be, and must want to see in your own leaders. And being tenacious as you commit to build the legacy that you deserve. The legacy that others will benefit from and want to remember you by.

The Real, Trustworthy You

So, how do you ensure trust? Rudyard Kipling provides the answer in his poem on page 52. Although written to his son and only child, his challenge is for us all, whoever we are: to constantly ask ourselves, 'Am I bringing the very best of myself, giving the most of myself in every particular situation?'

This requires maintaining awareness of oneself. For example, aware of the Larry I am being and portraying right now, of the prevailing situation and of others' hopes and expectations of me in this moment.

Human beings are naturally risk-averse. We all suffer from stress when faced with uncertainty, danger, fear, harm or failure and the potential opprobrium of letting ourselves and others down. Despite this, I have learned that one cannot build trust and be an effective leader if one is not at ease with oneself irrespective of the situation.

I have been in harm's way on a few occasions: while serving in the military and, earlier, with seconds to spare, narrowly escaping the murderous Khmer Rouge in Cambodia.

However high the stakes, or however anxious and even scared I have been, if I was to prevail, I had to let go. To move beyond myself, prioritise, engage with those around me and, in the best way possible, give them the clarity and confidence for us to move forward. I needed to focus on the task ahead and, if necessary, be prepared to adapt the plan to achieve it. And I needed to bring them with me and, together, execute as best we could.

Courage to Step Up and Do the Right Thing

What follows are stories where leaders, mostly from the world of business and often in challenging circumstances, have been able to step up, bring their very best and give their most, often exceeding the expectations of those around them. While many of the stories in this book relate to large organisations, each learning and practical tip is universally relevant. They are what true leaders practise every day, everywhere.

You will discover leaders who have a clear appreciation of what is required. There are humble leaders who acknowledge their shortcomings and welcome some external help. There are leaders who find the moral strength to rise to challenge, have a go and succeed. With an open mind and through their personal courage, they are willing to step outside their comfort zone and give their most.

Despite their status, these are ordinary people several of whom unexpectedly find themselves in extraordinary circumstances. They understand the importance of not taking themselves seriously. They resist the temptation to let their own needs or any prism of bias interfere with their judgement. Instead, they maintain a sense of proportion, remain calm and keep their composure. Critically, they are true leaders who, through their own authenticity, earn the trust and build the resilience of their followers.

Although the purpose of this book is to focus on good leadership, I cannot ignore examples of the opposite that confront us every day. As you will see, I also allude to people in leadership roles who are not meeting expectations. With a different attitude, a greater sense of awareness and a willingness to step up and do the right thing, I'm sure these people could also make a valuable and sustainable difference for those around them.

What matters is not only what we seem to the world but what we really are.

ATTRIBUTED TO ARTHUR SCHOPENHAUER (1788–1860) AND OTHERS

'It's too late for speeches'
Courage to show up and lead from the front

Maintaining stakeholder confidence is critical, especially when things are not going well and we are not delivering as expected. This was the case for a large global company that unexpectedly found itself facing a significant crisis.

Established over a hundred years earlier, it had lost its way. Too much diversification, too many entities in multiple jurisdictions. Then it made some acquisitions that turned out badly. Its capitalisation halved in less than 12 months and the stock price followed. There were other challenges. Health, safety, industrial relations and the environment were all areas where the company was failing to meet its obligations.

Its shareholders were baying for blood. They wanted the board of directors to resign and a change of strategy. The media echoed these calls on a daily basis with trades unions and environmentalists in support. The annual general meeting was approaching and a metaphorical bloodbath was likely. The company even arranged for its covert international security team to be in situ to protect the directors and senior executives, so extreme were the threats.

At such meetings, it's customary for the chairperson of a large public company to address shareholders from a carefully worded speech. This had been the tradition here, with the chairman standing behind a lectern and reading from an autocue. In my life, I have often found it necessary to challenge the status quo. I would do so again here.

I had been hired to advise the company and decided that this year had to be different. No autocue or teleprompter, no lectern, not even a formal speech. In the face of strong opposition from the in-house legal and communication teams, who typically see their roles as to protect and defend, the chairman and the board were persuaded that it was the right way to go.

'It's too late for speeches,' I told them. 'It's about the mood of the meeting and what happens afterwards. You have lost the confidence of the entire investment community, even the country. You will not regain it by the chairman reading out carefully prepared words from behind plates of glass.

'Your shareholders aren't your enemy. They are your investors, your owners, your partners. Many are current and former employees and others will be buyers of your products. This is about repairing a relationship which is now broken. This starts with you regaining their trust.'

Unfortunately, I did not give much thought to overall design of the stage at the meeting venue. To my surprise, when visiting with the chairman on the afternoon before the event, we found that, while the message about no teleprompter or lectern had clearly got through, a wooden, grey-painted battlement – there is no other word for it – was being constructed across the stage. Questioning its purpose, we were told the chairman and the board would be seated behind it!

'Who is the board going to do battle with tomorrow?' I asked the investor relations manager. 'I know there have been threats; they're being handled by your security people and the police. In reality, the audience will be made up of your owners. Yes, they are upset, even angry, but I very much doubt they will be taking pot shots at the board! This is about rebuilding trust.' The chairman wholeheartedly agreed and the production team then spent several hours removing the ridiculous barricade.

The day finally dawned and I joined the chairman for breakfast. Understandably, he was nervous. What lay ahead would be challenging. It was not just the prospect of facing 2,500 or so angry shareholders, of taking responsibility for the company's failings in the presence of his fellow board directors, or even of knowing his family would be out there somewhere in the crowd. His biggest challenge was overcoming his personal sense of failure at the pinnacle of what had hitherto been an illustrious career.

As his fellow directors took their seats at a row of plain covered trestle tables that had been installed overnight, the chairman walked right to the front of the stage where a small table and a stool had been placed. He spoke directly to the crowd without notes for just two minutes and then invited their questions. Five hours and 20 minutes later, the chairman and directors left the stage and joined their shareholders and others for refreshments.

No one else spoke from the stage that day. There were no speeches or visual media. Just one person, their chairman, with a clear and simple message. He reached out, engaged and shared his thoughts openly, extemporaneously and naturally with thousands of the company's investors, past and present employees and other stakeholders. All had arrived angry, upset, disappointed or confused. As a minimum, they wanted his resignation and many called for it.

Yet afterwards, wandering anonymously through the crowd helping themselves to the, by now, less than fresh sandwiches, tea and coffee, I sensed the mood had changed.

'Who would have thought our great company would be in the mess we're in today?' One shareholder said.

And another, 'Yes, but you've got to give it to the chairman. He showed guts, humility and patience as he stood in front of us. He listened and responded clearly and respectfully to every question. Some were very aggressive.'

'I agree. He acknowledged our pain, took the blame and apologised. He explained what had occurred and why. He gave a sense of the changes afoot and how the company will recover. I am going to stick with them for another year,' said a third, in a vote of confidence.

For You ...

The only thing we have to fear is fear itself.
FRANKLIN D. ROOSEVELT (1882–1945)

When under pressure or being challenged, we can easily become defensive. We tend to be fearful of the embarrassment – even shame – that failure can bring. We are often uncomfortable with the challenge of uncertainty and the need for change. In such circumstances, it is understandable to want to circle the wagons, keep one's head down, defend one's position and see everyone on the outside as the enemy.

This is not leadership. It is short-sighted behaviour stemming from a self-focused mindset that's more about protecting or justifying ourselves than acknowledging how others are feeling. As a result, we fail to connect with others and to bring them with us.

Such situations occur in organisations every day – the late report, the broken promise, the failing transformation programme, the missed financial target and tough questions from the boss, the ill-considered initiative that disappoints, and more.

When faced with such challenges, we must have the courage to open ourselves to vulnerability and embrace uncertainty. When things go wrong, we need to maintain our inner confidence and remain calm, step up, accept responsibility, be accountable, engage respectfully with our stakeholders, give our most and be our best. This is communicating as a true leader and it is what others expect of you and me every time.

AQ in Practice

- Have the fortitude to show up and lead from the front
- Be prepared to step up, take responsibility and be accountable
- Measure up to your stakeholders' expectations
- Acknowledge the disappointment, hurt and anger of others
- Have the strength to let go, be vulnerable and embrace uncertainty
- Maintain your inner confidence and composure; breathe and focus
- Give 100 per cent, be your best and give your most. Truth, hope and optimism are what others need from you
- Fear of failure, loss, being wrong or losing face are universal and stressful. Hold your nerve, acknowledge fear and fight it
- Looking ahead, ask yourself and your team, what could destroy or severely damage your organisation?

Your 21+90 Days Habit-Forming Challenge:

Let go of the script and have the confidence to express what you know to be true in your own way.

'The best community-focused company in South East Asia'

Aim for the best you can be – it's enough

Arriving at this pharmaceutical company's office in Singapore, Burns was intrigued by an array of dark wooden doors. Eight in all, they were placed along two of the walls surrounding the main working area. All were closed. Each appeared to have a combination lock and an adjacent intercom device. He casually asked the receptionist about them. She said that these were the bosses' offices.

Burns had been sent by the group's chief executive in Australia to work with this subsidiary's management team ahead of it being floated on the Singapore stock exchange. As he surveyed the 20 or so junior staff seated at workstations in the bland, open-plan space behind the reception desk, he thought about their managers in splendid isolation behind those doors. These were the company's senior executives with whom he had come to work over the following days.

After asking Burns to wait, the receptionist walked over to a young woman seated at one of the workstations. As the receptionist returned to her desk, Burns noticed that the young woman made a phone call. Then nothing. After about 20 minutes, the same young woman came to collect him. She introduced herself as Lou-Ann and they proceeded to one of the closed doors. Burns was surprised by what happened next.

Lou-Ann pressed the intercom and spoke into it in a language he couldn't quite grasp. A gruff male voice answered and Lou-Ann then punched some numbers into the lock. A click sounded and the door was unlocked. Lou-Ann held the door open and Burns walked inside. The door was closed behind him.

Gautham, the general manager, rose to greet Burns and motioned to a chair by the window through which the sun poured in. A conversation ensued and the working sessions with this manager and his senior colleagues were agreed.

The following day, Burns resolved to say something about the closed office doors to Gautham. If this business was to succeed as a public company and be worthy of ongoing investor support, it needed a working environment that was open, collegial and inclusive. None of these attributes were in evidence so far.

Gautham was indignant. How dare anyone question how he ran the business, let alone the office? Burns politely persisted and also raised the topic with the other executives. While he detected some willingness to listen, he made no progress. He asked them about the company's culture and if they felt anything should change. Seemingly not!

The weekend was approaching and, deciding on a radical course of action, Burns called our client, the chief executive, in Brisbane.

'Do whatever you think is right,' she responded.

Burns arrived in the office early on the following Monday morning. The staff were already busy at their workstations; he sat at one that had been made available and waited. It gave him a front-row seat for what was sure to be a spectacle.

Allowing himself a discreet smile, Burns watched the first senior manager arrive and head for his office. The executive looked puzzled as he stopped in front of the doorway. He then turned around and shouted at one of the members of staff. A young man looked up from his laptop, shook his head and went back to work. The executive disappeared into his office. Burns could hear him shouting at someone on the phone. This situation repeated as each of the other executives arrived for work.

Then Gautham arrived. He didn't get halfway across the work area before he too stopped and stared. Why was his office door open? Why were all the office doors open?, he shouted at Lou-Ann. She became upset as she explained she knew nothing about the doors. You see, the doors were not open; they were no longer there! The main work area was suddenly brighter and the first step towards building an open, inclusive and energised organisation had been taken.

Burns followed Gautham into his office and sat down. He explained that, with approval from head office, he had arranged for the doors to be removed over the weekend. And they were never coming back.

By the end of the week, Gautham and three of his colleagues had left the company. Burns could now get on with what he'd been tasked to do. Under new leadership, the company successfully floated on the Singapore stock exchange. Where it remained until a few years later.

This was when this story came back to me. Reading the morning news on the internet, I came across an article about a Singapore publicly listed pharmaceutical company. It had just been wholly acquired by its major shareholder, a Malaysian conglomerate. I smiled as I read on. After assisting the company to go public, we had been retained to facilitate a number of workshops with its senior management.

The first of these, located at a South East Asian resort, lasted three days. Its purpose was to develop a charter, a roadmap that articulated the Who (its brand and values), the Why (its mission or purpose), the Where (its vision), and the How (its strategy to uphold the values and mission and achieve the vision); and outlined the What (the necessary operations, initiatives and tactics) and the When (the short-term, achievable goals and measures by which the company would know how it was progressing).

The workshop's underlying objective was to align these managers with the strategy and encourage them to begin their journey towards becoming an effective, high-performing team of leaders. I imagine you may have attended similar events, although perhaps not all were situated on the edge of a palm-fringed, white sandy beach facing a sparkling, azure sea!

Together, the new company's chief executive, its human resource and communication managers and Burns put together an action-packed programme. It included several fun events as well as intensive plenary roundtable discussions and break-out sessions. What had caused me to smile as I read the report that morning concerned why the company was bought out so early in its public life. To understand, let's look at some of the workshop outputs.

In brief, the leadership team had decided their company's identity or brand was: 'An emerging pharmaceutical company with an Asian focus'. They then agreed its values (what it stood for) and the behaviours to uphold them. Next, they decided that the mission (why it existed) was: 'To enrich and improve lives through the reliable and responsible delivery of specialist health products.' In terms of their vision, they wanted the company to be recognised as: 'The best community-focused company in South East Asia, for the comfort and value we deliver to all our stakeholders.'

This clarity of brand, values, purpose and ambition enabled the company's leaders to pull together and develop the detailed strategy with which to move forward. Further workshops followed over the next two years. The chief executive and other senior executives visited some of the company's operations around the region to ensure that the message had got through and was being owned at the front line.

They were soon reassured when, on landing at a jungle airstrip in southern Borneo, they spied a large banner announcing *Stand up. Step up. Speak up. Make a Difference!* draped over the thatch-roofed terminal entrance. This was the motto adopted for the second workshop and clearly the local manager had been determined to carry it on beyond that event. Great!

This was reinforced at their subsequent meeting with the local manager and his direct reports. After everyone had briefly introduced themselves, the manager invited one of his team to 'value share'. This is where someone selects one of their organisation's values at random and describes a related behaviour they have recently observed, good or bad.

For You ...

There are two lessons here.

The first is about engagement, inclusion, trust and teamwork. As a leader, you cannot isolate yourself from your people. You must be visible and accessible. You must take every opportunity to acknowledge and connect with those around you, even if it's just a morning greeting or a meaningful enquiry about their well-being.

Most of this company's original senior managers, including the boss, were neither leaders nor team players. Their sole focus was on themselves and on bettering their personal status and wealth. Those who remained celebrated their new-found freedom and seized the opportunity to grow as true leaders and build a very successful enterprise.

The second lesson is how a diverse, multicultural and multidisciplinary group of managers spread across several geographies came together and resolved what they wanted their organisation to be. It shows how they defined their collective brand integrity, purpose and vision, agreed the standards that would guide them, determined the way forward to achieve their ambition and articulated the culture, the 'glue', that would ensure success.

It was this clarity combined with a genuine appreciation of their own humanity and that of those around them that enabled them to step up to leadership and achieve so rapidly. Critically, they became a first-rate champion team as opposed to a second-rate group of individuals.

Together, they created the business momentum and delivered the value that attracted their company's largest shareholder to act. In the words of the Malaysian conglomerate's chairman, which were reported on the internet that morning: 'This emerging pharmaceutical company with an Asian focus remains the jewel in our crown today.'

AQ in Practice

- Leadership is about disposition, not position
- Strive for the best you and your team can be
- Know who you really are and be your brand
- Values are a source of strength – stand up for them and live them
- Instigate random 'value shares' in your team and organisation
- Do not lose sight of the why – uphold your and your team's purpose
- Focus relentlessly on outcomes and pursue your vision
- Believe in yourself and there is a good chance others will too
- Loyalty works both ways and teamwork is everything
- Embrace diversity, celebrate difference and nurture your organisation's culture

Your 21+90 Days Habit-Forming Challenge:

At every opportunity, share your belief in and excitement for your organisation's or team's ambition with those around you.

'I think they will see it as more than just a line entry'
Humility takes guts

Some years ago, several large technology and associated companies got into trouble by making high-profile acquisitions. In many cases, those being acquired failed to deliver. Some even failed completely, with unhappy consequences for their employees and expensive ones for their new owners and creditors.

Jack, the chief executive of one of those large acquisitive technology companies, was preparing for the annual results announcement. Going through Jack's prepared remarks and slide deck, Burns noticed that Jack barely touched on what amounted to a significant write-off on account of a series of failed acquisitions and start-ups. The lost value amounted to almost half the company's net profit for the year.

After the chief executive had finished his run-through, Burns commented that the US \$1.6bn write-off might be regarded as more than just a line entry by the company's shareholders and market analysts. They would likely want to know what had happened and what was being done about it. They would also want assurances that a similar outcome would not occur in the future. Declaring his family to be a small shareholder, Burns challenged Jack to convince him why they should not sell their shares that very day (which, of course, insider trading regulations would have prohibited).

The chief executive took up the challenge and in less than three minutes, speaking off the cuff directly to his shareholder, explained the context and strategy, why and how these enterprises had been acquired, what had occurred and the lessons learned.

With a smile, Burns thanked Jack for his explanation and confirmed his family would remain a loyal shareholder. He then mentioned that his video camera had been running and invited Jack to look at two pieces of footage. The first showed the chief executive presenting the short, sanitised and on-message version that Burns had referred to as a 'line entry'. The second, just a couple of minutes longer, showed Jack communicating intimately, sincerely and powerfully as he shared the reality with his shareholder.

The obvious questions then followed: 'So, which one of these is the *real* Jack Tarnowski, Jack? Which one do you feel most comfortable with? And your shareholders? Which would your team, even your family, recognise and support? Now for the big question: which one will you go with tomorrow?'

Of course, the chief executive went with the second version. It showed the 'real Jack' sharing his thoughts confidently, authentically and, most important, credibly.

While the company's investor and media relations teams were annoyed with Burns for interfering, their boss's candour was vindicated. Following the annual results briefing, the company's stock price, in free fall for over nine months, started to recover. It continued to do so for the next 18 months and the company is still performing well today.

For You ...

Again, it takes courage to be vulnerable and confidence to be humble. Yet these are true leadership traits. Instead of making excuses, blaming others or hiding behind spin, admit mistakes and be willing to explain how they occurred and what you learned. By so doing, this chief executive, as we also saw with the global company's chairman at his shareholder meeting previously, reaped the benefits. And again, so did its employees and shareholders.

AQ in Practice

- Recognise that we human beings, however accomplished, are imperfect
- Have the courage to be vulnerable
- Humility in place of hubris, always; it's attractive and builds confidence
- You don't need to be right every time but you do need to do the right thing as best you can
- It is always best to admit your mistakes; imperfections are natural and powerful
- You must want to learn every day
- Accept that failure is part of your journey; pick yourself up when you stumble, refocus, persist and move forward

Your 21+90 Days Habit-Forming Challenge:

If you have made a mistake or upset someone, take responsibility, own it and apologise.

'What's the $900K for?'
Expectations before entitlements

I'm occasionally asked what I actually do. Jokingly, I respond that I metaphorically walk around carrying two implements. In one hand, a bicycle pump: most people I work with need some form of air in their tyres. In the other hand is a six-inch nail: when needed, it has the reverse effect!

One of my assignments involved a high-achieving, well-paid executive. Let's call him Roger. The brief given by his boss, Hameen, encouraged a 'take no prisoners' approach. Clearly, Roger did not need the bicycle pump!

Hameen saw Roger as her potential successor, but, to be considered, he would need to change his ways in some important respects. He needed to become more inclusive as both leader of his team and member of his boss's executive team, instead of relying solely on his technical skills and behaving as a champion of one – himself.

As I've mentioned, working with me is often described as being 'larry'd'. The unsuspecting Roger was about to understand what this can mean!

I approached the reception desk on Roger's floor in the imposing office tower. In a deliberately loud voice, I informed the young man in front of me that I had come to meet Robert. He responded by saying there was no Robert in that department. I insisted that I had an appointment with the division head, Robert Jones.

'Oh, you mean Roger!' he exclaimed.

'Yes, that's right, Robert,' I replied, somewhat dismissively.

Giving me an odd look, the receptionist picked up the telephone and spoke with his boss.

A few minutes later, a smartly dressed man in his late thirties appeared from a corner office. With a brief glance in my direction and a perfunctory handshake, he introduced himself as Roger Jones.

'Ah, good to meet you at last, Robert,' I replied, looking just past his left ear as I half-heartedly shook his hand.

'It's Roger,' he repeated, more forcefully this time.

'Roger, Robert, whatever. Where are we meeting?' I asked with little enthusiasm.

'Follow me,' he instructed and we headed to a windowless meeting room.

We sat down and looked at each other in silence. Roger's boss had told him why she wanted him to work with me. From what she had told me, I guessed he was none too happy about it. And, doubtless, his first impression of me would not be improving things!

'Don't hold your punches, Larry,' Hameen had insisted.

'Hey, Robert ... Roger, I was reading the company's annual report the other day. I noticed the remuneration report and the table showing the various senior executives' pay for the year. That was you earning US $1.9m, wasn't it? Wow, that's impressive! I must admit to being a bit jealous. May I ask you a question? What was the US $900,000 for?'

'Sure,' Roger began, puffing out his chest. 'My base was US $430,000, then the bonus, pension contribution, allowances, short-term incentive, long-term reward, sickness and holiday pay and ...'

'Thanks, Roger. Yes, I can see how it adds up. That wasn't the question I was asking. What did you actually *do*?' I interjected deliberately.

He repeated his previous answer, elaborating on the various components that made up his overall remuneration package. He also referred to his division's contribution to the group's profit.

'Again, thanks. But I still haven't got a clear picture of what you did; the difference or impact you really made.'

I continued, 'Our clients include one of the country's top consulting firms. In fact, I believe they're doing a lot of work around your organisation right now. I'm thinking, if you could not come to work for a while, Hameen or HR could pick up the phone to the firm's managing partner and, probably within a day or two, have a senior, highly experienced consultant filling in – for the equivalent of, say, US $1m annual pay. So, I'm keen to know why your shareholders are paying you almost double!'

Appearing less comfortable, Roger shifted in his chair.

'Before you walk out, Roger, let me explain. I'm sure you're doing a very good job. We probably would not be sitting here together if you weren't. As I have just suggested, the job itself is worth around US $1m a year. So, that's US $1m for you doing the job. I regard this as managing.

'The additional US $900,000? That's for leadership. By all accounts, you aren't yet earning it. This is where we're going to focus over the coming months, Roger. After all, you do want to be considered as a serious contender for Hameen's job when she's ready to move on, don't you?'

Nodding slowly, Roger stared in silence at the tabletop between us.

For You ...

The moral of this story is simple. As a leader, or potential leader, you must ask yourself each day, what's your mindset, attitude and overall purpose? Which 'Roger' are you bringing to work and why are you really there? How are you contributing to upholding your organisation's brand, values and purpose and pursuing its vision? Are you consistently looking for opportunities as to where and how you can contribute to the success of others? Or are you focused solely on you and your achievements, the task ahead of you and your aspirations?

It's never about the money, it's about the difference you make. Then the rewards will flow. Please think less about your personal ambitions and more about the broader context – about owning the situation and the effort you are putting in. You can never let a sense of entitlement cloud your view of your role and of who you are.

Instead, you must always be generous of spirit. Focus your enthusiasm on the expectation others have of you as a leader as well as a manager. Be determined to contribute to a legacy that your people really want to be part of. As a true leader, leadership is never about you.

AQ in Practice

- True leaders put the hopes and expectations of others ahead of their personal gains and entitlements
- Leadership is neither about the leader nor about personal championship
- Raise your self-awareness
- Technical competence is not enough for leadership
- Leadership is about the difference you make for others
- All leaders need to work on their emotional intelligence
- To fit in and succeed, your personal values and those of your organisation must align
- True leaders take what they do and with whom they do it seriously, not themselves

Your 21+90 Days Habit-Forming Challenge:

Every morning ask yourself, what can I do today to better serve my people and my organisation?

'They didn't really want me'
Awareness of yourself, others and the circumstance

Most office buildings have lifts (or elevators). When riding in one, I find myself smiling as I reflect on some amusing moments in these tiny boxes that travel increasingly vast distances.

It's funny, is it not, that despite the close proximity we share with our fellow travellers, we typically do our best to ignore them. This is the case even when we are employees of the same organisation. Others could be shareholders, or even existing or potential clients or customers!

The next two stories focus on the opportunities provided by these small vertical crossroads, and on what we may miss when we fail to look around us and seize them.

Burns is a student of lift behaviour. When travelling in them, he is often inclined to engage with total strangers. This is not something I would necessarily advise everyone to do but it can produce some interesting results.

Take the lifts at the headquarters building of one of the world's major insurers, for example. Oftentimes, Burns's departure from the building coincides with the end-of-day rush when the lifts are inevitably near capacity. This is when the mischief occurs.

'Have we had a good day?' Burns asks airily to no one in particular, nevertheless carefully observing his fellow travellers as they hurtle south.

'Yes, thanks,' cautiously replies one unsuspecting employee.

'Ah, well done you,' Burns replies, followed by: 'Have you achieved anything?', looking them right in the eye.

'Well, yes actually,' volunteers his surprised victim.

By now, he or she is desperately looking at the level indicator to ascertain how much longer this inquisition might continue before the lift reaches its destination, the doors open and they can escape.

'So, things are better now than they were at 8am this morning?' Burns asks. 'Well, thank you very much. Please carry on!' he concludes with a smile, usually neatly timed to coincide with the opening doors.

As the other occupants, who have kept their eyes firmly on their mobile devices or the floor lest they be next for Burns's attention, race out of the lift and head for the building's exit, they can often be heard asking their colleagues, 'Who was that person?'

'No idea but, with that accent, probably a board director,' replies one.

'Well, it was nice of him to thank Anne for her contribution. I wish our bosses did that more often, don't you?'

On one such occasion Burns was working in Hong Kong. Among our clients there was a young, newly promoted senior executive, Bao. On this particular day, the meeting went over the lunch break so Burns and Bao decided to pop down for something to eat. Many of the junior staff were doing the same and squeezed themselves into the lift. Hardly had the doors closed when, you guessed it, Burns opened up.

'Have we had a good morning?' Burns asked, scanning the young faces. A young man caught his eye and grinned.

'You have?'

'Sure. We're all working very hard and achieving lots,' he replied confidently.

Burns realised that he'd spied this person and most of the others earlier that morning. They had been sitting shoulder to shoulder with their heads down at what appeared to be long trestle tables that stretched down the middle of the office floor. Adjacent were the executives' bright and airy offices, many with views of the famous harbour below.

'You believe you deserve a break, do you?' Burns asked, smiling broadly.

Everyone, except Bao, began to laugh. When the lift reached the ground, the younger occupants rushed out still laughing among themselves. As Bao and Burns walked through the food court, Bao commented, 'That was embarrassing.'

'Really? What was embarrassing about it, Bao?'

No response. With hunger mounting and neither wishing to pursue the matter, they headed off to find something to eat.

A few weeks later, Burns was back in Hong Kong and bumped into Bao. 'You remember that young man with whom you spoke in the lift last month?' asked our client.

'Yes,' Burns replied.

'Well, you made your mark. The next morning, he and one of the others came up to me and asked, "Who was that guy with you in the lift yesterday?"

'I told them you're a consultant who works with the organisation from time to time.

'"Oh," they had both replied in unison, appearing disappointed. "We really liked the way he connected with us. We hoped he was a new executive who had recently joined."

'So, well done you,' joked Bao with little enthusiasm.

'Thank you – but you miss the point,' Burns replied. 'Yes, they wanted my openness, my friendly manner, my behaviour. But they didn't really want me!

'They want you and your senior colleagues behaving like me, reaching out spontaneously, connecting and engaging with them informally and displaying a sense of fun. Clearly, they felt appreciated that day and, I respectfully suggest, even empowered by my simple gesture.

'You can do that too, Bao. Indeed, to lead successfully, you must.'

For You …

The point in telling these 'lift' stories, and those that follow, is to remind you that you must seize every opportunity to give 100 per cent of yourself, to connect and engage with those around you. If you do not, why should they give you their 100 per cent?

I have often had clients write E E = O! at the top of each day in their electronic diaries: *Every Event*, however informal, provides an *Opportunity!* An opportunity to give your most and make a difference, even if simply to put a smile on someone's face! Why not? This is what true leaders do.

AQ in Practice

- Every event is an opportunity
- People want their leaders to make the effort to connect
- Be constantly, consciously aware of yourself
- Be aware of others and their expectations of you
- Read the situation, respond and behave appropriately every time
- Your attitude dictates the behaviours that create the culture that either drives or destroys your own and your team's performance

Your 21+90 Days Habit-Forming Challenge:

Every time you ride in a lift at your workplace, say hello and introduce yourself.

'Is he gesturing correctly?'
Trust starts with authenticity

It seemed that very few people trusted the chief executive officer. Even the board was beginning to think that they may have made a mistake in appointing him to the role barely one year earlier. Peter was one of those chief executives who had not learned the importance of under-promising and over-delivering. The newly minted acquisitions were already failing to deliver, and increasing competition was eating into the core business.

The executive floor had just received an expensive makeover and was now almost inaccessible to all but the privileged few who worked in the extravagantly titled 'Office of the CEO'. Even most of the group's senior executives, who reported directly to the chief executive, could no longer visit their boss without first making an appointment. The stock price was drifting and soundings from across the organisation indicated that morale was low.

Such was the situation when my associate James worked with Peter ahead of his first annual results briefing to the market.

'Do you think Peter is gesturing correctly?' enquired the group head of public affairs. Sally was new in the role, having replaced her highly regarded predecessor. She had worked with the CEO previously in another organisation.

'What do mean, Sally?' James replied.

'Well, I thought you would be commenting on Peter's body language. Is that not what you leadership people do?' she responded haughtily.

James laughed. 'Not exactly, Sally! You see, as I understand it, the market is losing confidence in Peter. It's less about his performance as a presenter and more about his performance as the chief executive officer.'

Everyone gestures naturally every day, some more or less than others depending on culture and personality. Gestures start in the brain. They are a way of expressing how we genuinely feel about what we are saying. Moving our hands naturally and spontaneously helps to engage our listeners.

Asking Peter to focus on his gestures would have encouraged him to focus on himself when he should be giving his all to his listeners. This was the only way they would trust and listen to him.

While we need to be aware that our body language is congruent with how we feel, it should never become the primary focus. If it does, we would be encouraging clients to act instead of interact.

'Shareholders, analysts, employees, the media and others will not be overly concerned about Peter's presentation effectiveness tomorrow, Sally,' James continued.

'They will be focusing on his effectiveness as the leader of this business and asking themselves three questions:

'First, do we believe Peter? Is he coming across as genuine, credible, with conviction, and do they feel he is capable? If so, they will listen.

'Second, is Peter speaking in a way which demonstrates his understanding of our concerns? Is he answering our questions respectfully, acknowledging our right to seek more information and even challenge him? Only now will they start to buy into him.

'And third, is Peter giving a clear picture of where the business is at today and how he is taking it forward despite the challenges? Is he explaining and taking ownership of the setbacks? And is he giving us confidence that the business strategy will achieve the goals he has previously announced and deliver on our expectations?

'Only if their answers to all these questions are yes, will they come along on the journey with him. If not, they won't.'

Politely ignoring Sally's dismissive demeanour, James refocused his attention on her boss. He sensed then that Peter would not remain long in his newly fashioned executive suite atop the building. Sure enough, six months later Peter was gone. And Sally? She followed shortly afterwards.

For You ...

Again, you will only succeed as a true leader by sharing your authenticity, credibility, competence, humility, empathy and understanding, coupled with reality, resolve and confidence – your humanity and your clarity.

This is true leadership and it starts with the right mindset and attitude. It's how you will bring your stakeholders along with you and succeed.

AQ in Practice

- Don't hide yourself away from your people
- Trust is founded on authenticity and openness
- Everything starts with your mindset
- Again, think disposition, never position
- Strive for your own personal excellence, not perfection
- Integrity is everything. It must govern your attitude and behaviour
- Face up and respond to reality
- Under-promise and over-deliver

Your 21+90 Days Habit-Forming Challenge:

Let go and really want to connect with those around you at every opportunity.

'It didn't appear to worry you, so I didn't let it worry me'

Keep calm and carry on

While a little risqué, one of my favourite anecdotes is also one of the most powerful.

One day I went to see the chairman of a large company in Sydney. He had contacted me on the advice of a colleague who suggested I could be of value. Since the chairman was running late, I went to the washroom. As I was standing at the urinal, a middle-aged man entered and stepped up a few cubicles away.

Without paying much attention to him – after all, there were more pressing matters to attend to – I then walked over to the row of basins to wash my hands. As I did so, I looked into the mirror in front in which I glanced at the man still standing at the urinal.

'That's the chairman,' I decided. As the man approached the basins, I could see that indeed it was. I went to dry my hands thinking, I had better say something. After all, I'm going to meet him in a few moments!

With my hands dry, I turned to face the chairman and said, 'Hello, Mr Nugent, I'm Larry Robertson.'

With a nod, the chairman responded, 'Oh, I'm sorry for keeping you waiting. Come along to my office.' Together we almost sprinted out of the washroom, through reception where I collected my worn leather briefcase, and on into a large office.

The chairman motioned me to sit in one of the easy chairs around a low glass coffee table at the window. The sunlight poured in and the harbour glistened 59 levels below. The chairman sat in one of the chairs directly opposite me and off we went in conversation.

Everything seemed to be going swimmingly ... until I made a painful discovery. I had been vaguely conscious of something white in my lower periphery vision for a while. I assumed it to be piece of paper. It wasn't. To my horror, I suddenly realised that it was my boxer shorts and, worse, what was inside was in full view. *Help!*

What I describe as the event, the self-focus-driven 'ball and chain' phenomenon (see page 212) then occurred. I momentarily lost my train of thought and stopped giving the potential client 100 per cent. Of course, it was too late to do anything practical about this embarrassing situation. I could hardly start fastening my fly buttons there and then. So, having grown up in Scotland where I often wore the kilt, I took a deep breath, crossed my legs and shifted my seating position slightly. Having recovered my poise, I carried on the conversation.

As soon as I bade the chairman farewell, I rushed back to the washroom and attended to those pesky buttons. My sense of embarrassment was still raw when I left the building.

Rather to my surprise, the chairman accepted my subsequent written proposal and we met a few weeks later for the first working session. As I was describing my proprietary Head + Heart model (see page 213), I commented to our new client: 'You must have thought me a little odd when we met the other day, Chairman.'

I often refer to my chairperson clients in this manner, not out of a sense of formality or deference but as a sobriquet.

'To my horror, halfway through our meeting, I discovered that my fly buttons were completely undone. I am very sorry,' I explained, sensing that my face was growing pink.

The chairman's calm yet friendly reply was interesting: 'Yes, I did notice. But it didn't appear to worry you … so I didn't let it worry me.'

For You …

This response is one of the strongest validations of AQ. Yes, I had wobbled for a few split seconds but quickly recovered my composure and focus. The ability to remain at ease when under pressure, whatever the circumstance, is critical. It's what I refer to as the swan on a lake – continuing to move forward with a serene, calm and purposeful disposition while our mind and our metaphorical legs are racing!

As you will gather from reading this book, I enjoy a good laugh – often at myself! Endorphin-driven 'belly' laughs come from being at ease and are propelled by deep breaths from our diaphragm. Conversely, when stressed, we take shallow breaths, speak faster and, in extreme circumstances, scream from our throat. I return to the importance of breathing in the True Leader's Communication Toolkit on page 227.

As this story indicates, managing unexpected situations as best we can while continuing to give 100 per cent of ourselves to those around us behaviourally, emotionally and rationally reaps a corresponding response. And it maintains confidence.

AQ in Practice

- Again, no one is perfect, no one
- Keep calm under pressure
- Just strive to give your most and be your best, every time
- Whatever the situation, focus on those around you, not on yourself
- What you give, you will usually get
- Stuff happens often when it's least expected; how you respond is what matters
- You must maintain confidence in yourself and infuse it in others
- Passion, energy, humour, adaptability and resolve are important leadership traits

Your 21+90 Days Habit-Forming Challenge:

When unexpectedly distracted, take a deep breath and double down on your focus on those whom you are with and why.

'Why haven't you brought the trophy home yet?'
Self-belief and the discipline to win

Other than when very young, and despite my love of working as a member of a team throughout my career, I've had limited experience of participating in team sports. I was more of a track and field person. I still love downhill skiing and occasionally persist on the tennis court with mixed success.

There's one thing I do know about every sport. As with all things in life, even the most gifted sportsman or woman cannot succeed on their own. They need a team around them: players, coaches, trainers, nutritionists, medicos, sponsors and so on. It's the collaborative effort of each person working together that wins the laurels.

When invited to work with the top players of a high-profile sports team, Burns was intrigued but also a little apprehensive. 'What can I bring these guys that they don't already have?' he asked himself. 'I don't even understand their code!' Yet, figuratively speaking, the club chairman insisted that Burns get on the field.

His brief? To help these players, all in their twenties and already earning many hundreds of thousands of dollars annually, communicate better with the media and the club's sponsors. On occasions, we have all seen or heard and, perhaps, winced as successful young sports people are interviewed by the media after a big win. Most speak too fast and every third word seems to be a non-word – *er*, *um* or *ah*. While excited by their physical success, we are often left little the wiser when they have finished speaking.

Burns had done his research. This was the one of the oldest clubs in the country. Most fans of this code, even if they supported another club, seemed to have a soft spot for this one. Throughout its long history, it had certainly produced some high-grade players whose names were synonymous with the sport. Despite this, it had been almost half a century since they had won the national championship. What was going wrong, he wondered? Surely more than their limited communication skills.

Following an initial session with the top dozen players, Burns divided them into three groups of four. Working in these smaller groups, he discovered that injuries were frequent and they were affecting play – what industry often refers to as 'high lost-time injury rates'. Even the captain, a big fellow with a strong reputation for his craft, had spent more of that season off the field than on it.

Burns asked him, 'So what are you doing while your team is playing, Ken? It must be very frustrating not being out there with them.' The captain replied that he would be in the coaches' box, taking notes. Surprised, Burns asked Ken to show him what he meant. Together they went into the stadium behind the clubhouse and climbed up to the box where they sat looking down on the pristine field below.

'You certainly get a great view of the field from here,' Burns commented.

'But you know, Ken, if it was me, I would want to be down *there*, as close as I could be to my team. My knuckles would be white from gripping the railings tight as my body reached for the turf. My voice would be hoarse from encouraging my mates. My spirit would take me out there onto the ground in every way I possibly could.

'Is that not what their injured captain should be doing, Ken? You've enough coaches and video cameras observing and recording every move from up here. Any critical feedback and advice can be given to the team at the breaks in play. Forgive me if I'm wrong.'

The highly acclaimed captain, around two metres in height and in his late twenties, began to nod. 'You're right,' he said with little enthusiasm.

It was then that Burns realised that they had the wrong man. Here, undoubtedly, was a champion player, but he was not showing the hunger that Burns expected of a true captain, albeit injured. While he could understand the captain's frustration due to his injury, Ken did not seem to even want to be in the thick of it with his team.

Burns's first advice to the club's management was to consider giving the captaincy to one of two team members that he had identified as having the right leadership potential. Neither was over 180cm tall. Nor did they have much of a track record as strikers. Each appeared to have escaped the notice of sports commentators hitherto. Both had shiny eyes, exuded enthusiasm and energy, shared ideas willingly and were clearly passionate about their sport, their club and their fellow players.

Ken rejoined his team on the field but, as the losses mounted, it wasn't long before the club replaced him as captain with one of these young men. The team went on to win three of the next five national championships. However, it was not only the team's leadership on the field that had been holding them back. It was also the leadership off the field.

Burns was perturbed by the injury rates. While the club's management (I've often heard sport administrators cheekily referred to as the 'blue blazer brigade') focused on the financial and social aspects of the club, they had literally taken their eyes off the ball. This failing had encouraged a poor culture where the discipline around physical training, nutrition, lifestyle and well-being was weak. Further investigation revealed that the coaches were required to handle multiple tasks and so were overworked and distracted. The close attention and support the players needed were missing.

Here was a once great institution in which many, within and externally, still passionately believed, and they yearned for it to regain its former glory. Yet it was clear that it had lost its soul, self-belief, passion and, with them, a will to recover. While conscious of its heritage, it had forgotten what had really made it great. It was now driven by a sense of hubris, believing its name, legacy and location alone meant that the local citizenry and sponsors would remain loyal and support it, whatever the results. Burns's challenge to management, asking why their sponsors and fans should bother to continue to support them, was met with a stony silence.

For You ...

I will end this story here. To give you a clue as to how this club rediscovered its brio, its spirit, how it re-established its sense of family, and how it regained its position as one of the most admired and successful sports teams in the country, please reflect on the pharmaceutical company's success earlier (page 62).

AQ in Practice

- It takes grit to look critically at yourself and resolve to lift your game
- Success comes from facing reality, being willing to adapt and maintaining self-belief and discipline
- Be sure to build on your strengths and work on your flaws
- To win, teams need fully engaged captains who are also team players
- Do not let down those who hold you up
- Culture is the glue that binds you and your people together
- Teaming is about the power of together
- TEAM = Together, Everyone's (unique) Attributes Maximised

Your 21+90 Days Habit-Forming Challenge:

Ask yourself, who am I really, why am I here and what worthwhile difference can I make for my team today?

'He didn't want you to see who he really is'
Engagement versus entertainment

My family and I once attended a performance of Noël Coward's 1930 comedy *Private Lives*. The play features a divorced couple who, while honeymooning with their new partners on the French Riviera, find themselves staying at the same hotel in adjacent rooms with adjoining balconies overlooking the sea. This production was being performed in a small, modern theatre. The stage and the front row of the auditorium were on the same level; the other rows rose gently behind.

Seated in the third row, our eyes and those of the performers were at the same level. As Elyot Chase, the lead male character, was well into one of his famous soliloquies, his and my eyes met. An interesting thing happened. Within seconds, as he continued speaking, the actor playing Elyot averted his gaze. He moved nothing else until he completed his piece and turned to his co-lead character and wife, Sibyl.

I smiled.

What had occurred? Recalling my own theatrical experiences, I've shared this story with professional actors who confirmed my suspicions. The actor in the role of Elyot Chase (I'll call him Marc) wanted me to perceive him as Elyot Chase, not who he really was – Marc. With me looking intently right into his eyes, I could see and sense the real person behind the make-up, the costume and the accent – Marc and not Elyot. When Marc realised, he broke eye contact and got me to re-engage with his character, Elyot.

For You ...

The point to appreciate here is that actors entertain, leaders engage. Actors create an illusion. They don't want their audiences to connect with their true selves. In contrast, true leadership requires you to play your real self. As I hope is becoming clear, being true to those around you requires authenticity, openness and credibility. True leaders are happy for their various audiences to see through the imagery, to get to know who they really are, to believe in them, and to come with them.

'Walk the talk'
Leaders are role models

Led by its board, its chief executive and her leadership team, a large manufacturing organisation was undergoing significant structural and cultural change. While waiting in the head office foyer on the ground floor at around 8.30am one morning, Burns was both surprised and disappointed to notice the chief executive's manner as she entered the building.

Without uttering a word, she swept past the security team and the receptionists at the front desk. She headed for what Burns later learned was a lift for the exclusive use of the company directors and senior executives. Even the uniformed security person who held the lift doors open for her was ignored. Apparently, the car park downstairs was also segregated. The directors and senior executives were able to park in a fenced-off area closest to the lifts.

What is all that about 'walking the talk', you may ask? As did Burns that morning. Here was an organisation in the throes of a major change programme. At its heart were the new purpose, values and behaviours required to create and sustain the inclusive culture that had been workshopped across the organisation and agreed by the board and group executive. Yet while the chief executive was a leading voice for the programme, little was in evidence from her that morning.

This story reminds me of Rollo. Rollo was a black labrador and a greatly loved member of my family for 13 years before he sadly died. He acted as my early warning system. After driving home from the station or airport at the end of a long day, I park my car at the wooden shed near the back gate and walk towards the verandah that surrounds the house.

Rollo used to lie outside the kitchen door. Although we could not yet see each other, I would already hear his tail wagging as it struck the timber verandah floor. He always recognised my footsteps and seemed pleased when I came home. As I continued walking around the verandah, the tail's pace increased and sounded more urgent, becoming a crescendo when I came into view.

As I got closer to the dog, either one of two things happened. Most times, with his tail still wagging furiously, Rollo sat bolt upright wanting a pat and a 'Good boy!'. However, on some occasions, the opposite happened. Without me uttering a word, the tail stopped and almost disappeared between Rollo's legs. He crouched down and began to resemble something closer to a dachshund.

This was a vital signal. Rollo had detected my mood and was mirroring it in his way. Just beyond Rollo were the French doors to the family room where my wife Mickey would often be working at her desk. While interested in how my day had gone, she would not want to be dealing with a preoccupied or grumpy husband! Rollo's response to my manner ensured, if necessary, that I was able to snap out of myself and instead give my family 100 per cent, as expected.

The chief executive in this story would have likely benefited from her own 'Rollo' at the entrance to the head office that morning!

For You ...

Whatever the pressure or circumstance, true leaders never cease to be role models everywhere, every day. As daily creator, carrier and custodian of the culture, a leader's duty is to be the same leader he or she wants to see around their organisation ... and their home.

Whenever possible leaders must be AVAA: Audible, Visible, Approachable and Accessible. Too few leaders seem to recognise the importance of this. Of course, it can be challenging in large organisations where technology might play a role. Nevertheless, every occasion however small is an opportunity to engage and make a difference, even metaphorically, if only to get a tail or two wagging!

Be open to and seek regular feedback from trusted sources around you. Your success will most likely depend on theirs.

AQ in Practice

- Leaders are role models every day, good and bad
- As a leader, you show the way every time
- You are the benchmark and you set the tone
- Treat others as you wish them to treat you
- Your family, friends, colleagues, customers and investors, and others, have expectations of the real you. Strive to meet them every time
- Ask a member of your team to observe you in meetings and give you feedback on how you engaged with and responded to your colleagues
- Be the leader you want to see, always
- Walking your talk starts with you
- And talking your talk will bring others with you

Your 21+90 Days Habit-Forming Challenge:

Greet ALL your colleagues, including cleaners, car park attendants, security staff, receptionists and assistants, with a smile and, ideally, by their first names whenever you see them. Occasionally thanking them for their contributions goes a long way too.

'He starts on Monday'
Imagination and going the extra mile

After the army and a few enjoyable months paying off my mess bill by selling expensive automobiles to pop stars, sheikhs and wealthy business people in Mayfair, London, I set my heart on advertising. Jobs in advertising agencies are not easily come by. Given my lack of relevant qualifications, I am often asked how I got a job at leading creative agency CDP.

I had done some research and gained interviews with a number of agencies. I was delighted to be offered a role at J. Walter Thompson and at another large, acclaimed international shop. However, those in the know kept telling me that CDP was the place to be. But how? It was not recruiting and did not respond to unsolicited applications.

Then I discovered that CDP held the army officer recruitment account. The current campaign at the time included double-page spreads in the major newspapers. The ads ran with the headline, '*We believe three years as an army officer can equate to three years at university*'. Underneath were the names and signatures of 50 captains of industry – the chairs and chief executives of many of the country's top companies – and academics from some of the leading universities. In the bottom right-hand corner was the signature of John Salmon, then chairman of CDP. Smiling, I removed and folded the ad from *The Times*.

I called the agency to ascertain the name of the army officer account director. The next day, I called again, this time asking to speak with Mr Nigel Clark's assistant. Truthfully introducing myself to Clare as Captain Robertson, I requested a meeting with her boss to discuss the account. She readily obliged and, suddenly, here was the opportunity to walk inside the agency of my dreams.

At 11am the following Friday, I was seated in a meeting room at CDP. My heart was pounding! Mr Clark eventually arrived and, after introducing himself, asked the reason for my visit. I explained I had a few questions concerning the current campaign. I then produced the ad and unfolded it on the table between us.

'Just confirming that this is the agency's current campaign, Mr Clark,' I began. He nodded, looking puzzled. He was doubtless thinking, who is this guy?

'Thank you. I have a couple of questions. First, is this the signature of the agency's chairman?' I said, pointing to the bottom right-hand corner. He confirmed it was.

'Second, when did the agency last put its money where its mouth is, Mr Clark?' By happy coincidence, I had discovered that Nigel was not only an account director; he was also the agency's deputy chairman. Beginning to look a little uncomfortable, he said nothing.

'I guessed so, Mr Clark. Here's your chance. I can start on Monday!'

Looking the deputy chairman right in the eye with a smile, I watched in silence as the penny dropped. It did not take long! Barely five seconds later, my new boss roared with laughter.

'Brilliant! Follow me.' We raced out of the meeting room, down the corridor and into a bright corner office.

'Barry, this is Larry. Give him a job. He starts on Monday.' And I did.

One of the agency's clients in those days was a well-known manufacturer of condiments and sauces. As a member of the account team, my involvement centred on producing great advertising to promote the company's products. At that time, I was unfamiliar with the science of brand management and the process of bringing products to market.

Cycling home one evening, I stopped at a familiar supermarket to buy supplies. Walking the aisles, I happened on the mustards section. To my surprise, the company's prized products were on the bottom shelf. I quickly put down my basket and removed a competitor's mustards situated on a shelf at eye level. Replacing them with my client's products, I put the competitor's mustards in the now vacant space below.

A couple of fellow shoppers stopped by and were about to pick up two of the competitor's mustards still at eye level. I handed them my client's products saying they were far superior. With a smile, they each took a jar and walked on. I continued my task of swapping the mustards.

Moments later, a man in a white shirt emblazoned with the easily recognisable supermarket logo approached. He introduced himself as Brian, the store manager, and asked what I was doing. I told him I worked on the advertising account and wanted to make sure my client's products were easily visible for shoppers. He laughed. While congratulating me for my efforts to support my client, he explained that products were deliberately positioned throughout the store according to a complex pecking order. He then politely asked me to complete my purchases and go home.

A couple of weeks later, I received a call from the client company's marketing director, someone I would not typically engage with in those early days. He had learned of my activities in the supermarket and was calling to thank me for attempting to reposition his products. Not long after, he gave the agency another of his company's well-known brands to advertise. The overall account continued to grow over the ensuing years.

For You ...

The true leader's daily mindset includes awareness, self-belief, humour and resolve. If you really want to succeed, you need to try to reimagine the possible. Don't let yourself be limited to the job description. Or be put off by no job! Seek out ways to cut through, have an impact and make a difference.

As a leader, you're in the help business. Ask yourself, what else? What else can you do to help your organisation, your team, your colleagues and your customers succeed? What's the competitive edge? This is true leadership thinking at any level.

AQ in Practice

- Back yourself, take a risk and, as always, strive to give 100 per cent
- Keep your eyes and ears open and use your imagination
- Be curious
- A bit of natural charm and wit can make the difference
- Make the effort to go beyond
- And be prepared to fail
- Thank people for their efforts, however trivial
- To succeed, you need people to support and sponsor you; as a true leader, you must do the same for those that follow you

Your 21+90 Days Habit-Forming Challenge:

Be consciously aware of yourself and what others expect of you. Ask yourself, what else can I do today to support them, surprise them and exceed their expectations?

'She is the best candidate'
Not every story has a happy ending

At the heart of this story are organisational politics, favouritism, fiefdoms and toxic cultures. I return to these cancers later. Unfortunately, too many organisations, spanning from government departments to global conglomerates, from public companies to professional services firms and sports organisations, allow them to thrive. The further up the line they occur, the more insidious and dangerous they are.

Such environments can allow some ambitious people to put themselves and their personal success before all else. While these people flourish, their attitudes and behaviours can destroy careers and, ultimately, even organisations.

In my experience, the root cause is scant adherence to organisational values and poor governance due to ill-informed, narrow-minded, over-populated or overworked boards. While comprised of directors who are intelligent and, for the most part, decent, many boards are made up of people with similar personalities, backgrounds, skills and connections. With a tendency towards homophily, their focus is often limited, even misplaced.

Nepotism can play a role too. Once in positions of power, some politicians, mandarins (senior bureaucrats), executives and others in senior roles enable like-minded people to follow them. The latter, whose positions and personal rewards depend on patronage, allow their inadequacies, insecurities and self-importance to guide everything they do. Their main concern is that they will be exposed and their reputations trashed.

I am not referring to 'imposter syndrome', which is not uncommon among those appointed to senior or high-profile roles. Such people can harbour self-doubt and lack a sense of worthiness. Once revealed, 'imposter syndrome' can be successfully addressed through support, including coaching, and reading the many books on this topic.

As I have described, on reaching the top, some executives create an 'Office of the CEO' or similar. Its purpose is to give the boss administrative support.

In so doing, these 'offices' do not themselves cause the behaviours I allude to. However, they can project a negative image and unwittingly fan the flames. The 'offices' are commonly headed by someone with the rather pompous title of 'Chief of Staff' and often staffed with former political advisors. Some have honed their craft in the corridors of parliamentary power, where the 'neither acknowledge, apologise, nor explain' dictum rules.

I cannot think of a government, irrespective of jurisdiction or political persuasion, that does not employ these obfuscating and divisive tactics. The behaviour is subtle but designed to ward off unwanted access, challenge and criticism. It also swings into action when the interests of the person at the top are likely to be threatened. Hardly a day goes by when the 'imperial guards' are not striving to maintain hypocrisy, deny dissent and overwhelm attempts to uncover the truth. Their weapons are typically secrecy, obfuscation, denial and spin.

I wonder how many founders of the new breed of entrepreneurial start-ups surround themselves with such an arrogant, expensive and often adversarial cohort. The real cost is the lack of open communication, humility, collaboration and, inevitably, trust. I have even heard well-intentioned leaders of some large, established organisations say they sometimes feel they're working in a bubble and are out of touch.

I observe that, where debilitating behaviours do occur, they are promoted by powerful people, usually men, with strong personalities who are capable of committing sheer bastardry. A potential descriptor that comes to mind is psychopathic. I have witnessed the results of their sickening activities.

Take appointments and promotions, for example. I've worked with many excellent candidates who have reached the shortlists for senior roles. Happily, some made it all the way to the metaphorical corner office. I have also worked with some of the world's leading recruitment and search consultancies that run the selection processes and determine the shortlists.

The CEO role requires experience, skills and attributes that are agreed upon by the organisation's board. A nomination committee is then appointed to assess internal and external candidates. These committees select the type of consultant I describe to assist them. Sadly, despite what would appear from the outside to be a robust and transparent process, the best candidates do not always win the prize.

It takes drive, competence and guts to put up one's hand for these roles, especially those that involve leading large global organisations. Relevant experience, maturity and, critically, the right leadership attributes are also prerequisites to being considered suitable. Qualifications and career success alone will not get you past the first post. It is the 3 Qs at the heart of this book that provide the answers regarding suitability.

Despite this, I can think of more than one occasion where the best internal candidate was unsuccessful. Why did they fail? You might be thinking it was because they lacked the right experience; not all their references were as glowing as expected; their psychometric assessment revealed an unattractive trait; their manner was incongruent with what was portrayed in their CV; or perhaps their interviewing skills let them down.

No, it was none of these. It wasn't anything they did or did not do. It was not what they said or how they said it. Nor was it what their referees said about them. In fact, they never stood a chance.

I'm reminded of the appointments of the chief executive officers of two global organisations. In each instance, there was a lack of transparency that involved the incumbent chief executive, aided by some of his close colleagues and a couple of pliant board directors, stitching up the process to ensure his man from outside the organisation was appointed. This enabled him to reap rewards as he continued to influence from behind the throne after vacating it.

These are stories about ego, greed, control and dishonesty. Most depressingly, they are about doing whatever it takes to ensure the best candidates do not have a chance of being considered seriously, let alone selected. They are also about boards being blinded by a strong chief executive and by the excitement and apparent prestige of appointing external candidates, often with disappointing results.

In one of these cases, the best candidate with the most compelling vision and strategy, as confirmed by the external recruitment consultant, was a woman. She was also among the group's highest producers globally. To thwart her chances, unfounded and unpleasant rumours about her behaviour with a colleague on a business trip were spread around the senior ranks. It wasn't long before they reached the boardroom.

Then allegations of exceptional and unauthorised expense claims were leaked to the media. These spurious claims persisted even after they had been investigated and fully dismissed by the auditor. Needless to say, despite the recruitment consultant's recommendation, this person did not make the shortlist. Ultimately, a crony of the incumbent chief executive was appointed to succeed him. It seems that, several years earlier, the same chief executive, then this woman's line manager, had allegedly made improper advances towards her which she had rebuffed.

Borrowing from actor Tallulah Bankhead's wonderful barb, I am confident that there's less to this man, despite the external trappings of success, than meets the eye.

Is this true leadership? You be the judge.

For You ...

Organisations speak proudly of their purpose and values, as they should. However, even robust boards can have little oversight of what really goes on. Many non-executive directors are inexperienced, too busy, unwilling to rock the boat while mindful of the requirement not to interfere with the day-to-day running of their organisations. No, it isn't easy to exercise good universal governance, but you must strive to do so in whatever way you can.

Compounding the problem is that many board directors' previous careers have been formed in a world where the primary measure of success is revenue; where, under pressure from major shareholders, profit can be placed ahead of principle. As important as data and metrics are, all too often these are the limit of their attention. Behavioural compliance and accountability with purpose and values end up taking a back seat.

Until recently, those who have been wronged, especially women, have typically said nothing. They knew they would not be taken seriously by what has long been a predominantly masculine environment where one was expected to bite one's lip and neither blame nor complain. Many felt that things would never change and gave up hope. Their best option has been to move on – what I've heard described as the silent surrender.

Whistle-blowers are encouraged to come forward but few organisations provide secure and independent places where they can speak up. Instead, these brave people are often vilified, punished and even sacked for their courage.

I've risked client relationships for calling out poor behaviour. I can think of chairmen and chief executives who have been reluctant to pursue such information for fear of causing an upset or a scandal. They've also been mindful of potentially losing a top rainmaker and even their own jobs.

As highlighted earlier, I fully support the call for gender diversity on boards and elsewhere but diversity doesn't stop there. Advancing and celebrating diversity of age, background, ethnicity, education, experience, skills and personality, as well as gender, at board and senior executive levels is critical. Not only is it the right thing to do but, as I experienced with CDP, it delivers the best organisational outcomes.

Thankfully, change is afoot.

Everywhere people call for more transparent leadership and, through social media, we have a louder voice. The spotlight is starting to shine into the dark corners. Shareholders, employers, employees, customers and society more broadly are becoming better informed about bad behaviour. They are questioning how these rogue activities can occur and demanding that the perpetrators be called out and punished.

Those at the top are now listening. Parliamentarians, mandarins, board directors and senior executives are finding their backbone. They are beginning to acknowledge their responsibilities, step up and take action as true leaders.

There also needs to be greater clarity and rigour about the purpose and function of the 'Office of the CEO'. A solution that I have seen work well is to make it a development opportunity for emerging talent. Not unlike my own role as ADC to the UK Chief of the Defence Staff years ago, appointees should serve no more than two years. This avoids any perception that it's a career in its own right.

AQ in Practice

- The best person does not always win
- Organisations are always bigger than individuals
- There is never room for ego or bad behaviour: let them go! No one is irreplaceable
- Be aware of and strive to overcome the biases and prejudices that you may hold
- Recognise talent beyond the limitations of your own horizons
- Diversity is not simply about numbers or quotas
- Real diversity comes in all colours, types, shapes and sizes; encourage it and benefit from the creativity it delivers
- Boards are responsible for organisational culture, behaviour and governance
- Imagine that a colleague or employee is a sister, brother, daughter or son of someone you know. Or even your own. How would you want their boss to treat them?

Your 21+90 Days Habit-Forming Challenge:

Be sure to offer your heartfelt congratulations and encouragement to someone, whoever they may be, on their achievements, however small.

AQ: The Quality of Authenticity in Summary: Being Our Trustworthy 'Who'

The four core AQ strengths, main traits and behaviours:

Character: Revealing our reality, essence and individuality

Authenticity: living and sharing our personal values, beliefs and feelings
Awareness: understanding and managing ourselves appropriately
Humility: recognising that no one is perfect, including ourselves
Integrity: knowing, saying and doing what is right
Courage: stepping up to a challenge even when we may fail
Vulnerability: revealing we are imperfect, uncertain or wrong

Confidence: Believing in ourselves and having others believe in us

Attitude: ours alone and up to us every time
Belief: what we stand for
Energy: how we build and drive momentum
Enthusiasm: infectious and so we must share ours
Adaptability: recognising when to do things differently
Optimism: giving others hope

Competence: Employing our capability and capacity

Skills: what we can do
Knowledge: what we know
Experience: what broadens our perspective
Acumen: how we analyse situations and apply insight
Judgement: how we decide
Intuition: balancing risk assessment with our gut feel
Creativity: thinking outside the box

Consistency: Doing as we promise every time

Values:	guiding our behaviour, always
Congruence:	being the leader we want to see in others
Role model:	walking the talk and talking the walk
Reliability:	being accountable and delivering as expected
Resilience:	persevering and maintaining course
Discipline:	sticking to the agreed rules

EQ – The Empathic Leader:

Sharing Your Respectful 'How'

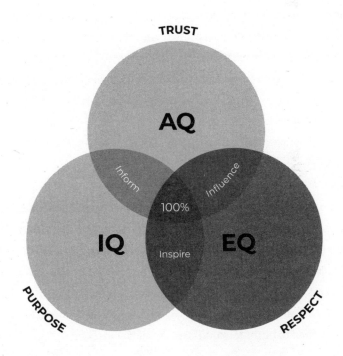

Once you are at ease, you can let go and give 100 per cent of yourself to those around you. This is what they expect and need of you as a true leader. It's what matters to them if they are to rely on you, feel valued and buy into you.

Very early in my military career, my commanding officer counselled me: 'Larry, the most important thing is to know, appreciate and value your men.

Take care of them and, through the power of human connection, respect and reciprocity, they will always be there for you.'

Of course, they were only men in those days and he was not just referring to knowing their names or roles. He meant understanding who they really were, as well as what they did.

The four strengths of EQ are engagement, empathy, encouragement and empowerment (your *pathos*).

Engagement

Engagement starts with an innate desire to reach out and spontaneously, genuinely and meaningfully connect with and seek to understand each of those around you. You must be aware of and strive to overcome your natural biases and prejudices. Yes, we all have them lurking beneath the surface. You have to want to involve all your people; to be curious about them; to understand what makes them tick. Let them feel safe, let them speak up and challenge you. Be sure they know they belong with you.

Empathy

Empathy requires observing and listening generously and without judgement. It means seeking out others' opinions, not just knowledge, noting how they are speaking and coming across, and seeking to understand why, as well as listening to what they are saying or doing. What motivates them? What are their concerns and fears? It's about appreciation, showing they matter to you and you care about them. In the words of author Stephen Covey: 'Seek first to understand, then to be understood.'

Encouragement

Encouragement is about you showing overt support and giving spontaneous feedback, including praise when due. True leaders are teachers, coaches and team players. They recognise that, to lead, they need to build a winning team. A team whose members don't just wear the same strip. They're fully present on the field, clear about their roles, want to play and to strive together for the goal in true collaboration. It's about celebrating success, being determined to learn from failure and push on.

Empowerment

Empowerment is motivating yourself and your people to succeed by creating meaning – the why (purpose) and the where (vision). Getting them to buy in and, together with you, to want to share responsibility for achieving the outcome, and to own and be accountable for their actions along the way. And it's about you relating to them, and supporting their personal contribution, development and growth. This is how you will earn and retain their loyalty. I return to the topic of loyalty later in the book.

Curiosity in Others and What's around You

Another important aspect of EQ is curiosity. Being curious encourages us to connect and understand people, to seek out their aspirations and concerns, and learn from them. This is sometimes the hardest thing for a leader because, as human beings, our natural instinct is to focus on ourselves and the task in hand, especially when under pressure. So, try to adopt a continuously curious mindset.

Of course, from time to time, you are likely to come across 'difficult' people who either disagree with your view or just do not want to engage. The temptation is to get frustrated with such people or even ignore them. Instead, you need to remind yourself that, while you believe your view is right, others have a right to have a view too!

If you are to have a chance of them coming with you, try to show tolerance and get fascinated in them instead. Everyone has their story to tell – carefully invite them to share it and discover what makes them tick. Challenging as it can sometimes be, working with people unlike you helps you grow. So, always look to play the ball with the person you're dealing with, and not the person.

The Importance of Listening.

Listening, which is more than just hearing, is another critical EQ skill. As I have pointed out, listening is voluntary; hearing is not. As leaders, if you want people to choose to listen and to buy in to you, you have to help them do so. Just because you are speaking is no guarantee they will. Perhaps you have already noticed this in your daily life? As I've indicated, the longest, most in-depth conversation each of us has throughout our lives is with ourselves. Almost every minute of every day, we are absorbed in our own thoughts and dreams. Occasionally, we even talk to ourselves. Really listening to someone else is hard, but if you are to learn, you must. It requires conscious effort and you need whoever is speaking to make it easy for you.

As I hope is becoming clear, you are not much of a leader when no one is listening. If they are not listening, they won't be following. As we have seen in the AQ section, this starts with them trusting you. EQ is about revealing your respect for them, treating them with courtesy, making them feel special and generating the raw components of successful teamwork: inclusion and belonging, coupled with the power and excitement of togetherness and purpose. For more on listening, please refer to Deep and Active Listening on page 241.

The following pages reveal how EQ is the second core quality of true leadership. Examples abound of leaders achieving real connection with others, of treating them with dignity, of motivating employees, embracing customers, persuading shareholders and engaging communities, of striving to understand what it's like to be them and responding appropriately and respectfully to what really matters to them. This is leadership communication.

The most important single ingredient in the formula for success is knowing how to get along with people.

THEODORE ROOSEVELT (1858-1919)

'Should I fire him?'
True leaders guide and support

No salutation. Just, 'Should I fire him?'

Entering Doha's Hamad International Airport on his way home, Burns had unwisely answered his cell phone. It was the president of one of our clients in Brazil.

'Oh, hi Ronaldo,' he replied. 'Sorry, can't speak now. May I call you back in about 30 minutes?'

This would not only allow Burns to get through security and passport control. It gave him time to reflect on the week he had just spent with the client's local general manager, the 'him' to whom the president referred, and the senior team. Had Burns given it, his immediate response would have been: 'No, don't fire him, Ronaldo, at least not now.' But he needed to get his thoughts together first.

These were exciting times to be in the Middle East. Oil and gas prices were high and governments, generally flush with funds, were spending large amounts on infrastructure, education, industry, tourism and other nation-building ventures. To profit from the numerous business opportunities, many Western companies had set up in the region.

The client in this story was one of these, a global property company which dominated its home market in South America. In recent years, it had expanded into Australia, China, Europe, North America, South Korea, Singapore, South Africa and the emerging markets. The company had appointed a highly successful operator to set up its fledgling Middle Eastern enterprise. This individual, Pan, was a rainmaker. He had established and built the business in Bangkok, whence he had brought some of his team.

Unfortunately, within months, it was clear that Pan was struggling to emulate his success in Asia. In his previous role, Pan had grown the business on the back of a small, tightly focused team of like-minded young experts whom he had personally recruited. Several had come with him to the Middle East. However, in his haste to grow the footprint and make an early impact on the bottom line as required by head office, Pan needed to recruit from local competitors and from outside the region.

The business expanded from the initial tight team to well over one hundred in a few short months. With their attention solely on deals, they had not had time to form into a cohesive, focused entity. The new recruits were used to their previous organisations' cultures, brought different work practices and, in most cases, had hitherto been in direct competition with each other. Their diversity, technical expertise and market knowledge went unharnessed. Inevitably, separate tribes, suspicions – and worse – developed.

While they each carried the same logo on their business cards, they operated as independent groups focused solely on what was important to them and what each needed to do to achieve it. Communication was minimal and collaboration non-existent. Pan was rarely seen or heard outside his immediate circle.

As the Middle East losses mounted, the group's board became increasingly concerned and the president asked Burns to investigate. It didn't take long for Burns to see that Pan, a smart, ambitious executive in his early thirties, was out of his depth. He spent almost all his time with a core group of young, formerly Thailand-based employees, seemingly trusting no one else.

Among the recent recruits, there were some highly qualified, well-meaning and focused young executives. They were excited to join the organisation and keen to make a difference. They could see many opportunities across the region but didn't feel empowered to pursue them. They were confused by the lack of clear goals and the strategic priorities to achieve them. In summary, there was a vacuum of leadership, purpose, direction, strategy and coordination. Burns also detected a very poor culture, low morale, little evidence of teamwork and no accountability.

After numerous conversations with a wide range of customers and employees, including several with whom Pan did not want him to engage, Burns began to form a clearer picture of what was happening or, in reality, not happening. This culminated in some tough conversations with Pan. These were followed by a day-long meeting attended by Pan and the top ten executives from across the business. While Burns understood Pan's discomfort, he shared his findings with everyone present and then facilitated a group discussion.

This resulted in a clear articulation of the business's identity: its brand and what it stood for, its values that were also aligned with those of the group. Together, Pan and his colleagues then agreed its role, its purpose in the region, and determined its vision, what success should look like. They settled on the key priorities to uphold their purpose and achieve their vision and what they each needed to do to make these happen.

Importantly, they also agreed the measures necessary to evaluate progress. Each person made three personal commitments which they all shared openly with their colleagues: first, how they would contribute to the business's financial success; second, how they would support each other; and third, how they would each role model the required leadership behaviours to uphold the agreed values and create the enterprise culture needed to drive performance.

The final step was to select a properly representative leadership team to support Pan. Given the business's short and chequered history and the personalities involved, Burns persuaded Pan that he and his executives should elect the leadership team by secret ballot. This resulted in a diverse, experienced team comprising five of those present and Pan.

Each member brought their own unique expertise and style. They committed to how they would work together to build a tightly focused and collaborative team. Individual responsibilities and personal accountabilities were agreed and the date for the first weekly leadership team meeting was set for the following Sunday, the start of the working week.

'No, don't fire Pan, Ronaldo,' Burns advised our client in Sao Paulo, outlining what had occurred over the previous five days.

'Give him at least three months ... and you must support him! Simply delegating is not enough. Frankly, it was unrealistic to expect Pan to build this business in such a short time frame without you setting clear expectations and providing guidance and support.

'I believe Pan's new team will rally round him. However, he'll benefit greatly from regular mentoring. Instead of reporting to you directly, why not have him report to Christina, the head of your European business in Lisbon? Part of her mandate and her KPIs (Key Performance Indicators) would be to help Pan grow as a true leader.'

For You ...

The quality of leadership is paramount. Just being appointed the leader will not cut it. As I've pointed out, leadership is never about position but disposition. Pan had no real experience of leadership. Working with a small team in his previous role allowed him to do what he did best: deals. Those around him had grown with him and became his trusted favourites. True leaders cannot allow themselves to pick favourites, let alone work with them exclusively, as Pan had attempted in the Middle East.

Instead of seizing the opportunity to engage with his new recruits, welcome their ideas and learn from their experiences, Pan had felt threatened by them. Had he been willing to trust them, delegate clear tasks and make them accountable, he would have quickly built a strong, cohesive and empowered team. He would also have bolstered their individual aspirations and self-esteem.

Another lesson here is the need to seek and accept guidance. Pan regarded Burns as a threat. His initial defensiveness, arising from his own recognition that he was floundering, and his fear of the consequences, made him unwilling to accept feedback and advice. Being a poor communicator, Pan also discouraged Burns from speaking with those whom he did not trust to support him.

Harbouring such anxieties inevitably results in insecurity that forces us to close in on ourselves. This encourages us to blame others for situations that, if we are to truly lead, we must acknowledge, take responsibility for, and be accountable for fixing.

To be a true leader, recognise that coaching and mentoring feature among your many roles. Based on Pan's previous track record and focusing on the growth opportunities across the region, Pan's boss had failed to appreciate that Pan was ill-equipped for the task he had been set and did little to support him.

Being technically proficient – even a highly valued rainmaker like Pan – does not automatically qualify someone for leadership. Pan's previous success had grown from applying his technical ability within his areas of expertise. He had not needed to appreciate the bigger picture or those within it. True leaders only succeed by giving 100 per cent of themselves and focusing on achieving their organisation's goals collectively. Recognising the multiplier effect of growing future leaders, they let go and empower those around them to succeed through delegation and empowerment.

EQ in Practice

- True leaders create the conditions for success
- Technical capability is insufficient for leadership
- True leaders develop their leadership by helping their people develop theirs
- Coaching and mentoring are critical leadership roles
- Give feedback and be willing to seek and respond to it, however challenging
- To build loyalty, true leaders need to respect, motivate and serve their people
- Take responsibility and then be accountable
- Beware favouritism, overcome prejudices and delegate more broadly
- When a team member is struggling, do not berate them publicly; instead, openly seek ideas on how to support them from the other members
- True leaders are multipliers and grow future leaders

Your 21+90 Days Habit-Forming Challenge:

New leaders and subordinates need advice, guidance and coaching. As their boss, it's your responsibility to provide it. And be willing to seek advice yourself.

'I don't want to be your friend!'
Curiosity and engagement matter

It never ceases to amaze me that people in senior roles seem to forget that they have not always been so. Status is one of my pet-hate words! Others are entitlement and privilege. I was fortunate in my upbringing and perhaps, compared to some, my family would have been regarded as privileged. But this was certainly not how I was I brought up. There was no sense of position or entitlement in my or my siblings' lives.

It has always been made clear to me that, coupled with self-belief, a good dose of humility and a respect for my fellow human beings are fundamental for a fulfilled and successful life. As I commented earlier, we will never succeed alone. We need others to choose to believe in us, support us and come with us. Again, nobody has to! Like listening, following is voluntary.

As we have seen in the AQ section, the first step is to be at ease with ourselves. Next, we need to make the effort to engage, listen and appreciate others – to discover what matters to them, seek to understand their dreams and their concerns and identify what makes them tick.

The tendency for most of us is to focus on the task in hand and to lose perspective, especially when the pressure is on. This is what my associate James found when working with François, the chief executive of a major European bank.

The bank was about to announce that it was seeking to grow its micro business loan book – lending to small businesses that were looking to borrow up to €2m.

James sat patiently as the chief executive ploughed through the dense script which had been prepared by the bank's communication department ahead of his upcoming media briefing.

'Frankly, François,' James sighed, 'I don't know why I'm listening to all this. Then I remembered, you're paying me.' Well, perhaps not after that interjection, he reflected, observing the bemused expression on our client's face!

James had been trying to explain the power of sincere, deliberate engagement. He was encouraging the chief executive to reach out, look him right in the eye and speak directly to him.

'Make me the most important person in your life right now, François,' urged James.

He was! There was no one else present, after all. Unfortunately, the client did not see it that way. He was entirely focused on the what, the words on the pages in front of him, rather than to whom he was speaking and why.

'Put the script aside and really convince me, François,' James encouraged.

'I don't want to be your friend!' the CEO protested.

'Really?' James replied. 'Let me put it this way. I understand you're seeking to increase your micro business loan book. My partner and I bank with a rival institution and, right now, we're talking about doubling our company's loans. If we proceed, it will take our borrowings to €1.8m, a not insignificant commitment for us. Why would you not want to be my friend now, François?'

Nodding slowly, he agreed that, as the sole representative of the bank present, he would indeed like James to be his friend and become a customer of his bank.

Thus encouraged, François moved from presenting and telling to communicating and sharing. His manner changed too, from overly formal to more personal, warmer, even intimate. He no longer simply informed James as before. Once he recognised the opportunity, François became a leader of thought and sought to influence his listener. And, yes, he even inspired James to consider changing banks!

For You ...

Existing and potential clients, customers, investors, advocates and employees are all around you. Your personal brand or reputation and that of your organisation is permanently on. Do you always measure up? Do you regularly see events as opportunities to explore, or merely as activities to endure? Is your focus too narrow, on yourself and the matter in hand? Do you overlook the need to really connect and engage with those around you?

True leadership is never about the event but the opportunity. For your own and your business's success to be sustainable, it can only be predicated on you reaching out to others and enabling theirs.

EQ in Practice

- Show genuine interest in others
- Be curious and seek to understand
- Make the effort every time
- Connect and move those around you
- Reach out and give more of yourself
- Think sentiment as well as substance
- Maintain perspective
- Opportunities are all around you

Your 21+90 Days Habit-Forming Challenge:

Treat everyone you meet as a potential customer, employee, owner or referee.

'This is why you're the boss!'
Connection through vulnerability and vision

We can become overwhelmed by situations and by the volume of information around us. We can also find ourselves taking positions where we become increasingly entrenched. In part, this is due to the encouragement of others such as well-intentioned (or sometimes not so well, as I've indicated in a previous story) professional advisors. It can also be due to our position and personality, which can influence us to see things solely from our own perspective.

Disagreements often start here. A wedge forms between the parties; it drives deeper, resulting in their interactions becoming more and more fractious. I imagine the backstory about the Firestone–Ford break-up, to which I referred earlier, took this path. The result was that a highly successful and mutually profitable business relationship ended with considerable unpleasantness over one hundred years after it had begun.

The newly appointed head of the Middle Eastern division of a large, global industrial conglomerate found himself in such a situation. A disagreement had blown up as a result of his business allegedly failing to fulfil an important aspect of a large contract with one of the Gulf state governments. The alleged misdemeanour had occurred a couple of years earlier and the new president was now having to deal with it. Worse, the matter was now in the hands of a high-profile, international law firm appointed by his head office in the United States.

The president's eyes glazed over as he sat back on the comfortable sofa in his office and contemplated another multi-page missive from the lawyers' Manhattan office. Soon his eyes closed and he began to dream. A vaguely familiar voice came into his head: 'You can put an end to this, Mohamed. This is why you are now the boss.'

All Mohamed's predecessors had been expatriates from overseas. This was the first time that the group had appointed someone from the region to lead the business. One of the reasons the board chose Mohamed was the new strategy that we had helped him articulate when he was being considered for the role. The mission he proposed for the business was for it to contribute to and participate in the professional, economic and cultural development of the entire region. His vision was for his business to be recognised as the leader in its category through delivering these impacts.

The voice continued as Mohamed dreamed: 'Do you really think you will win this conflict by pursuing the current course? Yes, yours is a large global enterprise and you have an impressive array of lawyers on your side. Do you not think this state government can hire some pretty fancy legal advisors too? They can probably afford to drag this out as long as they wish.

'This will likely result in not only a very long and expensive battle but a significant threat to your corporate brand in the region over the long term. It will also become a huge distraction as you set out to take the business forward in what are already challenging circumstances.'

'What do you suggest?' Mohamed heard himself whispering semi-consciously.

'Well, start by reflecting on why you were given this role, Mohamed,' came the response.

'You are born and bred of this region. You speak the language and understand the culture. You are passionate about the region's growing success in the world and how your business may best contribute. You're now its leader and you genuinely care about making a real, sustainable difference.'

'This is true,' Mohamed thought as he tossed and turned on the sofa, the increasingly familiar voice still in his head.

'Is that Burns?' wondered Mohamed out loud as the voice continued.

'Be the real leader you are, Mohamed. Step up and, yes, it's time to take a risk, and one without much downside. In fact, quite the reverse. You see, I imagine this state government sees your business as just a subsidiary of a large multinational run by executives who are parachuted in for a few years, have no long-term commitment to the region and whose sole ambition is to make as much money as they can before they return home.

'Now that this disagreement has arisen, through your Western lawyers you've been reinforcing this perception by playing hard ball. Unsurprisingly, the government is now doing the same. You need to change the game. Move from confrontation to conversation.'

The voice advised Mohamed to meet with His Excellency the sheikh, the head of the disputing government department. By making this personal approach and openly revealing the human face of his business, Mohamed was told the sheikh would be intrigued and willing to listen. Of course, arranging such a meeting would probably take time.

'I mean, really listen', the voice continued. 'Be determined to fully understand the sheikh's grievances. Without necessarily agreeing, you must acknowledge them and empathise with him. Resist trying to provide a solution too early. Your bosses and the lawyers must understand that, by letting his government down, your company has embarrassed him personally. Encourage him to share how he feels and show him you understand.

'Share something of your background. Then, explain your business mission and ambition. I am sure these are aligned with what the sheikh and his peers seek for their countries and the region. I am also confident that, hearing you speaking in his own tongue as you espouse your higher purpose and what it means for the region, he will start to see you and your organisation in a very different light.

'So, first, get the lawyers to back off. Then reach out to the sheikh's office. I suggest you work with your local advisor Yussuf to gain access to the sheikh himself. Yussuf has contacts at the highest levels within that government. It won't happen overnight. Be patient and persevere!'

Mohamed awoke from his fitful doze. Opening his eyes, he looked around: no one. The familiar voice had gone but he recalled every word and did as he'd been advised. He persuaded his overseas bosses to pause the lawyers' letters. After three months and several fruitless visits to the neighbouring state's government offices, he and Yussuf finally met with the sheikh at his palace. More visits and several conversations ensued and a deal was struck.

The outcome? The multinational settled out of court for a small fraction of the amount originally claimed by the government. The company's brand was safe and, without the distraction, the president was able to lead the local business forward to uphold his mission and pursue his vision. Today, the Middle Eastern division is the fastest growing and most profitable among all its group peers.

For You ...

We usually know the right, ethical thing to do. However, it's rarely the easiest way forward. All too often, we hesitate, become the victim of circumstance and increasingly risk-averse. Well-intentioned but narrow-minded and task-driven third parties become involved and play to our ego ... and our fears. Very soon, we are following rather than leading. We become entrenched, lose perspective and fail to see the wood for the trees.

This is when we need that inner voice that encourages us to reflect on our sense of purpose, on who we really are and the difference that we, as true leaders, must make. Then we need to take control and get on with it, even if it means taking a risk, eating some humble pie and, yes, perhaps failing.

EQ in Practice

- 'He enters through the other's door and comes out his own': St Ignatius of Loyola (1491–1556)
- Connection through vulnerability and vision
- Face a crisis head on and deal with it yourself
- Reputation is always more valuable than the bottom line
- Resorting to litigation is the last resort and usually the most expensive
- Everyone maintains relationships through meeting, engaging and conversing
- When you are prepared to give, you will often get
- Trust yourself: taking risks can bring rewards

Your 21+90 Days Habit-Forming Challenge:

However difficult the situation, strive to maintain interpersonal connections with colleagues, suppliers, customers, other stakeholders and family.

'May I make a suggestion, sir?'

Succeeding together

Memories of nearly failing the assault course in my first week of officer training and of the lesson learned remain with me today. At the outset, I was shown the course and then given three minutes to complete as many obstacles as I could. About a minute in, I was still struggling with the first. I was fixated and became increasingly frustrated. Eventually, one of the instructors told me to leave it and move to the next.

The lesson? While the overall objective does not change, the way to achieve it can and sometimes must. Recognising this and being prepared to adapt is critical for leaders to truly lead.

Almost a year later and just a few weeks into my role as a platoon commander, I was both excited and a little nervous. I was about to brief my 'direct reports', a couple of lance corporals and a lance sergeant. While roughly their age, perhaps a little older in one case, I was under no illusion that these young men were more battle-hardened than me. While I was now an officer, each of them had already been in uniform for several years having joined up in their teens.

A unique aspect of the military is how it builds up its people. Focusing on aptitude, personality, temperament and skills, it creates individuals at every level whose honed attributes, combined with specialist technical and leadership training, result in diverse and highly effective teams of leaders who easily adopt what is often referred to as 'shared leadership'. Like me, the people facing me were graduates of this process and now the leaders of my team. I was theirs.

Adding to the pressure was the hulking shape of my second-in-command, the platoon sergeant. Sergeant O'Connor was an experienced military man of few words who now sat to the side of the tent observing – was that a grin or a grimace? In his early thirties, O'Connor had seen several 'young puppies' like me come and go. All too often, he had rescued them from making total fools of themselves. Doubtless, he was wondering if he'd need to do so again that day.

Minutes earlier, with two of my fellow platoon commanders, I had been briefed by our company commander on the overall situation, the battle plan, our company's mission and, finally, my platoon's task. I had written it all down in great detail. Back in my tent with my notes, I had got out my still clean manual from the training academy to help me put together my battle plan. So it was that I now faced these three eager young men, each looking at me expectantly.

I described the situation, our battalion's role and our company's mission. Now for 11 Platoon, our platoon! There was silence as I ploughed on through my plan: 'Corporal O'Flaherty, I want your section to ...', 'Lance Sergeant Dwyer ...' and so on. I then invited their questions. There were none. The silence was deafening as they looked at me and then at each other. Still nothing.

I was about to encourage them to get back to their men and ready for the off when the youngest of the three spoke up. 'May I ask a question, sir?'

'Yes, Corporal Collins,' I replied.

The lance corporal ran through the key elements of my plan and checked that he'd got them right. I agreed.

'May I make a suggestion, sir?'

'Yes, of course,' I replied.

And with that, Collins, who was a year or so younger than me but had already served for at least four years, redesigned about half my plan. It quickly became clear to me that his suggestions were not only viable, they would also give us a better chance of delivering the outcome we had been tasked to deliver.

When the lance corporal had finished speaking, I thanked him and asked the others for their thoughts. They barely spoke but the looks on their faces told me that they were in full agreement with their colleague.

'Well, I must say that it all makes good sense, Corporal Collins. Thank you. I think we should adopt your suggestions.' I put down my notes, went to the board and sketched out the revised plan, checking with the lance corporal as I went.

'What do we think?' I asked of all three when I finished. They said nothing but all nodded and I could sense their relief. Corporal Collins had likely saved the platoon from almost certain disaster!

'Very good, sir. We will be ready to move in 30 minutes,' they replied in unison. Each rose and headed out of the tent to ready their men for the ensuing affray.

After they had gone, Sergeant O'Connor, who had not spoken a word throughout, looked me right in the eye and said: 'Well done, sir. Your first lesson in leadership... passed.'

For You ...

I think we can easily be confused by the word leadership. Phrases like 'leading the field' or 'leading the pack' suggest that the leader must always be out in front, the first across the line, the goal scorer, the sole winner ... or just located in the big corner office. That their ideas, words and directions cannot be challenged.

As we have seen, those in leadership positions cannot rely on personal competence alone. The role is multifaceted; true leaders are enablers and facilitators. They create the conditions for success. They gather the best people they can around them and determine the way forward. They provide the environment where their people feel both safe and empowered to speak up, to question when necessary, to collaborate and to contribute their all to delivering the best outcome.

As I've also pointed out, leadership is not championship and leaders are not perfect. No one is! Successful leaders are team players and the leader is rarely the most technically able on the team. Does the captain of a cricket or football team always score the most runs or goals? Of course not. To succeed as a true leader, you certainly need to strive to do your best. You also need to reach out and wholeheartedly engage with the others around you, be willing to learn from them and move forward together.

Respect is not about being in constant agreement but being willing to listen, acknowledge and understand disagreement. This story demonstrates the constant need for every leader to maintain self-awareness, to seek the involvement of others, to encourage different or even opposing views, to listen, be responsive, flexible and prepared to change. Based on information, perception and gut feel, the leader then needs to make a judgement and decide the course of action.

I have seen people in leadership roles trying to demonstrate that they're the smartest people in the room as they unilaterally seek to impose their solution. Perhaps you have too. I'm reminded of a comment attributed to Nobel Prize-winning geneticist and biophysicist James Watson and others: 'If you're the smartest person in the room, you're in the wrong room!'

When wanting to get the attention of a group of genuinely clever people, I sometimes do so by starting with: 'While conscious of being the most stupid person in the room, I wonder if ...'. It's usually true and it works! They listen and, quite often, accept my points of view. However smart you are, why not give this a go yourself?

You cannot know it all. Be comfortable enough to reveal your shortcomings and recognise the knowledge and experience of others. Seek out, listen to and be open to the opinions of those around you first before making a decision. This reinforces teamwork and builds loyalty, even if you don't agree with or adopt their ideas. It also demonstrates a healthy degree of humility. As I have already indicated in this book, and have stressed to several very senior clients over the years, humility is not a sign of weakness. It just takes awareness, courage and true leadership.

EQ in Practice

- True leaders play for and with their teams
- A high-performing team is about trust, purpose, goal, engagement, action, accountability and mutuality
- Again, it's always about disposition, never position
- Be willing to accept you don't know it all, nor do you need to
- Good ideas come from everywhere, especially the front line
- Be open and listen carefully to what others have to say, then decide, explain and move forward
- Strategy is a three-syllable word for plan. Either way, you need one but be willing to flex and adapt it as circumstances change
- Operations, initiatives and tactics are how you execute the plan and deliver

Your 21+90 Days Habit-Forming Challenge:

Make your people feel safe and encourage them to speak up, question your ideas and put forward their own.

'Every occasion is an opportunity'
Leadership is 24/7

We have been privileged to help organisations around the world prepare for some challenging competitive bids. On one occasion, our client's global president was due to join the team at dinner in Montreal on the eve of the pitch. The team had worked hard for several weeks. They had prepared copious printed materials. They had planned and rehearsed ahead of several meetings with their prospective client. Now they were just hours away from their critical final pitch to the prospect's senior executives.

Everyone was tired and also excited. While the opposition was certainly strong, our client was quietly confident that they had a good chance of winning. The private room had been booked at a local restaurant; both the pitch team and the support team were there. The local country general manager was the host.

Everyone sat around the rectangular table. The president, who had just flown in from London, was seated in the middle on one side; the general manager sat on his left and the bid team leader on his right. Burns found himself seated opposite the general manager. A young executive, a member of the pitch team, sat on his left and the local business development manager on his right.

As the dinner proceeded, Burns became increasingly concerned. The president spent most of the time looking at his mobile device. When he wasn't, he was in deep conversation with the country general manager. Occasionally he made a few comments to the team leader. Not once did he appear to look beyond his cell phone or his two most senior colleagues either side of him.

Burns could sense the disappointment around the table. He tried unsuccessfully to motion to the team leader that he might swap seats with a more junior member of his team. Other than the president and the general manager, everyone around that table had worked hard to get the company in such a strong position in this contest.

Yet here was their ultimate boss, who would be joining many of them in the prospective client's boardroom the next day and to whom each looked for recognition, support and inspiration – and he was ignoring them! Their local leader also seemed oblivious. Instead, he was taking every opportunity to monopolise his president to the exclusion of his own people.

A senior client once told me how she had not forgotten the impact of a chief executive or similar dropping by a junior-level meeting. Or just walking the floor and stopping to chat informally with a few employees at the water cooler or coffee station. She recalled the powerful effect it had had on her when she had been a junior employee.

In my military days, I would always judge the worth of a senior officer when visiting the troops in the field. At the risk of muddying his boots or uniform as he stepped from the helicopter, did he spontaneously jump into a trench or the back of an APC, an armoured personnel carrier, and readily engage with one or two of my young guardsmen? Or did he remain aloof, speaking only with my company commander, my fellow officers and me?

Back at the dinner, something had to be done. Having met the president previously and knowing he had been in Europe, Burns felt sufficiently confident to reach out across the table and ask him a question.

'How was your trip, Neil?'

'Fine, thanks,' came the response.

Having got the president's attention, Burns persisted. Gesturing to the woman seated on his left and directly opposite the president, he said, 'I'm not sure you've met Angela, a core member of the pitch team, Neil. She'll be seated next to you in the client's boardroom tomorrow.'

At last, the president made an effort to refocus his attention and engaged with Angela. Encouraged by this, Burns rose from his seat and spoke discreetly with the team leader suggesting that he swap seats with a more junior team member. Burns also motioned to the business development manager, Laurent, to take his seat next to Angela so that he would come within Neil's view.

The evening continued and everyone began to feel included, as they should. After all, other than Burns, each person present was an employee of the same organisation and, excluding the president and general manager, a hard-working member of this crack team that aspired to win the deal the next day. As they did.

For You ...

Whenever our senior clients are visiting one of their organisation's premises around the country or the world, we always encourage them to allow time to visit at least part of the local office, factory or plant. This provides the valuable opportunity to engage with more junior members of the local workforce and not just meet with senior colleagues and important customers.

On this topic, why not make a habit of walking around your own premises and getting to know some of your colleagues in other parts of the business from time to time? Even those visits to the restroom every few hours can provide the opportunity to take a different route when walking to and fro.

Sometimes senior executives are called upon with little or no notice to speak at company events or gatherings. Many are stuck for words. To help, we've encouraged them to put together a simple crib sheet which they can keep on their mobile device for easy reference.

I encourage you to do the same. It should contain your organisation's purpose, values and vision, its strategic priorities, the most recent publicised financial results and your own division or team contribution. It should also include a single, relevant message for the quarter supported by one or two pertinent anecdotes.

During the height of the Covid-19 pandemic, when restrictions required many of us to work from home, we regularly encouraged senior executives to connect with their most junior employees, informally and whenever possible. After the initial shock, receiving an unexpected telephone call at home from a 'big boss' can do wonders for morale, especially for those living alone.

EQ in Practice

- Good business etiquette demands that, as leader, you set the tone
- True leaders leave their egos at the door and make others feel number one
- Your people have expectations of you so don't let them down
- Make the effort to connect
- Communication is 80 per cent of a leader's job so be sure to carry and play your ACE: *Attitude to Communicate Every time*
- Senior leaders easily forget the positive impact they can make
- Be interested in everyone, not only the senior people
- Give each of them your individual attention wherever possible
- Don't get caught out! Put together your quarterly crib sheet – and keep it updated!

Your 21+90 Days Habit-Forming Challenge:

Make the effort to reach out to the most junior and newest members of your team or department and ask how he or she is feeling. Look them in the eye and really listen to their answer.

'Where did you get that tie?'
Pull, don't push

The corporate video had already blown its budget sixfold. And the rushes were still being worked on daily in the editing suite in Soho, London, often well into the small hours. My boss and account director at CDP was becoming very nervous. How would we make any money on this job? Worse, how would he explain a loss or even the possibility of a default to our managing director?

There had been considerable hesitation higher up the agency about this job. It was felt that this was not the sort of client we wanted in the fledgling corporate division. People were beginning to ask how we could have let it come to this.

The relationship began innocently enough. We had won the global advertising account of a major energy company headquartered in the Arabian Gulf. It was pretty heady stuff for our new start-up but, in many ways, alien to the 'mothership' CDP's more regular FMCG (Fast-Moving Consumer Goods), fashion and automotive clients.

Adding to the challenge was the client's marketing director. Living between the Gulf, the South of France, where he owned a magnificent villa, and London's Knightsbridge, Omar was certainly not typical of his ilk among the agency's other clients! Not only did he resemble his actor namesake, the late Omar Sharif, but he also fancied himself as a film director. In each location where the crew was filming, from Houston to London, Lagos to Doha, Kuala Lumpur to Darwin and elsewhere, Omar would arrive on location and make suggestions.

The highly regarded director and crew whom we had hired took it all in their stride. However, what had been planned as one or two days' shooting in each location ran well over. By the time filming was completed, the original schedule of 16 days had extended to almost five weeks. And now, what should have been a couple of days in the editing suite, down the road in Wardour Street, was already seven days at around 18 hours per day. I'm sure you get the picture.

Of greater concern was that Omar, while a fastidious payer during all aspects of the global ad campaign hitherto, had not yet paid the deposit for the corporate video. 'Has he actually signed the contract?' asked the agency's finance director. No one could be sure and no signed copy could be found. Clearly, we had a serious problem. Being partly responsible for the account, I realised that it couldn't continue unresolved.

To do so, we needed to think a little differently. Were we not the world's hottest creative shop? We thought about all the conversations we'd had with Omar and where they had taken place. We tried to identify what really mattered to him, not only as a senior executive but personally. Relationships were at the heart of everything he did. He would feel insulted if we started to chase him for the money or even suggest signing the contract at this stage. In his part of the world, one's word is still one's bond and a handshake its contract. 'Do you no longer trust me?' he would ask.

Omar was keen to become a member of a very exclusive, private social club in London where the waiting list was long and acceptance for membership difficult. I also remembered him talking with great pride about some high-fashion boutiques that he owned.

Under the eponymous brand 'Omar', these shops were located in several major cities and expensive resorts around the world. He had recruited a designer from Milan and often worked with him to come up with some of the accessories. Omar clearly felt he had a creative bent. I knew he had an ego.

It was agreed that I should travel to see Omar at his office in the Gulf. I stayed at the Hyatt next door and, after breakfast, went in search of a tie. My choice of hotel was deliberate, as was the decision to buy a new tie. One of the Omar boutiques was situated in the arcade below. With a very elegant and, yes, expensive silk tie around my neck, I headed for the company's executive suite at the very top of what was then one of the region's tallest buildings.

The view from Omar's office was spectacular. He smiled as he rose to greet me, looked me straight in the eye and shook my hand warmly. He could certainly turn on the charm. I noticed him looking at my new tie but said nothing. We sat down and spoke about his life – his family, his properties, recent travel and the business. As we moved on to the topic of the video, he suddenly stopped speaking.

'Tell me, Larry, where did you get that tie?'

Playing it cool, I replied 'What tie, Omar?'

'The one you're wearing now, of course!'

'Ah! Well, somewhat embarrassed, I realised this morning that I'd failed to pack a tie before leaving London. The hotel concierge advised that there were some shops downstairs and I would be sure to find something suitable.'

By now Omar was sitting on the edge of his chair, eager for me to continue, 'Go on,' he urged.

'After visiting a few shops, I came across a very smart boutique. It was beautifully designed with very elegant furniture and lighting. The assistant was charming and helped me choose this rather nice tie. Do you like it, Omar?' I continued.

'Like it? I love it! You see, I designed this tie and you bought it from my boutique. Look at the label on the reverse ... *OMAR*! Thank you.'

'Gosh!' I exclaimed, feigning surprise. 'You have excellent taste, Omar. Yes, it really is a very nice tie.'

For You ...

You may be finding all this a bit nauseous.

My point is simple. Again, get into your customers' – and your people's – shoes. Although less common nowadays, even wear their ties!

Strive to understand them and to see the deal or project from their perspective. Knowing what really matters to your customers, your clients, your people and your broader stakeholders is critical if you are to succeed in bringing them with you and achieve your ambition – and helping them achieve theirs. This is what true leaders do. Some creative thinking and playing an ego can also mean that you come up trumps.

As I've also reminded you, heart is just as important as head – or even more so. If we had sat down with Omar and tackled him on the unpaid deposit and exploding budget, or simply sent him a bill, do you think he would have happily paid up?

And the club membership? Yes, with some help, that was arranged too, but only once all the bills had been paid and the video was on-air.

EQ in Practice

- Pull, don't push
- Know what matters to your people, customers and other stakeholders
- Challenge yourself to think differently
- Human connection and instinct will help you win almost every time
- Never discount your natural, human charm ... and sense of fun!
- Be sure the feeling you're creating is the one you want to leave them with and have them act upon
- While all of us may justify with reason, we almost always decide on emotion
- People remember feelings long after they've forgotten the facts

Your 21+90 Days Habit-Forming Challenge:

Having done your homework, seize the initiative and give it a go.

'Where's the approval for the next stage?'
Perspective and patience pay

This story demonstrates patience, engagement, empathy, curiosity, mutual purpose, perspective and focus – all important true leadership traits.

Burns had been working with the Swiss division of a leading international consulting firm for a while. He greatly valued the relationship and they appeared to tolerate him. Soon after starting this work, Burns met with the senior partner, Alessandra.

'I really can't think why I'm still working here, Alessandra. I can only assume that, with so many brains around the place, you need my brawn to balance things out!' Burns said half-jokingly.

'Yes, something like that,' replied Alessandra laughingly. 'You see, we're highly process-driven whereas you are all about outcomes. We need to be challenged to cut to the chase and to focus on the why and the where, not just the what and the how. You bring clarity to situations and this, combined with your relentless focus on the human aspects, is valuable.'

It was Friday and Burns was meeting with two of the firm's young consultants in the Zurich office. 'You will be very proud of us,' exclaimed one of them as they entered the room.

'I'm always proud of you and of the opportunity your firm gives me to work with you all,' Burns replied to the young woman and young man in front of him. Neither was a partner but both would likely be soon. 'OK, tell me about it,' he continued.

'Well,' began Birgit, the senior of the two, 'we've been leading a team on a major transformation project with a large industrial corporation. Gabriel and I met with the chief executive officer and the head of strategy on Tuesday. The meeting had been scheduled a while ago. Its main purpose was to run through the final loose ends of the current project and to get their sign-off on the next phase.'

'The second phase is worth another two million Swiss francs in fees,' chipped in Gabriel. Burns detected a sigh of disapproval from his colleague. He fully understood the unwritten rule that the fees paid by the firm's clients and even its clients' identities were never to be disclosed.

Birgit continued, 'We had put together a very well-thought-through deck of slides, prepared with the firm's typical intellectual rigour, clear logic and process discipline. It was late, the client meeting was at 9am the next morning and we were about to pack up and go home when we both looked at each other and, in unison, shouted out, "Who, Why and Where *before* How, What and When!"'

Burns laughed on hearing one of our key tools being so confidently articulated by the young consultants.

'You see, we were focused on demonstrating the value we had created for the organisation as a result of the current project. We were also working on how to pitch the next phase. We had forgotten that a few things had changed since this meeting was first scheduled.

'Most importantly, we had overlooked the fact that the CEO and strategy director were planning to visit some of their subsidiaries and suppliers in Asia and the US. They were also intending to meet with several of their biggest customers and some of the larger institutions that invest in their business.'

'Happily, we remembered your advice and changed direction!' added Gabriel.

Birgit nodded. 'Yes, that's right. The next morning, we sat down in the chief executive's office and left the slide packs in our cases. I opened the meeting with, "Great to see you Damian, and you, Petra. How was your trip?"'

Their clients had replied with some short positive statements and then looked at Birgit and Gabriel expectantly.

Birgit continued, 'You'll recall that today's meeting was scheduled a while ago. The purpose was to update you on the current project and seek your go-ahead for the next phase. We've brought some materials along.

'Before we get into them, Gabriel and I would much appreciate hearing more about your trip. It sounds pretty full-on. I imagine some of your conversations with those whom you met may have influenced your thinking in some of the areas that we have been working on.'

With that, the consultants asked questions and probed further as they built on Damian's and Petra's answers. Listening carefully, they were able to get a good understanding. They learned how their clients felt about the trip and much of the information they were now sharing. Let's not forget, when we are building relationships, who does most of the talking? Not us, please!

Time went by, and, ten minutes before the meeting was due to end, the chief executive exclaimed, 'Wow, look at the time! We've not even got to your stuff, Birgit.'

'Not a problem', she replied. 'We have really enjoyed the past 45 minutes. Thank you. Importantly, we've learned a lot. Rather than rush through our slides now, we are going to leave you in peace to get on with your day. We'll head back to our office and review our materials in the light of what you have just told us. Maybe we can get together again later in a couple of days, Damian. Will that be OK?'

Birgit and Gabriel hastened back to their office in Irchelstrasse. There they met Klaus, the client lead partner. He was less than pleased on discovering that his colleagues had not returned with the new mandate approval as he had expected. Birgit stuck to her guns. She had taken quite a risk but knew it was the right thing to do. It was.

When she and Gabriel met with their clients on Thursday that same week, they presented a very different deck of slides. It had been updated with the new information gleaned from their previous meeting. It now contained more relevant detail and was better aligned with what their clients needed and wanted.

Shortly afterwards, they returned to their office and, with a spring in their step, went straight to see Klaus. Yes, the anticipated mandate had been approved and with a 30 per cent uplift in the proposed fee! No wonder they were feeling happy when Burns met them the next day!

For You ...

First, the backstory: A few years earlier, Burns had been working with this industrial company's previous CEO and his team. At that time, the company retained two highly regarded consulting firms; one was the firm in this story, now our client. Before long, the company decided to select just one firm. After a competitive pitch in which we were not involved, our client firm won.

Burns asked the industrial company CEO why. The latter told him that, while both firms had their strengths, the behaviour of the winning firm's managing partner had swung it. Over the previous years, he would occasionally drop by unannounced at meetings in his client's head office attended by some of his junior consultants and the client's project team. He would sit together with them and say little. He was there to support his people and to demonstrate that he cared. Significantly, the managing partner never used these opportunities to bother the client CEO or his senior colleagues. The latter would only discover later from their people that the firm's managing partner had unexpectedly joined them.

Some important leadership traits are listed at the start of this story. All are in play here. Others include the ability to see the bigger picture and the confidence to play the long game.

Like any relationship, business relationships take time to develop and nurture. Mutuality is at their core and whenever you start to focus on 'what's in it for me or us' ahead of 'what's in it for them', your trustworthiness and respect are questioned. As a result, you place yourself and your organisation at risk. As we've seen in the previous story, true leaders do not push. They pull.

EQ in Practice

- Perspective and patience pay
- Always place context and intent ahead of content
- Think and behave 'you' before 'I' and 'we'
- Be fascinated in others; listen and learn from them
- Silence with meaningful eye contact is inviting, reassuring and impactful
- Play the long game and be willing to change tack
- Before each meeting, ask yourself: who am I meeting with, why, and where must I take them?
- After each meeting, ask yourself: what do I need to do now and by when?

Your 21+90 Days Habit-Forming Challenge:

Be prepared to hold back, ask questions, listen, learn and, if necessary, flex before pressing on.

'Who is the most important HR person in this organisation?'

Every leader is a human resource officer

As a true leader, your sense of who you are, what you stand for and your purpose can never leave you. You must maintain a mindset that encourages you to keep your eyes, your ears and your mind open. Appraise every situation and judge how best to respond. Then deploy your authenticity appropriately as you engage with those around you in the manner they expect.

The key word here is appropriate. Let's consider these workplace scenarios.

1. If a finance colleague comes along with a worried look, you would enquire, 'Is everything OK?'

'Yes, I'm fine thanks but in a spot of bother. Our system crashed this morning. I have to get this report to the finance director by noon. Could you help?' she replies.

Of course, you're busy too and you sense this is going to require some hard graft with a basic calculator. Recognising your colleague's pain, you agree to help, roll up your sleeves and apply the most appropriate of your authentic traits to complete the task.

2. You are hard at work when there is a commotion down the corridor which gets louder. Suddenly, some workmates appear with bottles of champagne.

'We won!' they exclaim excitedly. 'Come and celebrate with us!' Despite the beckoning email inbox and the files piled in front of you, you jump up and head to the canteen, laughing and congratulating your colleagues as you go. Again, this is the authentic you, but deploying a different, appropriate set of innate traits as you put your own priorities temporarily aside and share in your colleagues' success.

3. The fire alarm sounds. Your first responsibility is your team's safety. You drop everything and move quickly to see that everyone has heard the alarm

and is present. You give clear direction regarding the evacuation routes. Your authority and your authenticity must be evident and appropriate in response, while calmly and genuinely showing selfless care for your people.

4. It's lunchtime. You are an external leadership consultant working with the chief executive of a communications company ahead of an important event where he will be giving the keynote address. The session is over and you both enter the lift and press 0. As it descends, the lift stops at various levels and you're joined by several employees. You're tempted to engage with them but are discouraged to do so by their boss's demeanour.

The first is a senior-looking executive who immediately enquires of her boss, 'Hello George, are you feeling better?'

'Yes, thanks,' comes the chief executive's expressionless reply, with no attempt to engage or even mention his colleague's name.

The lift continues its descent in silence. Another stop and the doors open again. Two more people enter, smile at their chief executive and are met with a brisk nod. Then another stop and a small crowd of younger employees enter. They are chatting noisily until they spy their boss at the rear. By now, George is deeply into his iPhone. Silence prevails until the lift finally reaches the ground level.

Being the last two to exit, you ask: 'George, have you got a moment, please?'

'Yes,' he replies.

'All this work we've been doing these past weeks is not about presentation skills. It's about leadership. You had a good opportunity to connect with some of your people just now. A couple even tried to engage with you and you brushed them off!' you say firmly.

'Ah yes, I've heard you raise your thoughts on leadership before. You really must speak with our HR people,' the chief executive responds dismissively.

Almost speechless, you follow up with, 'You just don't get it, do you, George? You are the chief executive officer. Who is the most important HR person in this organisation?'

5. In another building in the same city, a very different situation is taking place. The chief executive in this instance has recently been headhunted from overseas to turn this vast global conglomerate around. An engineer by background and with an already successful career behind him, Chuck took on what was considered one of the most challenging turnaround jobs in the world. Despite its great heritage and being hitherto regarded as a 'market darling', the company is in trouble and he has been hired to fix it.

You work in the corporation's head office and, in the lift at 12.30pm that day, Chuck encounters you and some of your fellow employees.

'Heading out to lunch?' he asks. 'We're obviously paying you too much!'

You and your colleagues look a bit taken aback. Laughing, Chuck asks, 'Hey, anyone got some good news for me? Have we had any wins this morning? I'm about to meet with some of our investors and I would sure like to give them something to smile about.'

A conversation ensues, the president and chief executive officer of this global conglomerate engaging energetically and warmly with some of his mid-level and junior staff. It continues as you all reach the lobby and head out onto the pavement.

Sitting down to lunch with the investors a few moments later, Chuck kicks off with the story of how a few of his people have identified a potentially significant administrative saving just that morning. 'This is one of the reasons why I took on the role, frankly – the passion of our people to get this business back on track.'

For You ...

As a leader, whatever the pressure, you need to respond appropriately to each situation that confronts you. Irrespective of the type or size of your organisation, as one of its leaders you are an exemplar. You set the tone. Every movement, inflection and comment are noted. It's vital that you respond to, meet and preferably exceed the expectations of those around you every time. In the words of author and professional speaker, Michelle Ray: 'Lead in real time!'

Strive to leave people better than you find them, whether that be better informed, motivated and inspired or simply feeling appreciated for their efforts that are contributing to something worthwhile. Putting a smile on people's faces is not so difficult. It's critical if you are to build loyalty.

Neither culture nor morale belong to the human resources department. Both fall squarely within the leader's domain. As I've indicated, if we give, we usually receive. Make the effort to give more of yourself and engage with those around you at every opportunity. Talk to them, listen and respond appropriately. Get to know their names and refer to them by name whenever possible. As I have mentioned earlier, I encourage senior executives, as they depart their office each evening, to greet cleaners and security staff by name and thank them for their contributions. This is what true leaders do.

EQ in Practice

- Every leader works in human resources
- Again, leadership is 24/7. Never miss an opportunity to engage and communicate
- Like you, everyone wants to be seen, heard and feel appreciated
- 'How are you feeling?', 'Are you OK?', 'Would you be open to ...?, 'I'd welcome your thoughts' are good ways to show you care and to build rapport
- A smile and a 'thank you' help too
- Be the leader you and your stakeholders want to see and hear every time
- Appropriate authenticity enables enthusiastic engagement
- Again, the best ideas often come from the front line

Your 21+90 Days Habit-Forming Challenge:

Be determined to leave your people better than you find them.

'I want at least 17.5 per cent return per annum'
Reality, humanity and collaboration

'At least 17.5 per cent!' bellowed his boss from Los Angeles and the line went dead.

'I've taken on an impossible task,' Corian sighed to himself as he contemplated another long weekend in the office.

Just a few months earlier, Corian had been sent to Shanghai to represent his American employer's global hedge fund. He had been excited at the opportunity. At just 33 with a double degree in applied maths and commerce from Sydney University and a master's in business administration from Harvard, he saw himself as one of those 'masters of the universe'.

Corian was not just above the average academically. He was also a concert pianist and spoke four languages including his native Cantonese. Corian had been born in Suzhou and, following the Tiananmen Square massacre in 1989, moved to Australia with his family when he was seven. Following Sydney and Harvard universities, he did a spell working for a well-known Wall Street investment bank in New York where he made his mark as an astute dealmaker. After a few years, missing the sun, he joined his current employer in California.

With this background, it made good sense for Corian's boss to send him to head up their fledgling operation in China. Corian arrived in Shanghai as the company's first local deal was struck. The municipal government had sold a 49 per cent stake in a large property portfolio via a public offering on the local stock exchange. It had been a controversial move since the portfolio consisted of public housing, shopping centres and car parks in low socio-economic districts.

Not surprisingly, there was a lot of public concern as to what this sale would mean for rents and prices. The prospectus had forecast a return of 8 per cent per annum. Corian's company had bought almost 30 per cent of the shares on offer, resulting in holding just under 15 per cent of the new public company. This had raised eyebrows. The hedge fund was not known for making modest returns. Its president, Corian's boss, certainly did not intend to this time.

Corian went to the window of his office in Pudong. Far below, through the rain-spattered glass, he could make out the bright lights of the famous Bund on the western bank of the Yangtze River. Representing his employer's significant shareholding, he had been appointed a director of the new real estate company and had attended his first board meeting that morning.

It had not gone well. Looking around the boardroom, Corian detected suspicion, even hostility. Each of his fellow directors was a government appointee and at least 65 years of age. His task, as had been made very clear in the telephone call, was to get the company to deliver more than double its projected financial return. To do so would likely require replacing the government-appointed chairman and chief executive.

Burns happened to be in town and, through a chance introduction, offered to help.

'You will not achieve what you want by taking them on, Corian. There are more of them than you. They each have had very successful careers and are entirely confident about what they're doing. They regard your company's shareholding as a nuisance at best and, at worst, a threat,' Burns advised.

'What should I do?' replied Corian downheartedly. 'You see, my boss will fire me if I do not shift the dial and deliver significant change.'

'I get the picture, Corian. Step back, look at the situation differently, think about the context and then reframe. The first thing to understand is that your fellow directors are not going to let you run all over them. They need to trust you, feel that you respect them and understand how your intentions may affect their mandate. Right now, they see you as a precocious young upstart who probably reminds them of their grandsons! Not surprisingly, they will not take you seriously, let alone listen to you.

'How do you build relationships, Corian?' Burns continued. 'You're not exactly friendless!'

Corian replied that relationships start by really wanting to connect and engage with people, treating them as individuals and making them the most important people in his life at that moment. That he must want to learn about them by asking questions, listening carefully, hanging on every word, and building on their responses. In other words, Corian confirmed, relationships are about them, not him.

'Agreed, Corian', replied Burns. 'Quite simply, stop being frustrated by these directors. Use your intuition and reveal more of your humanity ... get fascinated in them instead! Despite the pressure from LA, I suggest you try to take yourself a bit less seriously, let go and give them something of yourself. Be willing to declare your imperfections and behave as the notional grandchild they already perceive you to be.

'Go to their places and meet with each of them in person. Get them to talk about themselves, who they are, their lives, their achievements and what matters to them. Be curious and listen, really listen. Gently probe further, seeking to understand not just what they are saying but how and why.

'While you learn more about them, they will learn more about you. Not by you talking about yourself but through your demeanour, your questions and responses to what they are sharing with you. They will start to trust you and listen to you. As they start to feel your genuine interest in them, they will become more interested in you. Ultimately, they may even enjoy your company.

'Next, recognise that people love to give advice. What am I doing right now, Corian? You need to seek their advice as the elder statesmen they are, learn from their wisdom and respect them for it. As they warm to you, you can start to share some of your own ideas.

'Recognise that, after long and successful careers, their personal standings will be of great importance to them. If you can demonstrate that their reputations will not be at risk, that they will actually be enhanced by adopting your ideas for the company, they will be more likely to buy into your proposal.'

Corian listened carefully. While he was hoping for some form of 'magic bullet', he accepted that there wasn't one and realised that he needed to change tack. Working together over several months, Burns helped Corian plan his every move. He put the directors and their interests first, regularly meeting with each on their home turf – from southern England to Singapore and from Beijing to Hong Kong and Melbourne.

Corian built solid personal relationships by giving the directors the respect they wanted. He listened to their life stories, acknowledged their concerns and eventually, once mutual trust and respect were established, shared his dreams with them: 'Together, we can build a truly great company, the best real estate company, which all of us, and indeed all of China, will be proud of.'

Corian engaged with them, he charmed them, he inspired them and he won through. Within 18 months, the company was on track for 17.5 per cent return on equity. All this time, he kept in close contact with his boss in LA. While the latter was impatient for change, he maintained his confidence in his young employee. He also appreciated that any overt or hasty moves could damage his fund's reputation irreparably across the region.

For You ...

When working with corporations I still hear the mantra: 'Our primary focus is on increasing shareholder value.' My response is: yes, but how do you really achieve sustained, long-term shareholder value? Some form of corporate activity such as an acquisition, divestment or merger might impact the stock price favourably in the short term. Yet I imagine you can think of situations where such transactions had the opposite effect. I certainly can!

To grow your business, reflect on my earlier comment about the main reasons people leave organisations. With your organisation's values and purpose in mind, start with your people. See them for who they are, not simply for what they do. It's increasingly evident that those who feel their employers recognise that they have lives beyond the workplace are more engaged. They enjoy their work more and deliver products and services that delight customers who happily buy more. This results in increased revenues and greater profits for the business, which ultimately results in happy owners.

Furthermore, it creates loyalty at every stakeholder level. I encourage you to see that your people are happy, engaged, feel valued and are motivated by the difference they make for their customers and the business. As your business grows, so will the opportunities and rewards for everyone.

What goes around usually comes around. To get what you want requires inner confidence and a clear plan, a determination to engage with and value those around you, coupled with patience, persistence and the willingness to flex if necessary.

Again, try being fascinated in those whom you find frustrating! This is what true leaders do. Everyone wants to feel appreciated and has a story to share, so seek it out, listen and learn.

EQ in Practice

- See everything equally through the twin lenses of clarity and humanity
- Fully appreciate the context and maintain perspective
- Put together a circular 'stakeholder map' with you/your team in the middle and your stakeholders around the outside – identify the strength of each relationship and who owns it
- Your desire to make it meaningful for others is critical
- Understand what success looks like for all your stakeholders
- Again, put yourself in their shoes (and wear their ties!): what is it like to be them and what drives them?
- Be curious and still; ask questions, really listen without interruption and learn
- Think teamwork, and team with them
- And uphold 'Ubuntu'

Your 21+90 Days Habit-Forming Challenge:

Do not underestimate the power of human connection and employ yours every day!

EQ: The Quality of Empathy in Summary: Sharing Our Respectful 'How'

The four core EQ strengths, main traits and behaviours:

Engagement: Reaching out and giving our all

Connection: making the other person the most important in our lives right now

Relevance: asking ourselves 'why us?' and identifying what is in it for them

Curiosity: demonstrating our genuine interest and desire to understand and learn

Communication: sharing our ideas and seeking their feedback

Involvement: making it meaningful for them

Fairness: treating everyone the same way

Empathy: Focusing on feelings

Listening: how and when we learn from others

Understanding: about the who, the how and the why, not just the what

Acknowledgement: appreciating their feeling, issue or concern

Appreciation: what everyone wants occasionally, so show ours

Care: the sincerity we express and the experience they welcome

Feeling: how we behave and what they remember

Encouragement: Helping others believe

Support: being there for them

Praise: giving it when it's due, and publicly whenever possible

Collaboration: many minds and hands achieving more than ours alone

Team: playing for and with our fellow players

Coach: guiding them by sharing our feedback and knowledge

Inspiration: knowing that informing and even influencing are not enough

Empowerment: Giving others confidence in themselves

Meaning:	helping them understand the purpose and own the task
Loyalty:	what we give in order for us to receive
Responsibility:	understanding and embracing what's expected of us
Accountability:	accepting that the buck stops with us whatever happens
Delegation:	giving them and ourself opportunities to develop and grow
Motivation:	comes in many forms, not only material incentives

IQ – The Intentional Leader: Doing Your Purposeful 'What'

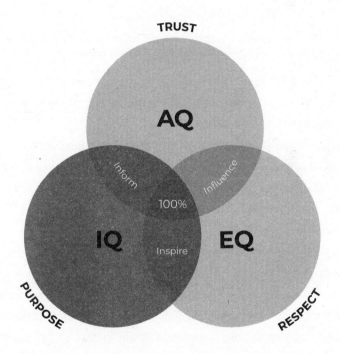

IQ starts with having a clear view of what the end state looks like. You need to own the game and be responsible for what it will take to finish; to move forward and be accountable for what happens along the way. It's where you're aiming to take your followers and what you are saying and doing (your *logos*) to get there. To ensure success, you need to think strategically with agility while maintaining perspective.

The oft-quoted military idiom 'No plan survives the first shot' is attributed to Field Marshal Helmuth von Moltke (1800–1891): 'No plan of operations extends with any certainty beyond the first contact with the main hostile force.' It reminds leaders that they may well be faced with unexpected complexity, challenges or changing circumstances along the way.

Robert Burns describes this phenomenon in his poem 'To a Mouse' (1785) as:

The best-laid schemes o' Mice an' Men
Gang aft agley

Leaders must acknowledge that, to achieve their ambition, the strategy and tactics may need to change. And, as I learned on that assault course at the start of my army career, they must have the courage and the humility to adapt and flex when required. However, whatever the pressure, leaders can never lose sight of their brand, values and purpose.

The twin lenses of clarity and humanity are fundamental to every aspect of life. Have the confidence to be clear about what you say and do and why, and what you intend to occur as a result. At the same time, recognise and manage human strengths and frailties, aspirations and fears – your own and those of the people around you.

When communicating, be clear about what you want your listeners to do. This starts with identifying the feeling you want them to take away. Yes, substance is always important but only where it's supported by sentiment. This is not only about making them feel good but what will encourage them to do good. In my experience, many people start at the wrong end. Instead of taking a deductive approach, they spend too much time 'in the weeds': focusing on their content and losing sight of their intent – and so do their listeners.

The core strengths of IQ are context, clarity, certainty and commitment.

Context

Context is about what's going on around you and maintaining perspective. It starts with who you are as an individual, a team or an organisation, what you stand for and where you are now: your core or brand; your values, strengths and shortcomings; and the prevailing situation facing you. Context is likely to include your audience, people, market, competition, investors, regulators, the economy and so forth. Context also covers why you exist, your role and the difference you aspire to make for your stakeholders: your purpose or mission.

Clarity

Clarity is the 'light on the hill'. It's about having a razor-sharp focus on where you're going and where you want to take those around you. It's what the intended outcome looks like for you and your followers – your mutual ambition or vision. When communicating, this is your simple headline message in a meeting, talk or when answering a question. It's the overarching single thought that encapsulates your big idea, the one that you want people to leave with, think about and act upon.

Certainty

Certainty is not always available. Providing it, as far as possible, to those around you, even if based only on intuition and belief, is how you are going to succeed. These are the core elements of the plan that forms your strategy and that will deliver the outcome you aspire to. When putting your argument, certainty includes the rationale, main points and supporting information that validate and substantiate your idea, point of view or headline message.

Commitment

Commitment is determining what you will actually do and having the resolve to get on with it. It's doing what you say you will do while remaining agile in how you set about achieving it. This includes the required initiatives, tactics, actions and behaviours you need to execute the plan, bring the story to life and deliver. It's also how you know you're making progress and reaching your goals along the way – the feedback, benchmarks, targets, measurement, results and KPIs.

I add two more Cs here.

Culture

While organisations require strategy, structure, policies and procedures to progress, it's the norms, behaviours and experiences that form the culture to ensure that they do. I am reminded of the dictum: 'Culture eats strategy for breakfast', attributed to management guru Peter Drucker and others.

It is culture that drives or destroys performance, rarely internal processes or external factors alone. As I've suggested, an organisation's strategy may need to change but success will only be achieved with a consistent, values-driven culture at its heart.

Culture is the living glue that binds organisations and it starts at the top. To flourish, a great culture must be constantly nurtured by leaders as its daily creators, carriers and custodians. As I have already demonstrated, true leaders set the benchmark and they consistently uphold it. This is even more important in the context of changing work practices such as the 4 Day Week and the work-from-home trends.

Challenges

Standing still and doing nothing is not a leadership option. Yet determining what to do and deciding to act is not always easy, especially when faced with confusion, complexity or uncertainty. Leaders face two sets of challenges.

The first is both tangible and rational. In the best way possible, this requires you to appreciate and interpret the situation facing you as well as all the contextual inputs. Then it's about identifying the most effective and most practical ways to respond and explaining what this means for your people. Once you have envisioned the 'light on the hill', you must develop the strategy to get there and how best to execute it, measure progress and be ready for what might hinder it.

The other area of challenge is emotional and ethical. This requires you to be aware of your personal biases, prejudices and preferences, drivers and ambitions – and your fears and shortcomings – and to resist being influenced by them.

Inevitably, you need to balance your mission with the possible consequences. Should the one override the other and, if so, which? In what circumstance might such a decision be necessary and permissible?

I've seen executives battle with this dilemma and follow the right course, sometimes at considerable risk to themselves and their careers. As I've intimated earlier, I have also witnessed the opposite. This is when senior people fail to step up and make the hard decisions. It can also be when they shamelessly pursue their personal ambitions in ways that are contrary to their organisation's values and purpose. Both failings can cost organisations dearly.

In this section, you will read about leaders who face both existing and unexpected challenges and who recognise the need for clear and sometimes urgent action. Each relies on the 'known knowns' such as their organisation's brand, values and purpose, and all are encouraged and supported by a strong culture.

Together, these attributes enable these true leaders to step up and do the right thing. Facing both known and even unknown 'unknowns', several had to make difficult decisions. By taking personal responsibility and seizing the moment, while mindful of structural limitations and organisational caution, they successfully get on with the job and meet all their stakeholders' hopes and expectations.

Effort and courage are not enough without purpose and direction.
JOHN F. KENNEDY (1917–1963)

'That's very un-"Main Co!"'
Creativity beats arrogance

'New Co' was not really a new company. It had been founded in poet William Blake's 'dark satanic mills' of England over 200 years earlier. The group's board had decided to sell this subsidiary by way of a public offering.

It wasn't the first time the group had taken this route with one of its now non-core businesses. Just a few years earlier, it had disposed of another manufacturing entity but with near-disastrous results. That 'new company' had been loaded with debt, and the safe, traditional sales campaign to attract buyers had floundered in its mediocrity and sameness. It no longer exists.

These lessons did not go unnoticed by this 'New Co's' recently appointed chief executive, Andy Krisp. Andy decided on a different tack and enlisted Burns's help.

'Ensure you are not saddled with debt and think differently about the investor marketing campaign, Andy,' he counselled.

With this clarity, Andy made a powerful case to the board regarding the debt, reminding the directors of what had occurred previously. Despite the pressure from many quarters including his boss, the group chief executive, Andy stuck to his guns, demonstrating both his resilience and his commitment to 'New Co's' success. Did they want this float to succeed, did they want to be proud of their former subsidiary as it made its way in the market? Were they really prepared to back their senior executive to lead it forward?

The board finally agreed with Andy's proposition. The go-to-market campaign was next. How would they sell a 200-year-old organisation operating in an old-style and dirty manufacturing industry seen by many as tired, and facing stiff competition from Asia as well as growing environmental challenges? Among its many product lines, the company manufactured metal roofing.

Andy invited Burns to join him at a hotel in east London where he had been holding an off-site with his leadership team. The executives had spent the previous hour discussing the marketing campaign for the company's forthcoming sale and had not yet identified what they felt should be the 'killer app'. This would be the essence of the company's market offering and would help it stand out to get the attention needed to secure a successful equity float.

The hotel's conference rooms were on the top floor and afforded a bird's-eye view of the Olympic Park nearby. Of course, the choice of this hotel was deliberate. The company had been a major supplier of materials for the construction of the many buildings that made up the venue for the much-lauded 30th Summer Olympiad.

Although the games had taken place several years earlier, the huge site still retained its energy. As Andy and Burns looked on from their vantage point, the main stadium, pool and velodrome appeared to hover above the ground.

Then it came. 'You know, Andy, steel's sexy!' Burns exclaimed. 'Look at those amazing girders, pylons and roofs of yours in front of us. They soar, they sweep, they ripple, they glisten, they float, they move, they energise, they entice, they excite! Yes, of course, they're functional. And they're also colourful, attractive, alive. Anyone would want to have a bit of that!'

They both laughed. They knew they'd hit on the line that would get the attention needed to demonstrate that 'New Co', while rooted in an old industry steeped in history, really would be a new, modern enterprise. It had a new leadership team, new values, a revitalised purpose and a clear vision. It was striving to build a culture of innovation, of inclusion, of 'one enterprise' collaboration and of energy, supported by a flat management structure and led by a youthful team of leaders. They were leaders driven by a desire to do the right thing for the environment and society as well as for their people, customers and shareholders.

As far as a steel company could ever be exciting, even sexy, 'New Co' fitted the bill. This encapsulated the brand promise it needed.

Not everyone was convinced, of course. Bursting to share the idea with the first executive they met on returning to the conference room, the CEO tested it with his new chief financial officer. Mary was speechless. 'You're both mad!' she retorted. Andy and Burns smiled. While Mary's response indicated there was work to do, they were convinced they were on the right track.

Despite her initial scepticism, Mary and the other members of Andy's leadership team bought into the rationale behind the 'steel is sexy' concept. Their excitement grew as the launch of the initial public offering approached. The 'Main Co' group communications department offered its services, which Andy politely declined.

Amid growing media interest, the big day dawned. At 8.30am, over 200 analysts and institutional investors began to file in to the main conference room at the Olympic Park. Andy had agreed to eschew the nearby City, London's financial district and traditional location for such events.

Several of the 'Main Co' group senior executives also attended, along with Andy's top team. Upbeat music filled the cavernous space and a video played as people entered, repeating every five minutes or so. The multiple screens were alive with fast-paced shots of steel roofs, gleaming structures, futuristic buildings. These were interspersed with dramatic scenes of steel furnaces, grimy smiling workers in hard hats and safety gear, happy customers and scenes from the London Olympics. It was loud, colourful and engaging.

At 9am, when everyone was seated, the doors closed, the music and video stopped and the room darkened. Just blackness and silence. Then a single spotlight shone on the centre of the stage.

'Good morning, everyone. I am Andy Krisp. Thank you for joining my team and me today.' Then a long pause. 'I am sometimes asked, why should I want to take on this job?' Another pause. 'Well, I believe that film says it all, as does this venue which we were privileged to help build. I find our steel products sexy!'

Andy stood still, smiling. You could have heard a pin drop. It was risky to speak such language publicly but Andy was determined to do so and it was clear the vast majority of those present loved it.

Before moving to the lectern and, with Mary and several of his team, introducing the formal launch of the public offering, Andy spoke off the cuff. He talked about his upbringing and early career, his journey to his appointment, his pride at his company's contribution to the Olympic Park, and his belief in all his employees, who would help take the business forward.

After it was over, the attendees filed out chatting loudly among themselves. Not everyone was happy. A serious-looking executive approached Burns. 'Hello, I am Matthew, the group head of communications. I believe you are responsible for this.'

Burns nodded.

'Well, it's all very un-"Main Co",' said Matthew haughtily.

'Thank you, Matthew. Isn't that the point?' Burns replied. 'Given what happened last time, if this public offering is to be a success, we have to do something very different. Equally important, Andy and New Co's management need something they can really believe in, get behind and drive forward together with passion, energy and commitment. They want to challenge the status quo. Sexy steel is their rallying cry. Let's support them and see how they go.'

The communications chief turned on his heel and left. The public offering was oversubscribed and, today, the stock price is more than 15 times its float price.

For You ...

Fundamentally I am a traditionalist. Yet, like the Scottish Bard, I will not hesitate to defy tradition and rebel when required. I learned in my time with CDP that a combination of clarity, creative thinking, intuition and being prepared to take risks and to fight for what one believes is absolutely necessary if leaders are to achieve the change they seek.

This is where you need to be mindful of the data and look beyond it. Remain focused on the outcome or vision and challenge yourself and those around you to constantly ask: is there a better way to get there? Almost always, there is! You must be willing to let go, embrace the need for change and innovate.

Again, focusing on reason alone will not suffice. Never forget the power of emotion. As true leaders know, it's what persuades! It's also sentiment that drives stock prices, rarely substance alone.

IQ in Practice

- Creativity beats arrogance
- Look beyond the facts
- Follow your belief
- Innovation starts with thinking differently ... is there a better way?
- Invite and respect others' opinions and persuade them to follow you as best you can
- Enjoy yourself and motivate others with your energy, conviction and enthusiasm
- Again, be willing to take risks

Your 21+90 Days Habit-Forming Challenge:

Focus on the feeling you want people to take away from all your interactions.

'We have a great little business down there!'
Principle, passion and purpose drive performance

Sometimes things just don't go right, do they? I am sure you have the occasional day or even week like this. It can happen with organisations too. This story is about a legacy business that had been in the doldrums for a while.

It was the oldest subsidiary of a large global conglomerate, so large that the group's board and senior executives had never visited their smallest entity in a far-off land. The only time that they may have been reminded of its existence was when the results were reported each quarter, but, being included in the overall division's numbers, they were hardly ever remarked upon.

Doubtless they knew that it operated an ageing plant and that its products faced a fickle market. They probably expected this small (relatively speaking) business to continue to flounder. It rarely broke even. Although it provided much-needed employment in the district, the local community constantly complained about its activities; the safety performance remained stubbornly below par; sick days were above average; and productivity was low.

Despite all this, the group was reluctant to dispose of it and head office sent Burns to work with the subsidiary's new general manager and her team. He still recalls his first impression: rundown buildings, peeling paint, weeds poking through the roadways, plants dead in their beds, unwashed vehicles with the company logo barely visible. Dirt and dust were everywhere, even in the reception area, as Burns discovered when he at last found it. The desk was unattended and the telephone on the counter went unanswered.

'What's the future for this business, Judith?' Burns asked on at last meeting the new general manager in her dingy office.

'What do you mean?' Judith replied, a little defensively. A native of the local town, she had worked for the company since gaining her engineering degree. While proud of her appointment, she was unsure of her capability to meet expectations. Unsurprisingly, she was suffering from what is often referred to as 'imposter syndrome' (I touched on this earlier).

'Well, I'm sure you have been warned: I can be an acquired taste!' Burns continued. 'You see, Judith, as a shareholder of your parent company, I'm really wondering why bother. As I understand it, your business is barely breaking even and has actually lost money in six of the past ten years. Employee injury rates are high and morale is low. The local community wants you to pack up and go away. And, while yours is a cyclical market, your customers appear to be fickle at the best of times.'

'Oh, you've done your homework, haven't you?' replied Judith, looking uncomfortable.

'Yes, and I'm here to help if you would like me to,' Burns assured her.

'OK. I'm listening,' she said cautiously.

'Well, I'm very outcome-driven, so let me put it this way. If I were to bump into Bob, your group president, the next time I visit the head office and tell him I've just been working here, how do you think he'd respond?'

'He could frown and, without any enthusiasm, say, "Oh yes, we do have a little business down there." Or instead, Bob could smile and exclaim, "Lucky you. We have a great little business down there!" Which one would you want it to be? And which do you think it would be if I were to have that conversation tomorrow?'

So began the turnaround that, 15 months later, resulted in markedly higher employee engagement, among the lowest absentee and injury rates across the entire group, happier neighbours, more satisfied customers talking about longer-term contracts, and the bottom line returning to a more positive trajectory. Furthermore, the group board decided to allocate US $50m for much-needed capital expenditure. Even the flower beds were replanted!

And Judith? Following the successful turnaround, her career progressed rapidly. Before long, she was transferred to Pittsburgh to run one of the company's joint ventures with a US manufacturer.

So how?

It required repositioning the brand, developing a new plan and creating an all-encompassing strategic narrative. This involved many discussions with employees across the business to understand what was working and what was not. There were also meetings with representatives from the local community and conversations with customers.

These meetings formed the foundation that enabled Judith and her senior team to look beyond the prevailing grim reality and to reimagine the possible: 'What could our business aspire to be, say, five years from now? What would we want it to be known for – its brand identity, values, purpose? What would our ambition be for our business and what difference could it make for our employees and our community? And how will we achieve this?'

The desired culture, one that would ensure the company's success, was also discussed and captured in a few simple words. This last step was critical because, as we have seen, while strategy shows the way ahead and principles and values guide it, it's the mindset and attitude of leadership that results in behaviours that create culture, good and bad. Again, it's culture that ultimately delivers strategy and drives performance.

Judith and her senior team then worked on the narrative through which they would communicate the new company story to employees, group colleagues, customers and beyond.

As she developed the organisation's new brand, strategy and narrative with her colleagues, Judith's confidence grew. She wholeheartedly engaged them, shared her beliefs and discovered their personal motivations. She encouraged their individual skill sets and made full use of their experience. She energised them to believe in themselves and in their workmates. Soon she had built a strong, cohesive and focused leadership team.

Once Judith and her colleagues had agreed the desired 'who' (identity and values), the 'why' (purpose) and the 'where' (vision), they worked on the 'how' (key strategic drivers) along with the 'what' (initiatives and operational changes) to deliver them. Then they settled on the 'when' (the short- and medium-term achievable goals) to measure the company's progress and align them with their own KPIs.

Together, they focused on the opportunity and how best to move forward. They realised their potential and identified what they needed to do to achieve their ambition for the business. They built a true legacy organisation, with a clear purpose that everyone could relate to; an organisation of which they themselves, their people, their group colleagues and even the local community became justly proud. Following its transformation, it's a business that can prosper for a long while to come.

For You ...

Can you clearly articulate your own, your team's and your organisation's story for the future? And what you want your business to be known for? Have you formed the plan to deliver this?

Have you defined the culture and behaviours needed to enable it, and how you will nurture them? As a true leader, you are the creator, carrier and custodian of the culture. Your own and your team's success, and failure, start at the top – with you.

IQ in Practice

- Principle, passion and purpose propel performance and profit
- There's always an opportunity to make a real difference
- It starts with clarity – creating your personal and organisational story
- Who you and your team are and why you exist – your brand, values and purpose, which bind you together
- You need to have those around you believe in themselves and the opportunity
- Involve your people to determine what the culture should look and feel like
- Then, as pathfinder, engage all your stakeholders and make it happen

Your 21+90 Days Habit-Forming Challenge:

Most things are possible if you really believe in them, so strive to enlist the support of those around you to achieve them.

'You both want the same thing'
Seek the higher intent

Industrial relations are not something about which I have any great expertise. You might have already surmised this, given my suggestion that the birth of the union movement may have been mitigated by true leadership.

I firmly believe that, if leaders are doing their job properly, they should be able and willing to engage and motivate their people at every opportunity. By connecting spontaneously and directly, true leaders create and nurture a strong culture where people feel safe to speak up when things aren't going well. True leaders respect their people's desire to voice their opinions; and they listen without necessarily agreeing.

Unfortunately, from my observations having worked with a very wide range of organisations, some with workforces of over one hundred thousand and others a lot less, it seems that some leaders are reluctant to engage with their people outside of formally orchestrated events.

All too often, this results in a communication vacuum. Like any vacuum, it does not remain empty for long. In some instances, the more militant unions and anti-business voices, keen to test limits and exercise power, seize the opportunity to reach out directly to workers. This results in disharmony between an organisation's executive and the workforce and, sometimes, in industrial action.

Burns once found himself in such a situation. The majority of the company's workforce had been on strike for almost two months when he was summoned to help the chief executive prepare for an important board meeting. The dispute had become increasingly hostile, with picket lines positioned at the gates of all the company's factories around the country. The disruption didn't stop there. Several smaller businesses that relied on the materials produced by our client to create their own products were shutting down due to the lack of supply. The overall effect was starting to impact the national economy.

Burns felt emboldened to raise it with our client: 'How much longer is this strike going to last, Jonathan?'

'When those rabid lefties come to heel,' came the chief executive's response.

Burns smiled and pointed out to the Princeton University-educated client that unions, along with his workers, inevitably and justifiably featured among his stakeholders.

He persisted: 'When did you last have a conversation with Gerry Longbottom?'

'Look, we've got the best industrial lawyers on this and it's going through the courts. Don't worry yourself about it. I need your help with next week's board meeting. It's going to be tough,' replied the CEO.

'Fine,' Burns continued, 'but as a long-standing supplier and supporter, I would like to see the company get back to work as soon as possible. So, to my question, when did you last have a conversation with the union leader, Longbottom?'

'Well, yes, I did meet Longbottom once. It was a couple of years ago. We didn't say much but he seemed a reasonable kind of guy. I am really annoyed with where we're at now,' answered Jonathan contemptuously.

'Doubtless Longbottom has a few agitators around him who are making the running. They see you and your fellow executives as grossly overpaid and completely out of touch. Your Ivy League background doesn't help, I'm afraid. It reinforces their perception of privilege and arrogance,' Burns replied.

'You need to meet with Longbottom and let him experience the "real Jonathan". You see, I believe you both have rather more in common than you realise. I know you well and have assisted with many of your public utterances. I have also read quite a bit about Longbottom. I think it's time for a quiet chat.'

The chief executive sighed. He was exhausted. The conflict, the business uncertainty, the sometimes hostile media coverage, the calls from the larger institutional investors, not to mention the daily conversations with his chairman, were all taking their toll. 'As I said, the lawyers are handling it,' he almost whispered.

'I hear you and I'm sorry to keep on about this, Jonathan. I genuinely believe you have an opportunity to get a quick resolution outside of the court process. I want you to meet with Gerry Longbottom alone.'

The chief executive managed a laugh. 'What will we talk about, pray?'

'You should speak about what you both believe in. You're each so focused on winning this battle that you've taken your eyes off the war. It's a bit like you're standing on opposite sides of a mountain and all you can see are the cols immediately above your heads,' Burns explained.

'If you would both only stand back, each of you would see that there's a lot more mountain above those cols. Step back further, you will ultimately see the summit. Then, as you look around, you will notice each other, both fixated on the same point way up there in the sky.

'Both of you are actually aiming for the top of the same mountain. At present, you cannot see it. Nor can you see each other. I think you should talk about the mountain peak – what you both believe in and what you both strive for – your mutual higher intent. Then you should seek the path to reach it together.

'You're both passionate about British manufacturing. You both regularly attack the government's tariff reduction policy. You've each spoken out against the World Trade Organization. I suggest you start there.'

Jonathan was persuaded to allow his assistant Veronica to call the union boss's office. By chance, Gerry Longbottom was there and Jonathan came on the line. It was a big risk but Jonathan realised that he had to do something. As the chief executive, and with the beliefs that Burns had reminded him of, he was in a unique position to give it a go.

'I think it's time we met for a quiet, confidential chat, Gerry,' said Jonathan. 'Neutral territory, no advisors, minders, lawyers or media please. Just the two of us.'

Burns couldn't hear Longbottom's response but, judging by Jonathan's demeanour, it was positive. Jonathan added that they both lived in neighbouring suburbs and suggested a discreet local café.

The meeting was arranged for the following Saturday afternoon. When Jonathan arrived, Gerry was sitting in the corner alone. He had kept his word. Both men shook hands and talked for several hours. There is no record of this conversation. At 8am the following Tuesday, the strike was over.

For You ...

This is what I refer to as discovering the higher intent, the mutual purpose that people can believe in and get behind, and that delivers an outcome that everyone is willing to live with and work towards.

This is another example of the power of leadership communication: balancing clarity and humanity. It requires the ability to have strong beliefs, to be courageous yet humble; the will to seek out, understand and acknowledge the views of others; and then to find a way that enables both parties to move forward together.

The overarching concept here is *win-win*. It's about recognising that there are times to compete and there are times to cooperate. It's about acknowledging that there are always times for making the effort to communicate. As we saw in the story about Mohamed in the Middle East, it's about being sufficiently brave to initiate the difficult conversation. This is how real transformation begins. You will not be a true leader if you fail to do so.

IQ in Practice

- With disagreements, suspend your personal beliefs and ambitions
- Again, look at the bigger picture, the situation and the context
- Identify what you can agree on and seek the mutual higher intent
- Remain calm, avoid blame, listen and show empathy ... not easy, I know!
- Achieving an outcome is what leaders do
- 'Win-winning' is better than 'lose-winning' and even 'lose-losing'
- Leadership often involves taking risks
- If you're not bringing others with you, you're not leading
- If you're not leading, you're not progressing

Your 21+90 Days Habit-Forming Challenge:

As with most communication technology, email is transactional. The expression and discussion of views are better achieved through conversation, preferably in person; if that's not possible, then by phone.

'You didn't come here to turn out the lights after 160 years'

Stand up, speak out and make a real difference

Memories of the Global Financial Crisis remain in many people's minds, and perhaps in yours too. We were fortunate in Australia. A solid regulatory framework and a robust banking system had been born out of the tough early 1990s 'recession we had to have', as it was described by Paul Keating, the then Treasurer and later prime minister. These were coupled with a prudent central bank and a China hungry for raw materials that carried the nation through relatively unscathed.

Not all businesses were unaffected. An Australian-based international construction company, partly financed by one of our clients, got into difficulty. All the creditor banks came together in a consortium to help the company remain afloat for as long as possible. Our client, a subsidiary of a European global bank, was one of the smaller members of the consortium and had little say in how best to proceed. Ultimately, the largest banks pulled the plug and the construction company went under, resulting in heavy losses for both shareholders and creditors around the world.

This was the situation as Burns walked into our client's building in Collins Street, Melbourne. He reached level 39 and was soon walking through the executive floor behind the reception area. The receptionist had directed him towards the chief risk officer's office; he was scheduled to spend time with her that morning. Seeing Burns, Kurt, the country managing director, came rushing out of his office.

'Hi. Can you pop in for a few minutes, please.' It was not so much a question, more a command. Hardly had Burns entered Kurt's office when he was asked, 'Have you seen our stock price?'

'Sorry Kurt, no,' Burns replied. Why would I look up the DAX (the German stock exchange)? he thought to himself. Of course, this was not good enough. He should have done so, just as every advisor should always search the internet before meeting with their clients to ensure that they are aware of what's happening in their client's world.

'*Katastrophe*,' Kurt responded in his native tongue as he swung the large desktop screen towards Burns. A red line descended sharply to the right – the bank's stock price was in free fall. He could now understand Kurt's consternation and his unusual sickly pallor. The bank, one of the world's largest, had thus far been viewed as having escaped the worst of the crisis. Clearly, no longer.

'What are you telling the troops, Kurt?' Burns asked.

'What can I tell them? I've received no information from head office in Frankfurt,' he answered.

'You can't wait for that, Kurt. I'm sure it's not going unnoticed that you are sitting in this goldfish bowl of an office, staring at that screen with a look of death on your face. You need to say something.'

Kurt looked uncomfortable. Speaking in public, even to small groups, was not his forte. He preferred email.

'Apart from your exposure to this construction company, is the bank still performing OK here? Are you making money?' Burns continued.

'Yes,' he replied.

'Well, tell them that, Kurt. Tell your people that, while you cannot control the stock price, the bank is performing well. Remind them that this was among the first non-British banks to set up in Australia. That it has helped to build the nation's infrastructure from the earliest days following European settlement and continues to do so. Remind them of some of the successes across the bank: for example, in securities, custodial services, equity raisings, debt markets and syndications.

'While you cannot predict the future, you can remind them of the past, of the bank's brand, what it stands for, what it has achieved, and your vision for its future in this country. Give them something to believe in, Kurt! The bank will get through this.'

With that, Burns reminded Kurt that he had come to see his colleague, Ingrid. He promised to return immediately afterwards and suggested that Kurt invite Julian, the bank's communications manager, to join them. Together, Julian and Burns would craft an appropriate set of words for Kurt to share with his leadership team. They would also put together a short email for Kurt to send to all staff. Next, they would formulate the storyline for some 'town hall' style meetings over the coming days as more clarity emerged from head office.

'Meanwhile, please log out of that website and get back to work, Kurt!', Burns urged with a smile.

Over the next few days, as the Australian subsidiary continued to perform well and the local media made little mention of its membership of the bank consortium, Kurt and his team fronted meetings with every employee around the country.

Unfortunately, the group's stock price didn't recover. Kurt was summoned to meet with the bank's executive chairman and board at a hastily arranged global strategy meeting at the spa town of Baden-Baden in southwest Germany.

Discreet enquiries with Kurt's immediate superior in Hong Kong caused more concern. To save money and in view of the worsening situation around the world, the board was considering closing the Australian operations. The latter's involvement with the now defunct construction business and the ensuing losses had been the final straw for what was the financial behemoth's smallest and most distant outpost.

'We can slim down the Australian business and run it all from Singapore,' was one of the stories emanating from Hong Kong. Of course, it didn't take long for the bank's local employees to hear the rumour. Clients also began asking questions. Kurt called Burns.

'My dear Kurt, I do not believe you came here to turn off the lights after 160 or so years. Your career has several more years to run and it will not be enhanced by having "The last head of the Australian operation" added to your hitherto impressive resumé. You must go to Germany to fight for your business, for your colleagues' jobs ... and for your career.' Burns appreciated that nothing could be further from Kurt's comfort zone!

Five days later, Kurt and his finance director travelled to Baden-Baden. Kurt presented his case so effectively and with such impact that the chairman leapt to his feet, clapping loudly.

'*Hervorragend!*' shouted the chairman. 'Magnificent, Kurt!' The group's executive board also stood and enthusiastically joined their colleague clapping.

'*Die inspirierendste Rede, die wir seit vielen Jahren in dieser Bank gehört haben!*' – 'That was the most inspiring speech we've heard in the bank for many years,' continued the chairman. The Australian operation had been saved and it continues to perform well today.

For You ...

As the saying goes, when the going gets tough, the tough get going. Kurt did, despite the pressure and his initial reluctance. A risk-averse manager all his life, with a bit of encouragement, he recognised his responsibility as the local entity's leader and faced the challenge head-on. He stepped up and put himself on the front line as a true leader. He realised that it would not be enough simply to reassure his bosses. He needed to persuade and move them.

Through his personal conviction and passion, and with a very real awareness of the needs of his employees and clients thousands of kilometres away in Australia, Kurt persuaded his senior colleagues and the many sceptics around the bank that he could right the ship and lead it forward.

Kurt's success in Baden-Baden ensured the continuation of the fine tradition of contributing to Australia's economic growth that the bank had begun all those years ago. This is true leadership.

IQ in Practice

- True leaders do not make excuses, and nor do they blame or complain
- In tough situations, step forward, take ownership, do what needs to be done and be accountable for the outcome
- Rise above your own fear and remain calm for those around you
- While attending to the immediate need, don't lose sight of the bigger picture
- Again, an organisation's leaders are its communication and human resource officers
- Communication is the leader's primary role, especially when faced with a crisis or uncertainty
- You can't predict the future so focus on the situation and what you can control
- Your people look to you for confidence, clarity and perspective
- See every occurrence as an opportunity; it's how you will build your own legacy

Your 21+90 Days Habit-Forming Challenge:

Remember that, as a leader, you must always be AVAA: Audible, Visible, Approachable and Accessible, especially when times are tough or uncertain. This isn't hard but too few leaders seem to recognise its importance.

'We try harder'
Biggest does not always mean best

Not long after hanging up my army boots, I began my advertising career.

I was in awe of CDP. As I touched on earlier, this was an extraordinary enterprise. I was excited to have joined the team and desperate to learn my new craft. I had loved my life as an army officer but this was so different. Yet much of what I had learned while in uniform helped me here, even the vocabulary. One had to understand the context (perspective and prevailing situation), the audience (target) and the purpose (mission), and to determine the overarching message or concept (objective), the strategy and the execution steps as well as how to measure results.

Of course, teamwork was also critical. I appreciated even more the vital need to work with others, to collaborate, to share, to encourage others to speak up, to listen, to probe, to challenge, to welcome the ideas of those around me, and to team together and be excited by the opportunities that diverse thinking brings.

Is this not what diversity, equity and inclusion are really about? It's not just the physical aspects of looking, sounding and being different, or complying with quotas. It's the power that's generated by celebrating and harnessing genuine human individuality. This means encouraging and embracing each person's unique beliefs, skills, experiences and ideas.

One of my agency accounts was Hertz, then the world's largest car rental company. Their logo even used to feature the icon #1. They were an exciting client to work with in a very competitive sector. Their main rival was Avis, whose slogan in those days was 'We try harder'. Introduced in 1962, it was at the heart of a famous ad campaign by US agency Doyle Dane Bernbach.

Years later, in my current role, I found myself reflecting on this when working with a global technology company that was desperate to hold on to its 'World's Biggest' status.

This tech company had grown largely by acquiring other businesses. Shortly before my involvement, it acquired a well-known rival. The purpose, so investors were told, was to add to its capabilities and grow market share.

As is often the case in such situations, shareholders were assured that the acquisition would create synergies and be accretive over time. While little of this proved to be the case, it did increase the acquirer's annual turnover by a few billion dollars. This meant that the company remained ahead of its rivals in terms of size and global dominance, for a while at least.

Sitting down with the company's new president, I asked a simple question: 'So, Matt, what will you do with the organisation?'

The president was taken aback. What an odd question, he must have thought. I waited for Matt to answer. He didn't take long.

'Be the biggest, of course!'

'Really? I think you are already the biggest, Matt. How much bigger is biggest?'

'Well, yes, we are. And we plan to remain number one in all our markets,' said Matt as he looked through the window to the midtown Manhattan skyline.

'How big is your market share in this country – 40 per cent?'

'Yes, about that.'

'Well,' I responded, 'I'm wondering how much bigger you can get before someone starts to raise some questions ... the FTC, competitors, media, even customers.'

'Humph ...' snorted Matt. Was that arrogance? Or perhaps fear.

'Let me make a suggestion, Matt.' I stood up and walked towards the whiteboard on the office wall. Taking up a thick black marker, I wrote: **BIGGEST**.

I then picked up a thick red marker and put a line through the letters ~~IGG~~ and turned to Matt.

'You see, I think that is a far more aspirational goal. BEST could well be the biggest, but BIGGEST is not necessarily the best. Biggest is so old hat, so "baby boomer"! It's like having the biggest house, the biggest boat, the fastest car, the largest share portfolio and best wine cellar and so forth. Then what?'

I went on to explain that the trouble with focusing on being number one is that there is only one way to go when we're not. Inevitably, our energies are all about hanging on to the position rather than constantly challenging ourselves – how do we innovate, transform and be our best?

'Sorry, Matt, but the recent acquisition is a case in point. What did it cost? Seven billion dollars? Yes, it gave you a step up in revenue. It temporarily bought some space between yourselves and your nearest competitor. But numbers aren't a vision, they're an outcome.

'Where are you today, just three years on? Your stock price has not moved significantly and your primary competitor has drawn level in terms of capitalisation. The cultures of your organisation and the one you acquired have always been markedly different. Unsurprisingly, most of those senior executives you bought with that company, including its founders, are now in the money and checking out,' I continued.

'Biggest is finite and inevitably creates an unhealthy focus on ourselves – almost to the point of panic as we allow ourselves to be solely metrics-driven. As the great investor Warren Buffet advises: "Games are won by players who focus on the playing field, not by those whose eyes are glued to the scoreboard."

'I like "best" because it's an aspiration to which we can all relate but we may never actually achieve. It also applies to everything we do, as an individual, as a team and as an organisation. It's being best in terms of safety and quality, people engagement and retention, customer satisfaction, community relations, environmental practices, peer and market recognition, social enterprise, achievement awards and, yes, performance, profitability and return on equity.

'Very few of today's employees are baby boomers like you and me, Matt. Thanks to the internet, the next generations are globally savvy. They seek meaning in what they do. They want to feel they're making a worthwhile difference. They are challenging our generation, the institutions we represent and many of the standards that have guided us. They are asking about purpose; about what success really looks like and how it can be achieved sustainably. I sincerely believe these people would rather work for an organisation that aspires to be the best in its field, not simply the biggest.'

Matt nodded. 'You have a point,' he conceded, perhaps thinking of the many challenging conversations with his own teenage children.

'Although it's so much easier for businesses to measure things. Was it not management expert Peter Drucker who is credited with saying: "You can't manage what you can't measure"?

'We like to apply this to quantifiable, tangible metrics like revenue, margins, profit numbers and stock price, which are readily there for all to see. It's largely how we're rewarded. We also have employee and customer satisfaction surveys and net promoter scores,' he concluded.

'Fine and dandy, Matt,' I replied. 'As important as these quantitative measures are, they alone will not bring sustainable advantage. You also need to focus on the more difficult, less visible qualitative drivers such as morale, loyalty, quality, sentiment, reputation and the culture that underpins them. It's these critical factors that will deliver you long-term, sustained performance.'

'Without wishing to discount Mr Drucker's expertise, the clue is in the moniker "management expert". I am talking about leading, not only managing. Success, and failure, starts with an organisation's leaders and the quality and the culture those leaders uphold every day.

'How do you measure culture, Matt? Put simply, you can't, at least not in the precise way you would expect. For example, while the metrics you mention may be indicative that not all is well, you cannot rely on them alone. Equally important are staff retention and gross turnover. You will also sense it. You will experience it every day, as will your people, your customers and other stakeholders. You see, culture is the glue that holds it all together and drives, or destroys, quality and performance. If it's not kept strong, the various components will fall apart.'

Matt was now listening.

For You ...

Avis discovered the power of the underdog. It gave its people the pride to believe in themselves and their business. It gave them the confidence to celebrate its strengths and to challenge itself to do better. And it gave them the resolve to continue striving to delight its customers. 'We try harder' was the true purpose that described the unique experience Avis aspired to give its customers, and they bought into it. It was also a none too subtle way of having a laugh at its larger competitor's self-important positioning.

This recognition created a powerful culture that drove Avis forward to close the gap with its arch-rival Hertz, even before the latter filed for Chapter 11 bankruptcy in 2020. Avis's success was realised by a positive force founded on a determination to differentiate itself by the 'who, why and where', not simply the 'how, what and when'. While it's no longer used by Avis, the slogan 'We try harder' helped to build the solid foundation that continues to underpin the rental car company's success today.

To beat the competition and win, organisations of every type need true leadership.

IQ in Practice

- Biggest does not always mean best
- To achieve success, answer these questions in this order: who, why, where, how, what and when
- Be clear about your brand and its promise
- Keep abreast of and respond to society's changing expectations
- Trying harder and working smarter pays off
- Focus on the qualitative as well as the quantitative
- Have some fun at your competitors' expense

Your 21+90 Days Habit-Forming Challenge:

Ask yourself and your people, what do we really want to be known for? And then remind yourself and them again, and again!

'I am pleased I don't own shares in your company'
Lead as well as manage

I sometimes wonder how I've survived in this business so long! While I espouse authenticity and rarely pull my punches, I can also forget my own advice to include the descriptor 'appropriate', as in *appropriate* authenticity, as I described earlier. As we have seen, leaders need to measure up and respond appropriately to every situation with which they're faced.

This story illustrates the need for leaders to step forward and truly lead, even when the natural inclination might be to hold back and manage. The other point here is to see every event as an opportunity – an opportunity to influence and inspire, not simply to turn up and inform.

It was the day before the annual financial results briefing. I had worked with this company for a number of years, often with the chief executive and finance director ahead of important investor briefings. While high profile due to its long and chequered history, the business was no market darling. The story always seemed to be the same: managing the business prudently, controlling overheads, cutting costs and so forth. Sitting in their boardroom that afternoon, I decided to say something.

'You know, Will, I am pleased not to own shares in your company. This is the sixth time we've worked together ahead of an important market briefing. I am of course grateful to be invited to do so but I'm not sure why: the narrative doesn't change. Frankly, why don't you simply close the whole thing down, turn out the lights and give your shareholders their money back? After all, the stock price has barely moved beyond its very narrow range in over five years!'

The CEO shifted uncomfortably in his seat. Steph, the finance director, looked down at the files in front of her, and Dion, the investor relations manager, smiled nervously in my general direction. The silence was deafening.

Finally, Will asked: 'What do mean? What do you want us to talk about?' He was clearly tired. I also detected a hint of annoyance.

'Well,' I continued less forcefully, 'you're running one of the world's oldest telephony companies. Is that not something? By all means talk about what you've been doing with the company this past year; they will expect that. Please also talk about where you're taking it. You see, it seems to me that you are waiting for Fonavibe, your biggest competitor, or someone else, to walk in and take you over. I think it's time you spoke about taking the fight to Fonavibe, Will.'

'I'm listening,' the CEO replied wearily. His colleagues began to relax.

'Thank you. I am sorry to bully you but you know me and this is important. We need to position you as the true leader of this business, not simply its managing director. We need you to talk about your plans. You kindly invited me to speak at your strategy off-site a few months back, yet there's no mention of your strategy here. This is what I suggest you do.'

Thirty minutes later, when Will had left the room, Steph and Dion began to laugh.

'You're impossible,' said Steph, grinning, 'but well done you. I cannot imagine that anyone has ever spoken to Will like that. Given Will's stellar career in management consulting and as dean of a leading business school, he's used to calling the shots.'

'Yes, I accept that, but running this business, any business, is different,' I responded. 'It's about leadership, not just management. First, Will has to demonstrate pride in the organisation. Why did he take the job on, for God's sake? I hope it wasn't just for the money. Given the recent performance, he won't have earned many bonuses and his share options must be almost worthless.

'Will must talk about what's unique about Teleffona; what the organisation stands for; where he's taking the company; and, in outline, how he and his team will arrive there. And he must give a sense of why people should want to work and invest here. We discussed all this at that resort down the coast just a few months ago. I left pretty excited! Didn't you both?'

Will needed to not only inspire the market, but also to lift company morale. He needed to put a spring back in the step of his workforce, many of whom joined this organisation because of its illustrious history, because of the skills they would learn and because of what they hoped it would do for their careers.

However, given the recent performance of the business and the growing pressure from the competition, morale was as low as profitability. Will needed to share his belief in his team and give them, his people, his investors and his customers hope!

Unsure if I was now persona non grata, I sent Will a short note on arriving home that evening. I was relieved to receive a call later from his assistant Fiona. Will wanted to see me in his office at 6.30am the next day, just three hours before the investor briefing. The light of the rising sun was streaming into Will's office as I entered.

'I have given a lot of thought to what you said yesterday and your subsequent note. You're right. I need to step up and tell the Teleffona story, who we are and where we're going, and to explain some of the exciting things we're doing.'

I smiled and listened in awe to the words that the CEO had put together. Yes, Will is certainly one of the smartest people with whom I've had the privilege of working. Not only had he captured the essence of my challenge the previous day, he had also crafted a story with a combination of elegance and power that was compelling. Not for the first time in this role, I felt a tear welling in my eye.

'I have another meeting soon, Will, but I'm going to reschedule so that I can attend your briefing. Is that OK with you?' It was one of those rare occasions when I saw Will's habitual pensiveness fall away and in its place was a broad smile. He suddenly appeared years younger. 'Sure,' he replied.

'Many thanks, Will. Now let's refine this and work on how best to deliver it.'

Later that morning, when the 130 or so investors and analysts had departed, three of Will's executive team came up to me.

'I have never seen Will like that!' said one with a look of near incredulity.

'Why hasn't he done this before?' asked another.

'He was awesome! There's no other word for it,' added the third.

The briefing had begun with Dion welcoming everyone, outlining the agenda and explaining the emergency evacuation procedures. Then the screen went blank. Will strode out in front of the audience without notes, a discreet lapel microphone in place.

He began: 'As I was preparing for today, I was reminded that this is the sixth time I have fronted such an event, presented our results and talked about how we are managing the company before asking our CFO Steph to take you through the numbers.

'You will have seen the overall result that we posted on the internet this morning. Yes, Steph will explain the detail and I will give you my overview of the business and what I believe lies ahead. Before we do, I want to share some thoughts with you.'

A slide with a quote from author James Kerr appeared on the screen: 'Vision without action is a dream. Action without vision is a nightmare.'

Will paused for what must have been at least eight seconds as he scanned the audience before him. Everyone looked up from their information packs and, noticing the slide, waited for the chief executive to speak. No one stirred.

The screen darkened again and Will began. 'I thought I'd start by telling you why I am so delighted to have this job. I thought I should remind you what a great company this is. I thought I should reveal something of our plans for the future. And I thought I should explain how we're embracing the growing media convergence challenge and are ready to seize the opportunities it offers.

'I also thought I'd take this opportunity to send two clear messages to our owners, our people, our customers and, indeed, our competitors: first, we are still very much in business 133 years on; second, we are determined to be here in another 133 years.

'And finally, I thought I should leave you in no doubt as to my personal resolve and that of my executive team, each of whom is here today, to continue to be worthy of your support as we move forward.'

By now, Will had moved into the audience, engaging easily with one person at a time as if in regular conversation. From where I sat at the back of the room, the atmosphere was almost evangelical.

The focus on Will and what he was saying was intense. He continued for another five or six minutes, bringing the crowd with him, before moving to the lectern at the side of the low stage and signalling for the slide show to resume.

For You ...

This is leadership communication ... the art of bringing people with you. Much to everyone's surprise, Will achieved it that day. So can you. You just need to remind yourself that, as a true leader, you must take every opportunity to reach out, engage with those around you and bring them with you. Irrespective of the situation and whether speaking with a group or just one individual, share your beliefs, tell your story, be clear about the destination and give them hope.

IQ in Practice

- Lead as well as manage
- Never lose sight of who you are, what you stand for and why you do what you do
- Reveal your true self and your inner confidence
- Put aside formality and engage naturally
- Talk about your team's difference and the difference you can make together
- Vision is the 'light on the hill', the endgame, the collective ambition where you and your colleagues are headed
- Maintain a 'can-do' spirit, help others to share your optimism and keep going to the very edge

Your 21+90 Days Habit-Forming Challenge:

Remind yourself every day, who you, why you and where you – your personal brand, your purpose and your vision for your business, your team and yourself.

'We had never been in a meeting like it'
Head and heart every time

'I am pretty certain I speak for my fellow directors in saying that I have never been in a meeting like it!' exclaimed the chairman of the nation's largest retailer. His comment was immediately echoed by two other directors on the board. The remainder were soon nodding in agreement. And so, the company's new auditor was chosen.

You may be wondering why I'm referring to winning business mandates in a book about leadership, and why I have dedicated a section to pitching later in the book.

It's because the same true leadership qualities are required. Leadership starts with leading the thinking of others. Similarly, we need to lead our prospects' thinking. We will not succeed if we just inform them. We need to influence and inspire them to choose us. As already highlighted, this is what true leaders do.

Returning to the story, let me give you a sense of the context. Shortly before it announced it was reviewing its audit arrangements, the retailer had appointed a new chief executive. The choice of this outsider was a surprise to most observers. It was more easily understood by those closer to the organisation. They were fully aware of the board's ongoing frustration with their company's regular appearance at the bottom of the sector's quarterly customer satisfaction tables.

The board had now recruited a leader from overseas with an impressive track record in lifting both employee engagement and customer satisfaction. His mandate? Get us to number one! Some five or so years later, he did.

It had been many years since there'd been a change of auditor. The selection had been an exhausting process for the four big accounting firms who had taken part. Round one took out two, including the incumbent, and it came down to the remaining two firms, one of which was our client.

Burns's first question to its partners had been: 'The board wants its organisation to be number one in employee engagement and customer satisfaction. How do you help them get there?'

Burns will never forget the look on those very experienced accountants' faces. 'Customer service? Seriously? We're auditors and we are going to offer them the best audit,' they exclaimed.

He laughed, 'Of course you are! And what do you think your competitors are going to offer, the second, third or even fourth best?'

Burns continued, 'Yes, this organisation needs the very best audit and I have every confidence you can deliver it. But they already have an auditor and have not yet expressed a definite desire to change. On the other hand, they want to be number one in employee engagement and customer service. They are presently the retail sector's number five in both. This is your opportunity – to help them not just with what they need but with what they actually want!

'In the first round, your task will be to get them to decide to change auditor, along with ensuring you remain in the race.'

Despite its poor track record in the engagement and satisfaction surveys, the retailer's legacy from when it was previously owned by a huge US conglomerate ensured it was already the nation's leading retailer in terms of number of customers, market share and capitalisation. While it had not overtly expressed any dissatisfaction with its current auditor, it needed, even deserved, the nation's leading audit, thought Burns.

'What does the nation's leading audit look like? Indeed, why stop there?' he teased his new friends. 'What does the world's leading audit look *and feel* like?'

Thus challenged, the firm's crack audit team got to work. As the country's biggest audit, the prize was worth every effort on account of the prestige, let alone the fee.

They entered the first round, painting an oral picture around the retailer's aspiration, introducing the factors that could disrupt this journey and suggesting that, if they wanted to remain the market leader, they surely needed the leading audit, and asking: what might that be?

Having posed the question rhetorically, the team deftly answered it, homing in on areas where they sensed the incumbent was failing or, at least, not fully delivering.

They were through to round two. Now for the *coup de grâce*.

'What actually are employee engagement and customer satisfaction?' asked Burns. The accountants decided they are about the employee and customer experience at every touch point with the company – in its supermarkets and other outlets, on the telephone with its call centres, online ordering and deliveries, and, of course, its products. Experience is about heart as well as head. It's about the feelings and the facts.

'OK. What's the feeling we want your audience, the company's directors, to experience during your pitch and remember afterwards?' Burns continued.

Everyone laughed. 'We want them to love us!' said the team leader. Clearly, Burns was getting to him.

'You're absolutely right, Raymond,' he replied. 'You must give them an experience such that they will want to work with you, whatever.'

The 'whatever' turned out to be prescient. Informal, internal advice from our client firm's contacts at the retailer suggested that, on a number of measures, they were running second. Not good news, especially as there were just two runners in this race! The pressure on participants in such large and high-stake tenders is always intense and understandably so. This news, coming just days before the final pitch, was particularly unwelcome and the team's anxiety was palpable.

Maintaining confidence is critical, but beware over-confidence. A regular dose of 'why will we *not* win?' is a useful antidote to stem the latter. But this news, from a well-placed, trusted source within the prospect client organisation, was an unexpected blow.

There's rarely an instant cure in such circumstances, although a hug can help! While Burns has given several on occasions, it did not seem appropriate just then. Instead, he took the team to the car park below the office. As you might expect, there was a wide range of automobiles.

'Look around you,' Burns urged. 'Every vehicle you see here does the job. It starts; it stops; it conveys people from point A to point B. Given the speed limits, the difficulty with parking and the tax, insurance and fuel costs, one has to wonder why anyone would choose that Porsche over this Hyundai. Yet people do. Why?

'The experience. The unique value that each of these products creates for its owner. Some might quantify that in terms of safety, others in terms of performance, prestige, economy, design, carrying capacity, resale price, sustainability and so on. What experience must you give the retailer's board to demonstrate your understanding of the special, unique value they desire and you will give them?'

Two days later, Burns did give each team member a hug as they set off to the company's headquarters just ten minutes' walk away. Wishing the leader luck, Burns spied him tucking his prepared notes into his jacket pocket.

'Just go in there and woo them, Raymond. You don't need instructions on how to do that, do you?' Hardly, Burns thought. The team leader was one of the most charming and elegant business people he had come across. With a grin, Raymond reluctantly handed over his notes.

Later that day, the competitor firm had their chance with the company board. Then both firms waited. Days followed, then a week, followed by another and then another. At last, our clients heard the news. They had won! Their opponent was understandably devastated. All the more so because, as we learned later, the losing firm was convinced that its team had won even before it entered the boardroom those few weeks earlier.

As we also learned, the retailer's subsequent feedback informed the losing firm that, while each of its team members was clearly skilled and well prepared and their presentation was very professional, the audience never really engaged. This was because they had been captivated by our client's pitch and were still reflecting on it several hours later.

While not really comprehending what they'd been told, it answered the biggest question in the minds of the losing team on the day: 'On any other day we would be nailing this, so why are we not connecting with this audience now?'

For You ...

Let's return to the comment by the retailer's chairman. Given the information that they were likely running second, what was it those auditors did that day to win the chequered flag?

The answer: they connected with both head and heart ... the very words they had chosen for the title of their proposal. They identified not only what the retailer's board needed but what it wanted. Instead of giving them a slick, data-driven, technical presentation, they had a warm, informal and meaningful conversation with their listeners. They came across as a powerful and engaged team of professionals who clearly enjoyed working together and genuinely wanted to help the company succeed.

As true leaders of thought, the successful team took their audience on an exciting and inspiring journey. They gave them an enduring emotional experience, not just an expert exposition. This is what true leaders do everywhere, every day.

IQ in Practice

- Head and heart every time
- Instead of just focusing on what you think your customers or people need, strive to understand what they actually want
- Put context and intent before content, and focus on the outcome
- Work on the experience ahead of the explanation – what you want people to feel, not just know
- Successful team members play together and support each other
- Excellence is not the same as perfection; the former is necessary and attainable, the latter is not
- Every organisation is made up of people who do business with people

Your 21+90 Days Habit-Forming Challenge:

Determine the experience you want to give all those with whom you interact every day. Afterwards, ask yourself what experience you actually gave them. If you're not sure, ask.

'Do you really want to be known for destroying the last untouched original landscape?'

Winning by helping your opponents do the same

Harry is an old school friend of my associate James. He once lived in a delightful early European settler's farmhouse on an urban fringe in Ontario, Canada. Despite the population growth in recent years and the resulting expansion, the valley where the property was situated had been largely untouched since European settlement.

With the help of his friendly bank manager and the support of the local community, Harry and his family worked hard to restore the once derelict 18th-century stone house and its rare collection of vernacular timber outbuildings. Guided by organic principles, they created an impressive garden, which was increasingly visited by garden lovers from all over the world. They also ran a small herd of cattle.

Then disaster struck. A wealthy property developer bought a large vacant block of land opposite. The site dominated most of the hills overlooking Harry's farm. Any development there would not only destroy its charm but also the integrity of the landscape.

The site's zoning allowed for the proposed development and the battle lines were drawn. On one side were the experienced and determined developer and his advisors, one branch of the descendants of the original family that had first settled there in colonial times, and half the local municipality's councillors and most of its staff. Opposing the development was Harry, his family, a second branch of the original family, many local residents and various heritage bodies.

The battle had raged for almost three years – in the municipal chambers and in the village at the centre of the controversy, where anonymous letters would regularly be found in letterboxes up and down the winding country lane. The two branches of the original family were at loggerheads and the occasional community meetings held in the church hall inevitably ended in acrimony.

This was the situation James found when he went to stay with Harry and his family. While Harry was already active on social media, James advised him to raise the stakes by involving the traditional media, from the local paper to the national broadsheets, radio and even television. James also encouraged Harry to commission an expert report on the heritage values of the area. The author discovered that Flashpoint Hill, the hillside where the bulk of the development was proposed, was central to 'one of the last surviving unspoilt original landscapes'. The developer responded with his own report, which was quickly discredited by heritage bodies.

A few weeks later, when James was back in Melbourne, Harry emailed to say that there still seemed to be no end to the impasse. James wasn't so sure. While the councillors' support for his friend continued, albeit on a knife edge, the municipal staff were still recommending approval. At some stage, he felt, the developer would call the councillors' bluff and head to the provincial environment court.

Similar to Australia and the United Kingdom, these courts have a reputation for ignoring the more qualitative arguments such as heritage matters. Instead, they tend to uphold what's permitted by the zoning. James feared that this would result in disaster for both his friend and the environment. He called Harry and proposed a radical course to resolve the matter once and for all.

At around 9.30am the following Sunday morning, Harry telephoned his nemesis, the property developer, at his home. The phone was answered promptly and the conversation went like this.

'Hello Elliot, it's Harry.'

'What do you want?' came the gruff reply.

'Well, you've certainly given me a few sleepless nights. I imagine I have done the same for you. I've been thinking it's time for us to have a chat.'

'What about?' asked Elliot.

'I believe we have rather more in common than we've been prepared to admit, Elliot,' Harry continued.

'I'm listening,' responded Elliot without a hint of enthusiasm.

'Thank you. Rather than speak on the phone, would you be open to meeting at your place? I could come over this morning, say at 11am, or between 2 and 5pm this afternoon. Which would best suit you?'

Once Harry had established that Elliot was at home that day, James had advised offering several times when to meet. This is an old sales device; it is less likely the prospective customer will refuse all the options.

'11am works,' answered Elliot.

'Fine. See you then, Elliot,' said Harry, ending the call.

With James's help, Harry had done his homework. Elliot lived in the midst of several hundred hectares just a few kilometres down the road. He was immensely proud of his property and was rumoured to be planning a development there one day. He had a close-knit family. Each of his sons and daughters lived in various houses on his large estate. Elliot was also a successful cattle breeder, with his cattle grazing not only there but also on several other properties he owned.

Elliot was also proud of his standing in the community. His support and generosity for numerous worthy causes was well recognised. With Elliot's focus on his reputation, James found it amusing how he had done his best to avoid the spotlight just as Harry had invited the media to shine it.

Yes, Elliot clearly preferred to do things his way. And he did not like to lose. Yet it seemed that this development proposal was not the only one that was causing Elliot headaches. Furthermore, there had been talk in the district that his backers were applying some pressure.

With all these factors firmly in Harry's mind, he drove through the impressive gates at the entrance to Elliot's home. He continued on slowly, drinking in the open farmland, the grazing cattle and the various buildings scattered across the landscape.

During James's stay, he and Harry had taken a walk on the proposed development site. They had sat on the highest part of the block and looked around. It dawned on them that, if it had to proceed, the development could be achieved far more efficiently and without creating a devastating impact on the landscape. They scribbled a simple 'mud map' and returned to Harry's home with a spring in their step. James urged Harry to share it with Elliot, although he sensed his friend's reluctance.

First of all, however, Harry telephoned Noah, the mayor, to arrange a meeting. Unlike his predecessor, who had ejected Harry from the municipal chambers, Noah had been one of Harry's consistent supporters long before his appointment as mayor. With a margin of just one vote, Noah had managed to hold back the development thus far. However, he knew he couldn't do so for ever. Noah was relieved when Harry called to discuss a potential solution.

The mayor welcomed Harry's suggestions and agreed that if Elliot could be persuaded to alter his proposal he would encourage his fellow councillors to support it.

Elliot came out from the house as Harry parked his ancient pickup, especially chosen for this vital mission. Extending his hand, Harry greeted Elliot and attempted to look into the latter's eyes. He needn't have bothered. Elliot was one of those people who typically looks down as they shake hands. Not a great start, Harry thought, but better than the last time they met. It had been at the local butcher's shop. Harry had offered a friendly greeting, only to be rebuffed by Elliot as he stormed out of the shop muttering.

Bill, the butcher, said he had known Elliot all his life and had never seen him in such a state. 'You've certainly got under his skin, Harry!' Bill joked, running his finger along one of his extremely sharp knives.

'This place is magnificent, Elliot,' began Harry. 'I've often driven past those impressive gates and longed to see inside. Before we have our chat, could we take a drive around please?'

'OK,' replied Elliot, motioning Harry towards the shiny, late-model Jeep Wagoneer sitting in the drive. They drove around, stopping at closed gates that Harry opened and shut without being asked, his boots and jeans becoming heavily muddied in the process. Along the way, Harry was able to ask about Elliot's family, admire the various houses and other buildings across the estate, inspect some prize-winning bulls and a couple of thoroughbreds, and even visit Elliot's pack of greyhounds.

Harry also dropped snippets of his own upbringing into the conversation. He had grown up in the Scottish Highlands where his family had bred Angus cattle and maintained a large flock of black-faced sheep. Harry wanted Elliot to see him as a country lad, not a classic NIMBY (Not In My Back Yard) who had recently moved from the city and was trying to impose narrow inner-city standards on his neighbours.

When they returned to Elliot's home, he invited Harry in for a cup of tea. Harry sensed he was making progress but declined saying, 'Thanks, Elliot. Rather than disturb your family, why don't we sit on that bench over there in the shade.'

'OK. What's on your mind?' began Elliot as they sat down together.

Harry had been careful not to mention the proposed development while touring Elliot's property. 'Well, it's just as I suggested on the phone, Elliot. We have lots in common. You see, we both love this country. What you've achieved here is magnificent,' replied Harry.

Elliot nodded in appreciation as Harry continued. 'My family and I are simply trying to do the same on our much more modest bit of dirt over the hill. We've made a lot of progress but, to ensure we can leave even half the legacy that you undoubtedly will here, we need your help.'

'What do you want me to do, Harry?' asked Elliot. It was the first time the developer had used Harry's name. As they say in Australia, there seemed to be movement at the station!

'Well, I would love you to pick up your shovel, pack up your bulldozer and leave us alone, Elliot!' replied Harry with a grin. 'Of course, I know you won't do that. Property development is what you do. It is in your blood and, by all accounts, you are pretty good at it. I understand that.'

Harry continued, 'I'll cut to the chase. I recognise that the zoning allows for a development on that site. I believe we can achieve a far better development, one we can all be comfortable with and even proud of.

'Given all you've achieved in your life, I don't think you would want to be remembered for destroying one of the last surviving untouched original landscapes, would you?'

As Harry fixed him with a firm gaze and gentle smile, Elliot blinked. 'Show me,' he said.

Harry scratched out the mud map from a few weeks earlier in the gravel at their feet. He pointed out the easier, less expensive access, the way the houses could cluster around an existing lake in the style of a small hamlet in the valley behind, leaving the historic landscape untouched. Observing Elliot's growing interest, Harry mentioned he had already spoken informally with the mayor who felt the councillors and staff would be willing to endorse this solution.

Harry paused. After a couple of minutes' silence, Elliot suddenly stood up, put out his hand and, to Harry's surprise, looked him right in the eye. 'Thanks for coming over, I'll be in touch.'

With that, Elliot turned and walked towards his front door. Harry got back in the pickup and, allowing himself a slight smile, headed home. He sent Elliot a short, handwritten note thanking him for his time and the opportunity to visit his home.

The following Friday evening, Harry's cell phone rang. It was Elliot.

'Hello, is that you, Harry? I'll be on the block at 10 tomorrow. I've something to show you.'

'Fine,' replied Harry.

At 10am precisely Harry walked across the road, through the old farm gate and up the gentle rise towards the familiar Jeep. Next to it stood two men. One was Elliot. The other Harry recognised as Elliot's architect, Jackson. Harry had certainly had some run-ins with him in the municipal chambers!

'G'day eh, Harry', said Elliot. 'I think you know Jackson. We have something to show you.'

Spread out on the car's hood was a large map. Harry could not quite believe his eyes. Eighty per cent of the proposed dwellings had been relocated, just as he had recommended the previous Sunday. Of course, while thanking them both, Harry pushed Elliot to move the remaining sites but the latter would not budge.

Fair enough, thought Harry. He was mindful that the development could not be stopped entirely. As James had counselled, 'To gain anything, you must give something. Go for a win-win, Harry.' An 80:20 result was certainly better than nothing and, in reality, was more of a win-win for Harry's family and its supporters ... and the landscape.

For You ...

Successful negotiation is never about one party getting everything they want.

The skill in any dispute or negotiation is to understand not only what you think your opponent needs but what they actually want. Discover what really matters to them.

While Elliot was a long-standing, successful property developer, money alone was not his motivator. Achieving a quick outcome, enhancing his reputation, being appreciated for his achievements, and his family – these were what really mattered to Elliot.

The strategy for Harry was to unearth these hidden personal drivers and find a way to achieve an outcome that everyone could live with and work towards: a true win-win. And, as you will have noticed in the conversation between Harry and Elliot, Harry subtly changed his approach by using 'we' in place of 'I' and 'you'.

These are techniques you too can adopt, whatever your particular circumstance. It's what true leaders do.

IQ in Practice

- In negotiation, find out what really matters to your opponent
- Influencing is about getting people to think and feel differently
- To persuade, you must seek to understand wants, not only assume needs
- Show your genuine interest in what interests them
- Again, flattery can be a useful device
- Real change occurs when both heads and hearts are engaged and mobilised with a common purpose
- Have the confidence to make a move, even when you may fail
- Playing the long game takes patience and some luck
- The outcome is the only measure of success

Your 21+90 Days Habit-Forming Challenge:

'When I am getting ready to reason with someone, I spend one-third of my time thinking about myself and what I am going to say, and two-thirds thinking about them and what they are going to say.' Abraham Lincoln (1809–1865). Please give the president's advice a go.

'Don't go wobbly on me now, George!'
Clarity and humanity

When the pressure's on and the stakes are high, we need true leadership. As I've said before, this starts with a clear sense of self-identity and self-awareness, asking oneself: 'Who really am I and what's expected of me in this role?' Reflecting on my strengths and shortcomings, I remind myself: where do I typically 'go' under pressure?'

The coronavirus pandemic, which first appeared in late 2019 and continues to affect the world today, created the perfect storm for political and business leaders around the world. Initially, uncertainty prevailed, giving rise to enormous pressure on lives and livelihoods, revenues and budgets and causing panic for many and misery for many more. As the pandemic spread, so did the financial uncertainty.

Lee had recently been appointed general manager of the Singapore office of a Hong Kong private equity group. A few years earlier, the group had acquired a locally based media business that had been struggling. Once the necessary changes had been made, it had been the private equity group's intention to sell this investment. The growing pandemic had tied their hands and the media business had remained on their books.

It included a group of regional newspapers and radio stations across South East Asia, Australia and New Zealand as well a media business in Alabama, United States. The latter had been acquired the previous year. With the growing health and associated economic crises, its market share and revenues were dropping and it required hands-on, day-to-day management. The responsibility for this had been given to Lee who was now spending a lot of time on all-night video calls from across the Pacific Ocean.

The private equity group's directors were becoming very uncomfortable about their portfolio, with the media business causing the most angst. Board meetings were occurring twice weekly, with directors either attending in person or joining virtually from around the globe. The chairman was from Cape Town, a bull of a man, intimidating both in stature and intellect. His fellow directors, all male, came from the cream of the world's financial, legal and corporate firms.

Egos abounded as, increasingly, did fear. These 'masters of the universe' were not the kind of people who were used to losing. This is where they now found themselves, with the value of this investment, and others, dropping rapidly as the twin crises mounted.

While the media business was holding almost US $300m in cash, it owed over US $1bn to a consortium of regional banks. Those most exposed were pressing for early repayment. The group's backers were becoming progressively nervous, with some seeking to cash in and others looking for a special dividend. Hedge funds were shorting the stock and the media could smell blood. Commentators across the region and on both sides of the Pacific rarely omitted a reference to their competitor's situation. This wasn't all.

A large Japanese investment bank, associated with the private equity group, was pressing to do a deal. A prized regional television station was in trouble and coming to the market. 'What a bargain,' extolled Maverick, a New Yorker and one of the bank's vice presidents based in Singapore. Mav had become a close friend of Lee and, doubtless, had an eye on the potential bonus! The TV station would be a great fit, thought the private equity group's directors. Despite the ongoing challenges, they were also tempted by its fire-sale price.

Board meetings were now held daily, with Lee required to give regular updates about the media holdings, either in person or virtually. His physical and mental exhaustion grew as he tackled the growing range of demands in Asia, Australasia and the US.

Should he keep his friend Mav happy by recommending that the board proceed with the TV station purchase? The cash in the bank could easily cover it. Should he acquiesce to the growing chorus from the creditor banks and repay some of their dues? The reduced interest burden would certainly help cash flow. Should he advise the board to pay some form of special dividend to the shareholders? The major ones were well represented around the board table and keen for an early distribution.

On top of all this, what to do with Alabama? As much as Lee was an experienced turnaround agent and was genuinely excited by the business, he was not a US media expert. While the company's media operations on his side of the Pacific were still just paying their way, the North American radio and print advertising markets were in trouble. This was due to many small- and medium-sized businesses closing and laying off millions of workers. Worse, the original owner of this business was still employed but, nearing retirement and with the bulk of the sale price already banked, she showed little interest in remaining engaged.

By chance, Lee came across an email from my associate James in his inbox. It reminded Lee of those conversations he used to have with us when he was working for his previous employer in Melbourne. Echoes of my foghorn-like voice banging on about clarity and humanity entered Lee's head:

'Be very clear about brand, purpose, vision and the plan, Lee. Keep them simple. Be true to and back yourself while mindful of others' expectations. Maintain awareness of yourself and those around you and avoid presenting; communicate instead! Be curious, ask good questions and listen well. Be resolute, determined and persistent. Be prepared to fail and, if you do, own it and learn from it. Then pick yourself up and move forward. Standing still is never an option!'

'I would really like a chat with them right now,' Lee heard himself say out loud. He pressed the reply icon at the top of his MacBook screen.

The Australian government's pandemic-related travel restrictions were at last easing and, the following week, James found himself in Singapore. The city state had been one of our regular haunts before the advent of Covid-19. When I had first visited while in the army many years earlier, Beach Road really was at the seafront!

Neither James nor I are financiers but our initial advice was: 'Don't buy the TV station, Lee. Don't give in to the shareholders' or the banks' demands. Keep the cash in the bank!'

As a priority, Lee needed to speak with each board director individually to better ascertain their personal views. And he urgently needed to find someone with radio and print experience who could travel to the US.

Lee was also encouraged to meet with all the creditor banks, virtually and in person when possible. The company was not in default and was fully adhering to its bank covenants. Lee then sought the chairman's approval for three interviews with selected regional finance journalists.

On James's return to Australia, he was stuck in hotel quarantine for two weeks but we both still met with Lee by video call early each morning. Working with Lee, we mapped out the strategy for the day, including preparing for every meeting, in person and via video, with directors, employees, the US team, the banks and the major shareholders. Lee even found time to catch up with his friend Mav and to explain why the TV station deal was not possible at that time.

The media business survived. It was ultimately sold by public offering on the Singapore stock exchange. Lee became its chief executive.

For You ...

This story highlights the importance of relationships. Lee was juggling a number of stakeholders, most with competing interests. Everyone was under considerable pressure, particularly Lee, who consistently had to rise to every occasion and give his most and be his best.

The quote in the story heading is a favourite. It's attributed to the late Margaret Thatcher, the former British prime minister, when visiting then US president George Bush to discuss the West's response to Saddam Hussein's invasion of Kuwait in 1990. The president was apparently displaying some reluctance to mount a military response. Lady Thatcher, taking him by the arm as they walked together in the famous White House Rose Garden, reportedly urged 'Don't go wobbly on me now, George!'

Bush didn't. Later that year, the Americans led an international force that ejected the Iraqis from Kuwait in what became known as the First Gulf War. True leaders do not wobble!

IQ in Practice

- When facing complexity or uncertainty and you don't have all the answers, you still need to do something
- Total certainty is rare; dig deep and, with whatever information you can muster, use your acumen and your intuition to form your own
- Keep your cool, prioritise activities according to what's urgent and then what's important, maintain perspective and be mindful of the future
- It comes down to judgement – doing what you believe to be the right thing and doing it as well as you can
- Acknowledge your limitations and be willing to seek advice
- Understand with whom you're dealing and where they're coming from
- Involve and delegate to others, setting clear tasks, expectations and timelines
- Maintain your confidence and share it with those around you
- Communicate, communicate, communicate!

Your 21+90 Days Habit-Forming Challenge:

When the pressure's on, stand or sit still with both feet apart and firmly planted on the ground and follow the breathing exercise described on page 35. Then say what needs to be said and do what needs to be done.

'What's the story there, mate?'
Always focus on the end game

'Start with the end in mind.' This is one of the many pieces of advice offered by author Stephen Covey, whom I quoted earlier.

I first understood the importance of this concept as a young army officer. I also learned that inner confidence, a clear understanding of the objective and a relentless focus on the desired outcome, while maintaining execution flexibility, are true leadership essentials.

Burns pointed this out to the new chief executive of a leading South Africa-based international trading conglomerate in their first meeting. Burns had been invited to attend the rehearsal of the company's annual results announcement due the following morning. He was excited; we had long wanted to work with this institution that had almost failed during the Global Financial Crisis. The organisation had been rescued thanks to some deft moves by its chairman, who had appointed the first overseas chief executive, a highly experienced Scotsman, to lead it through the crisis.

His job done, the Scot returned home. His successor's appointment greatly surprised the market and the conglomerate's stock price, still volatile, took a tumble. Having spent most of her career with the Reserve Bank of South Africa, Karyn wasn't in the mould of a traditional chief executive of such a multidisciplinary organisation. As a highly regarded senior economist, she had helped to guide her country through its greatest economic challenge since the Great Depression. Risk and prudent financial management were now the trading company board's focus and, in the directors' eyes, Karyn was the right person for the job.

Burns sat patiently as Karyn and her finance vice president went through their paces. The projector whirred as the seemingly endless supply of PowerPoint slides flashed by. At last, the end came and they joined him at the back of the conference room. Also at the table were the group head of communications and his investor and media managers. Only the latter already knew Burns.

'What do you think?' asked Jabu, the communications chief.

Burns took a deep breath. He thought the presentation had been awful. Of course, he didn't want to destroy the new chief executive's confidence given that the main event was just hours away. Burns also reminded himself that this was our first opportunity to work with this organisation. Unsurprisingly, he did not want to screw up before he'd even begun. Yet he had to be true to himself, uphold our purpose and meet the expectations of the young media manager who had invited him to the rehearsal. There was silence as Burns felt the five pairs of eyes boring into him.

'Well, thank you for allowing me to join you here this evening, Karyn,' he began, looking the new chief executive right in the eye. 'Before I answer Jabu's question, may I ask you one?

'Imagine it's 11am tomorrow morning. You have just given that presentation and answered those questions. As an analyst with the local office of Goffmann Sax, I've attended your briefing and, as I leave the building, one of my buddies from global investor Franz Bloch sees me and says: "Hey, what are you doing in this part of town?"

'To which I respond: "Hi Michal, I've just attended the Morenstorenhoff Group's annual results announcement." "Oh, really. What's the story there, mate?" asks my friend.

'How would you want me to answer, Karyn?' The former senior economist and now chief executive nodded. 'That's a good question!'

Karyn's brow furrowed as she stared motionless at the table between them. She was thinking deeply about her answer to Burns's challenge. So much so that her communications chief began to look concerned. 'Who is this jerk?' Jabu was probably thinking, glancing at Burns: 'How dare he put my new boss under such pressure?'

In contrast, the media manager was almost certainly saying to herself: 'This is precisely why I wanted Burns to attend the rehearsal.'

'OK, here's your answer,' the new chief executive announced at last. 'I would want you to say that the group really has turned the corner and it's still in safe hands.'

'That's a terrific answer, Karyn. I can understand you wanting to get those thoughts across tomorrow,' Burns replied. 'After all, just a few years ago, Morenstorenhoff was on the verge of lodging a bankruptcy filing under the 2008 South African Companies Act. The board made some dramatic changes, including the appointment of your predecessor.

'He's now departed and, given your background, people are wondering, "Who is this new CEO? Has she got what it takes? Is the company really OK?"

'Putting my insider obligations aside momentarily, if I were to be stopped as I leave the building this evening and asked the question that I've just posed, I'm not sure how I would answer. It certainly wouldn't be as clear as you were just now, Karyn,' Burns continued.

'However, now that we know what you're aiming to achieve tomorrow, let's take a look at what you're saying and how you're saying it.

'Let's agree that your answer to my question, succinct and confident as it was, is simply a concept, a claim. That's fine. As I've said, I fully understand your wanting to make that assertion. We just need to ensure that it's believable and memorable.'

Over the next few hours, they worked with the Larrymid, so named by a former client (see page 219), to clarify and structure the flow of the presentation. This also helped to identify the issues and prepare answers to the likely questions. The visual support was greatly reduced, with the excess going into a separate slide pack that the audience could take away. After the scripted speeches had also been reduced to short bullet prompts, the two executives moved from presenting to communicating. It was a long night!

While the investor briefing went well the next morning, the best part of this story occurred several months later. Burns was working with some analysts at the Johannesburg office of a leading Wall Street investment house.

'Any of you FMCG [Fast-Moving Consumer Goods] or finance analysts?' he asked the group.

'Sure!' responded two of those present.

'Thanks. By chance, were either of you at Morenstorenhoff's annual results briefing a few months back?'

'Yep, we both were,' replied the older of the two. Burns realised he was Sammy Dipankar, then the country's leading FMCG analyst.

'What was the story there, Sammy?' he asked without a hint of irony.

'Well, it was reassuringly good. Karyn, the new chief executive, is relatively unknown to the market. Nevertheless, she impressed us with her candour and confidence. The numbers are starting to look strong again too. We feel the company really has turned the corner and it's in safe hands.'

Burns stifled a laugh and said, 'Great! What were the pre-tax profit and the return on equity?'

'I can't recall precisely,' came the response. 'Of course, we have those details in our models.'

For You …

I have reminded you that, like most things in life, the stock market moves on two axes – substance and sentiment. Initially, Karyn and her advisors had focused too much on the former without appreciating that the latter will endure far longer, even in the most analytical minds. They needed to tell their story if they were to sell their numbers successfully.

Data alone is meaningless and can easily be misinterpreted by the receiver. The leader's job is to assess information and fashion it to influence his or her listeners. I describe this as recognising that the sizzle is as important as the sausage; if the former entices and the latter satisfies, the taste will linger longer!

True leaders always start with a clear view of the desired end state. This almost certainly requires the confidence to say less yet convey more – following the KISSSS principle is always best: Keep It Short, Simple, Specific and Structured.

IQ in Practice

- 'If you don't know where you're going, any road will get you there', paraphrased from Alice in Wonderland by Lewis Carroll (1832–1898)
- Again, think intent before content and outcome before process
- Be sure to get your story straight before you tell it
- Identify the overarching headline message or theme that you want your listeners to take away and to remember – and keep it simple
- Establish the logic-flow to support the message and bring it to life
- In people's minds, feelings last a lot longer than facts
- Perceptions are real to those who hold them and must be managed

Your 21+90 Days Habit-Forming Challenge:

Before every meeting, be aware of who will be there and why, and identify what you want to happen – what you want them to think, feel and do afterwards.

IQ: The Quality of Intent in Summary: Doing Our Purposeful 'What'

The four core IQ strengths, main traits and behaviours:

Context: Maintaining perspective and seeing the bigger picture

Reality: awareness of who we are, who we're with and the situation

Opportunities: recognising the difference we can make

Change: inevitable, and fundamentally what leadership is for

Challenges: appreciating what may hinder us

Risk: identifying what could go wrong or we could get wrong

Governance: oversight, checks and balances, and the 'smell test'

Clarity: Keeping it simple, specific and attainable

Brand: the who – our essence, what we stand for and want to be known for

Mission: the why – our purpose and the difference we make

Vision: the where – our big idea, the headline, the 'light on the hill'

Higher intent: the mountaintop – the one thing we can all relate to and strive for

Strategy: the how – the building blocks upon which we base our idea and form our plan of action

Tactics: the what – the activities, initiatives and operations that bring our plan or story to life and and enable us to execute it

Certainty: The essentials to validate our big idea and enable our success

Resources: our qualified and experienced team, required materials, finance and more

Structure: our logic-flow and weighting of the plan elements

Culture: the glue that binds us together and either drives or destroys our performance

Environment: what allows our desired culture to live or die

Priorities: determining what's urgent and important and how best to proceed

Goals: the milestones along the way that keep us on track and on time

Measures: when we know we're succeeding or not

Commitment: Without it, even our best ideas or intentions will come to nought

Alignment: getting everyone in the boat and rowing together in the same direction

Innovation: constantly challenging ourselves and others: is there a better way?

Focus: sticking to the vision, managing complexity and avoiding distractions

Decisions: sometimes difficult but making them is always necessary

Execution: getting on the field and, together, kicking the ball towards the goal

Outcome: the endgame and knowing we gave our most and did our best, win or lose

Part 3: The True Leader's Communication Toolkit

The single biggest problem in communication is the illusion that it has taken place.

A Strategic Issue

As I have attempted to illustrate, organisational success and failure start at the top. To excel, organisations need confident, articulate leaders who are able to influence and inspire others by consistently communicating their values, wisdom, passion and vision.

As a true leader, this requires you to have two overarching communication objectives. First, make sure that your own natural character and personality strengths come across so that you are seen for who you really are. Only in this way will you gain the trust and confidence of your listeners. Second, ensure that you share your thoughts in such a way that they will be listened to, understood, believed, remembered and acted upon. Put simply, to truly lead you need to reveal what's in your head and in your heart.

This is not about changing you or your own personal style. It is about employing some straightforward, practical tools to help you perform at the top of your own game consistently, whatever the pressure or circumstance, just as you have seen exemplified in many of the scenarios I've shared with you.

Relating to your listeners is the starting point to successfully engaging them. This begins with a plan and ends with you giving your best to every audience, large or small, every time. Of course, it's not just about speaking in public or to the media. What I'm referring to is the basic, crucial requirement to communicate openly, to listen actively, to understand and to respond appropriately.

The ideas in this section will help you reflect on much of what I have covered. They will also give you many of the tools with which to lift your own communication effectiveness and truly lead others' thoughts and actions.

Presentation or Communication?

I had been invited to speak to a few hundred executives at their company's annual conference. The topic was presentation skills and, while grateful for the opportunity, I groaned and thought to myself, 'Really?'

I walked onto the stage and stood motionless in front of the crowd. It was the end of their second day and, judging by the full agenda, it had been a long one. The previous day had apparently been similar and the next would be little different.

I scanned the audience in silence for several seconds. 'So, who has been giving presentations in the past couple of days?' I asked. Several hands were raised. 'And tomorrow?' More hands raised.

'Well, it seems you don't need much help from me! But, as I'm here, I'd like to share some simple words of advice: when it comes to giving presentations ... whenever possible, please don't!'

There was an audible gasp around the room. The group's head of human resources, who had hired me, began to look very uncomfortable.

I continued, 'To help you understand why I've just said that, hands up those of you who've ever sat in an auditorium like this, or even a small meeting room, and occasionally switched off while someone is speaking about their particular topic, just as I'm doing now.'

I raised my own hand and within seconds everyone followed. I'm sure you would have done the same had you been there.

'Please keep your hands up and look around the room. This is why we shouldn't give presentations. No one's listening!

'So, what should we do instead?' I posed to them.

Let me share with you some of what I told them.

Presentation, originating from the Latin verb *praesentare* (to reveal), is a one-way process, as in, for example, offering a present or gift. I am not sure about you but, however perfect it always seems to me, my gift-giving is a bit hit and miss! Within moments of it being unwrapped, I can soon tell when I've missed the mark.

It's the same with presentations. I see many presenters who have carefully prepared and rehearsed their presentations, often over several weeks, and even dressed for success, only to have their words fall on deaf ears.

I have also observed that most presentation advice appears to be premised on some kind of special model of excellence. To succeed, we're told that we have to be perfect and do it a certain way. The focus is almost exclusively on the speaker – the giver. From how they stand, move and breathe, what they wear, where they look and how they gesture, to the content of their visual support. This is largely wrong. It's never about perfection. It's simply about us each giving our personal most and being our individual best. That's enough.

Yes, we need to be appropriate. Critically, we must also be our real, natural self in every circumstance. What I refer to as our appropriate authenticity.

Earlier, I wrote about a senior communications manager who appeared to be more concerned about her boss's gestures than whether anyone actually believed him. I recall another 'expert' whom I recently observed advising how his boss should position her head – 'slightly more angled to the right' – and how to place her hand – 'a bit closer to the table edge'. Just nonsense, frankly.

This comes back to managing instead of leading. As we have seen, managers need to inform, but leaders must inspire. Managers convey facts, which alone are meaningless; leaders give them meaning. Managers focus on their content; leaders on their intent. Managers transact; leaders transform. Managers present; true leaders communicate.

As in every aspect of life, leadership success is about the strength of relationships. When speaking, if we are to influence the thoughts and inspire the actions of our listeners, we must set out to build and maintain a relationship with them. This applies whether speaking to a crowd of several hundred or even thousand, a small group or one to one.

How do we build relationships every day? Not by presenting, spouting endless data or running through a pack of slides! Instead of focusing on ourselves and our content, we focus on our listeners and our intent. We communicate with them.

Communication also derives from the Latin, in this case *communicare* (to share). It's a two-way process, with the listener being in control and determining the pace. As I have pointed out, listening is voluntary – listeners do not have to listen! The challenge for leaders and speakers is to have people choose to listen and continue doing so.

As I also mentioned earlier, the biggest conversation in our lives is with ourselves. Each of us thinks all day; we dream at night; and, occasionally, we even talk to ourselves. Listening to someone else requires conscious effort because our brains are already preoccupied with our own thoughts!

Furthermore, the average, overall speaking pace is 120–160 words per minute. According to the *Harvard Business Review*, our listening capacity is higher and our thinking capacity is far higher still. Our brains therefore have spare capacity! Not surprisingly, we become easily distracted due to listening to ourselves internally. As a result, we often 'switch off' momentarily when trying to listen to someone externally.

As a leader and a speaker, if you are to succeed in consistently engaging people, having them buy into you and come with you, you need to be aware of the listening process. Remember: if people aren't listening to you, they are not following and you are not leading.

But to return to the story, I caught up with our human resources client a few days later. He told me that, yes, my 'disruptive presentation' had indeed made an impact. So much so that every executive who spoke the next day did so very differently to their colleagues on the previous days. They used very few slides, told stories, connected with the audience and moved them. This is another example of the power of effective leadership communication.

The Head + Heart model on the next page illustrates the engagement process and highlights the difference between presentation and communication. On the right, underpinned by the core principles of mutuality – mutual trust, respect and purpose – you see that communication is about the two-way opportunity to connect with and move listeners – the intent. I represent the listener's mind as a heart. This is to remind us that communication is about feelings as well as facts. We remember the former long after we've forgotten the latter!

On the left, you see how presentation is one-way speaker- and content-driven – the event. This is illustrated by the 'ball and chain', which acts like a hidden weight around the speaker's neck, pulling attention away from their listeners and onto themselves instead. This phenomenon grows when under pressure.

Engagement with Head + Heart

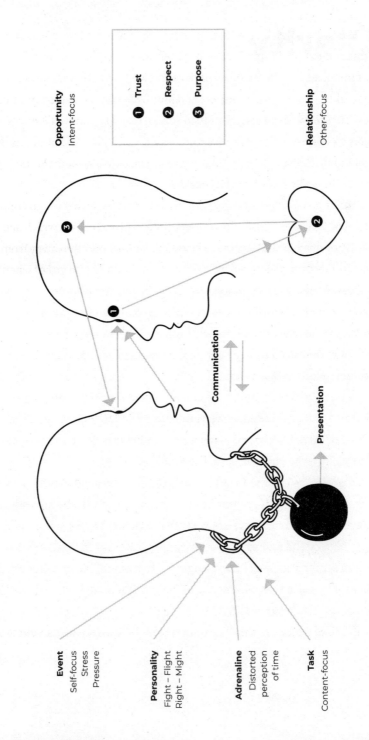

Opportunity
Intent-focus

1 Trust
2 Respect
3 Purpose

Relationship
Other-focus

Communication

Presentation

Event
Self-focus
Stress
Pressure

Personality
Fight – Flight
Right – Might

Adrenaline
Distorted
perception
of time

Task
Content-focus

Clarity:
Head

Clarity of strategy and structure forms the basis of successful leadership communication.

One of our biggest challenges is to stop people focusing on content too early. They seem happiest when they are writing volumes of words or preparing endless slides. Instead, before writing a word or opening their computer software, they need to step back and think intent – Who? Why? Where?, then content – How? What? When?

I have never heard anyone be congratulated for being complicated, muddled or long-winded. Have you? I often need to remind clients and myself of US politician and playwright Clare Boothe Luce's observation that 'Simplicity is the ultimate sophistication'.

Of course, as I learned working with CDP, capturing the essence of what it is that we seek to convey in simple terms is not easy. It's why advertising art directors and copywriters are among the most highly paid in their industry. They understand and apply the persuasive powers of rhetoric and imagery.

As a leader, you must have a single, clear, overarching message for each of your communications whether oral or verbal. Then support it with a few key points and bring them to life!

To achieve this, use the Preparation Steps below and the Larrymid on page 219.

Who, Why, Where

This is fundamental. Here's the first question you need to ask yourself, or your boss if they have asked you to set up or participate in a meeting: What is its purpose? Why you? Who will be attending? And what is the expected outcome?

1. Establish the objectives of the meeting or talk

- Who are you; who are the others (your audience/listeners) and what's their situation?
- Why are you here? Why are they here?
- What are their expectations of this meeting or talk, and their expectations of you? What's in this for them?
- Who are the decision-makers and influencers, if any?
- Where must you take them? What do you want them to think, feel and do afterwards?

2. Aim to achieve rapport

You may be familiar with the proverb: 'different strokes for different folks'. You need to relate to your audience by understanding what makes them tick! To do this, you must first research and analyse them. Then build a bridge. So, ask yourself:

- What does it feel like to be this person?
- What about their background; their values and beliefs; their likes and dislikes?
- What do they want? (e.g. hopes/aspirations/needs/concerns/issues/fears)
- What is their level of knowledge of the topic? And how do they feel about it?
- How do they feel about you/your team/your organisation?
- Also, as far as possible, consider their personal style/preferences. To help, please refer to the Communication Styles model on page 226.

3. Identify the essence

Write down a single phrase or sentence which addresses the objectives and encapsulates your overall idea, theme or headline message. This provides the focus of your talk. To discover this headline message, ask yourself:

· Returning to the first step above, what do you want these people to think, feel and do afterwards that will meet both your objectives and their expectations?
· To achieve this, what is the overriding, top-of-mind thought/idea/perception you want them to take away?

Now, with your overarching theme/message in the centre, form a mind map as you build your content following the steps below.

How, What, When

4. Keep it simple, short, structured and specific – KISSSS

Limit yourself to three key points to support your theme. This is the hardest thing to do. We all like to demonstrate our knowledge! It is far better that your listeners clearly remember your three points than be overwhelmed by an avalanche of thoughts and remember nothing! You can always supply written material to support your points. And be sure to frame your argument in both language and style to suit your audience and its preferences.

5. Flesh out your key points

Use a logical flow to support and expand an argument, for example:

· Situation	→ Challenge	→ Answer	→ Consequences
· Problem	→ Options	→ Solution	→ Impact
· Trends	→ Analysis	→ Recommendation	→ Advantages
· Purpose	→ Programme	→ Execution	→ Outcomes
· Needs analysis	→ Product/Service	→ Features	→ Benefits
· Background	→ Current performance	→ Future expectations	→ Results

6. Consider contrasts

Using contrast for emphasis can assist your listeners' understanding of your key points, for example:

- Chronological: Time-based (e.g. yesterday ... today ... tomorrow)
- Geographical: Place (e.g. New York ... Mumbai ...Auckland)
- Focal: Changing perspective (macro to micro or vice versa)
- Analytical: Issue/problem (alternative solutions + recommendation)
- Aspects: Features/facts (what it is)
- Functions: Benefits (what it does)
- Consequences: Value or difference (what it delivers)
- Alternatives: On the one hand ... and on the other ... (comparison)
- Extremes: Highest ... lowest (compromise/the best way forward)
- Priorities: First ... second ... next ... and finally ... (ranking)

7. Link with everyday transition phrases

These help to connect parts of your talk, for example:

- First of all, let's look at ...
- Which brings me to ...
- Moving on, let's consider ...
- I believe another important issue ...
- Finally, I would like to ...
- That covers ... (consider inserting 'mini-summaries' after each major point)
- So, bringing all this together, what have I been talking about today?
- In a nutshell ... (i.e. overall summary)
- If there is just one thing I would like you remember ... (i.e. conclusion)
- Why this is important and what it means ... (i.e. benefits and consequences that link to your headline message)

8. Check the 'So what?'

Be clear about the difference between features, benefits and consequences, i.e. Why are you sharing this with your listeners? How does it affect them and what does it actually *mean/achieve* for them? Again, what do you want them to think, feel and do as a result? Similarly, when answering questions (see page 248), be able to supply proof of your arguments. Reviewing your preparation thus far, use this checklist to evaluate and unpack each of the key points that support your headline message. Your key supporting points could be claims, facts, features, reasons, explanations, priorities, solutions and recommendations, for example:

- Proof: How/why is this so? Give reasons, evidence or examples by way of validation.
- Relevance: How does it relate to them? Use analogies, anecdotes, humour.
- Benefit: What does it mean for them and how does it affect them?
- Consequence: What is the real value, impact or difference for them?

The LARRYMID

CONTEXT Situation / Market / Opportunity / Problem / Complication / Identity / Values / Audience / Purpose = The 'Who' & 'Why'

**CLARITY /
CONCEPT / CLAIM**
Belief / Big Idea /
Headline / Vision /
Higher Intent / Offer /
Message / Solution
= The 'Where'

CERTAINTY
Explanation / Rationale / Support / Strategy
= The 'How (come?)'

CONTENT + COLOUR
e.g. Detail / Proof / Evidence / Examples / Stories / Tactics /
Initiatives / Efficiencies / Resources / Culture
= The 'What'

CONCLUSION + CONSEQUENCE + CALL TO ACTION
Incl. Summary / Benefit / Implication / Value / Goals / Results
= The 'So What?' & The 'When'

Then share **Concisely** & **Conversationally**,
with **Conviction** & **Charm**!

CONTEXT Situation / Market / Opportunity / Problem / Complication / Identity / Values / Audience / Purpose = The 'Who' & 'Why'

LISTENER &
STAKEHOLDER
CONFIDENCE

9. Summarise your logic-flow on a page

Having created your mind map and before settling on any visual support (e.g. slides), prepare a simple, linear run-sheet on a single page using the deductive approach shown in the Larrymid above, as follows:

- **Context** (whom you will be speaking with, why and their current situation): Identify your topic/audience and introduction/opening to get their attention/paint a picture/use an image/tell a story/share a personal experience/set some bait/get your listener thinking. Be sure to relate the opening to your purpose and overall message/theme. Introduce the agenda if necessary.
- **Clarity** (where you want to take them): Your single big idea/core message/theme/claim (the first 'bookend').
- **Certainty** (how you will get them there): The three key points to validate and support your big idea/message.
- **Content and Colour** (data/examples/anecdotes to bring your key points to life): The three sub-points (max) to prove/illustrate each key point.
- **Conclusion** (e.g. 'So, let me bring all this together'.)
- **Consequence** (e.g. 'In a nutshell ...'): Return to your headline message – the feeling/theme/claim linked to opening (the matching, second 'bookend') and the final thought/what this means/the value/the way forward/the call to action.

Bring your story to life

10. Illustrate your talk

This is how you will really engage your listeners and help them remember what you are saying. It's the 'colour' to which I refer above. Be aware of the VAK (visual, auditory and kinaesthetic) pathways to a listener's mind and heart. Every audience is made up of people with a dominant pathway, just as you and I are. Where possible, use visual (e.g. 'looks like'), auditory (e.g. 'sounds like') and kinaesthetic (e.g. 'feels like') phrases to explain your points and to get your audience to sit up and listen.

Sharing examples, employing metaphors and telling stories are the true leader's best visual support. We relate to stories. They touch the heart and contribute to the emotional experience, so that any meeting or event becomes more than data-driven exposition. As we saw in the final IQ story earlier, even the most analytical people remember feelings long after they've forgotten facts!

A range of visual aids such as slides, videos, models, diagrams, boards, placemats, brochures and so forth can also be good ways to illustrate your points. These can also keep your audience on track and help its understanding of your ideas.

However, recognise that such aids inform; true leaders influence and inspire. When used, visuals should support your talk, not drive it. They should assist the audience, not replace you. As a leader of thought, *you* are your most important visual aid and the imaginations of your listeners are theirs.

So, resist building your talk around visual aids and be selective in their use. As I advise above, prepare your mind map and one-page storyline first before deciding how best to bring your talk to life. Put your points across by saying them first and use stories, examples and visual aids to reinforce as necessary.

All support must earn its place. If in doubt, ask yourself: Why do I want to tell this story or show this slide, model or chart here? What is it actually saying, demonstrating or proving? What will the take-away be for my audience? Is there a better way to achieve this? Oftentimes, the most impactful aid is a simple sketch or diagram drawn spontaneously with a thick black marker on a whiteboard or flipchart. The story in the IQ section where I described writing BIGGEST on a whiteboard and crossing out IGG is an example.

While visual aids can form an important dimension for any talk, too many speakers treat them as a prop or even their proxy. They can also distract if not properly managed. As always, the basic rule is to keep your visual aids simple. Images, diagrams and physical objects work better than words. If you need to put words on your slides, limit them to no more than a dozen and ensure they can be read at the back of the room!

Every talk should be capable of surviving on the oral content alone. You may be unlucky enough to lose the materials on the way to the meeting or encounter a power failure moments before you're due to start. Like any tool, technology is not foolproof!

A story to bring these points to life

A few years ago, a global resources company got into trouble. The share price collapsed and the board replaced the chief executive officer with an engineer from overseas. Mario had successfully turned around two similar organisations in South Africa.

The new chief executive's first investor briefing had been scheduled and I worked with many of the senior executives who would be speaking that day. I knew the company's investor relations chief, Elias, well. He and his team worked into the small hours night after night preparing reams of PowerPoint slides for the chief executive and the other speakers.

After welcoming over 200 analysts and institutional investors and giving the standard safety advice, Elias invited his new boss to the podium. The slides started to roll. After a couple of minutes, the chief executive stopped talking and called out to his colleague.

'Hey, Elias, can you get someone to turn this stuff off, please? I think everyone already has the slide pack. If not, they can collect it at the end.'

Speaking directly to the audience, Mario continued, 'I imagine the main reason you're here is to get the measure of me. You may be wondering: Does he really know what's going on with this organisation? Is he up for the task ahead? Can we trust him to deliver? You will best answer those questions by not being distracted by what's on that screen behind me!'

I smiled broadly and almost clapped. This was precisely what I would have recommended had I been asked; although I did feel for my friend Elias!

Clarity in Summary

As a former soldier, I am reminded of this amusing World War I anecdote that illustrates the importance of communication clarity. It may be familiar to you.

The message allegedly sent from the front line: 'Send reinforcements, we're going to advance.' The message that ultimately reached headquarters: 'Send three and fourpence, we're going to a dance!'

Use the Preparation Steps and the Larrymid. Understand your audience's situation, needs, wants, preferences and expectations. Be clear about your purpose and your overarching message or big idea. Build a logic-flow in support. Put it together as a story that paints a picture of where you're going and explains how you are taking your listeners there.

Bring it to life! Illustrate your argument and support your points by showing the value that comes from appealing to your listeners' hearts as well as to their heads. And beware over-reliance on technology!

If we are to achieve the two objectives of spoken communication that I mention above, we must maintain the undivided attention of our audience. Always remember: our message is not just the facts, but how we *feel* about those facts.

With PowerPoint or Keynote, the most valuable tool is at your fingertips: when you press the B key, the screen goes blank. This enables you to interrupt your 'slide show' occasionally and have your audience refocus their attention fully on you and what you're saying. We also encourage clients to build in blank or minimalist slides to achieve the same outcome.

Humanity:
Heart

Every spoken communication, informal and formal, is fundamentally about the quality of the engagement.

If you have ever felt nervous before speaking with a group of people, you're not alone. Even the most experienced among us question themselves ahead of important events. As a member of the Professional Speakers Association, I regularly hear declarations from even the most proficient members like: 'I doubt myself each time I go on stage!'

Nerves arise because we sense we are about to be judged. Naturally, we do not want to let ourselves, our boss, our colleagues or our broader audience down.

In such situations, I imagine you have been told, 'Just be yourself.' This is good advice but not quite as simple as it sounds. It requires you to be prepared, to know the circumstances of your listeners and to be the most and best of the real you – authentic, relaxed, affable, personable, yet also confident, focused, appropriate and effective. The stories in the 3 Qs sections demonstrate this.

Again, You Are Your Brand

What do you offer and what do you want to be known for? Are your appearance, demeanour, manner, style, clothes and, most importantly, your mindset and attitude commensurate with these aspirations?

This starts with the first impression. Be aware of how you are walking, standing and sitting. Generally, pull your shoulders back and walk, stand or sit tall! Feel and look as if you really want to be there 100 per cent. Reach out, connect and engage with the other person and, if appropriate, smile. Looking straight at them, shake hands firmly with your hand *and* with your eyes, and don't be in a hurry to disengage.

As we've seen in the AQ section, impressions apply to every encounter, informal or formal, whoever they are with. They last a long time and need to meet expectations. Constantly ask yourself, 'Who are these people and why are we all here? Am I feeling and showing that I really want to be here? Right now? If not, why am I actually here?'

In communication, as with most things in life, what one gives one usually gets back. So, again, always try to give 100 per cent of yourself if you want 100 per cent of them!

Managing the Pressure

As I've indicated, our thinking capacity exceeds our listening capacity. If anything, what your listeners remember is less about what you say than about how you make them feel. To have the best chance of being listened to and having your points remembered, you must give them time to reflect on what you're saying, how you're saying it, and what it means for them.

In most situations when we are engaging with others, for example in normal conversation, our attention is naturally and comfortably focused on them. In stressful situations when under pressure, tired or feeling threatened, confused, nervous or angry, we revert to our individual personality type and unwittingly focus on ourselves.

A lot has been written about personality types over the past hundred or so years. Having studied several methodologies, I have adopted a straightforward approach which acknowledges some of Carl Jung's theories. Please refer to the Communication Styles model on the next page. It is not exhaustive and should be treated as a guide only.

Based on an individual's natural level of assertiveness and responsiveness, the four leadership communication styles I describe are purposeful/driving, considerate/amiable, organised/analytical and inspirational/expressive.

Communication Styles

Outcome /
Task-oriented

Transformational
Big picture / vision / mission / values /
belief / meaning / change / motivation

Outcome /
Feeling-oriented

Extroversion & Inspiration

Directive
Project & task
-driven / clear /
firm / overcomes
inertia / factual /
less awareness
of self & others /
unemotional /
presentation

Left brain oriented

**PURPOSEFUL /
DRIVING**
Clarity / intent / curiosity /
focus / confidence /
decision / urgency /
action / assertiveness /
control / direction /
change – seeks
performance & results

**INSPIRATIONAL /
EXPRESSIVE**
Concept / imagination /
enthusiasm / pride /
spontaneity / risk / fun /
responsibility for team /
opinion / warmth / novelty
– seeks recognition &
excitement

**ORGANISED /
ANALYTICAL**
Logic / systems /
structure / plan / discipline /
efficiency / detail / caution /
evidence / reflection /
measure – seeks accuracy
& predictability

**CONSIDERATE /
AMIABLE**
Empathy / care / team /
support of & interest in
others / co-operation /
mediation / steady / status
quo – seeks harmony
& collaboration

Right brain oriented

Participative
Relationship
-driven /
emotional /
encouraging /
brings out best
in people /
greater
awareness of
self & others /
conceptual /
communication

Introversion & Information

Transactional
Detail / process / rules / short term /
caution / incremental improvement

Process /
Data-oriented

Process /
Feeling-oriented

Each of us displays a blend of these. In my experience, one or two are typically more dominant. In my Head & Heart model on page 213, I have applied the commonplace descriptors 'fight' and 'flight'. I have also added two more, 'right' and 'might'. Each of us needs to be aware which of them relate to us and how they manifest when we're under pressure. Fight is about self-justification, flight self-preservation, and right self-perfection. With tongue slightly in cheek, I describe 'might' as self-delusion!

When stressed or anxious, our amygdala, which I referred to in the Self-Leadership chapter, swells and our individual personality type takes over. Adrenaline now flows into our bloodstream, thinning the blood and drawing oxygen from the brain. This phenomenon accentuates the physical over the rational, affecting our thinking and the ideas we want to share.

Adrenaline is our friend when sprinting 100 metres but not when speaking. It causes us to lose sense of time. We move and speak faster without realising; we overload our listeners with content and risk leaving them behind. The result? The 'ball and chain' (again, refer to the Head & Heart model on page 213) kicks in, our focus shifts to ourselves, on what we're saying or doing (our content and the task) instead of with whom and why (our listeners and the purpose). As a result, we fail to bring them with us (the lost opportunity).

A common manifestation of this situation is to use 'filler' words and phrases such as *um, er* and *you know*. Driven by the subconscious rush and the physical need to make a noise (it is what speakers do!), we insert these without thinking in order to fill the gap. As true leaders, we must become more comfortable with silence. As alluded to above, listeners cannot and will not listen to constant noise. Speakers need to help their listeners listen. Recognise that fillers are vocalised thinking pauses and do your best to cut them out by saying nothing instead.

To help, exaggerate your pauses with deliberate, one-to-one eye contact. Pausing provides the opportunity to think about what you really want to say and to whom. And it enables you to breathe deeply, draw more air into your lungs and speak with more gravitas. While often uncomfortable for speakers, pauses are natural for their listeners. They allow them to keep up and ensure a natural, appropriate and listener-friendly delivery style. Pauses also create greater and more lasting impact.

Listeners Drive the Process

As I have pointed out, just as the follower chooses to follow, the listener chooses to listen and thereby determines the speaker's success. In the True Leader's 6 Ps Drill model on page 232, the listener's mind is again shown as a heart. Around it you will see what resembles a string of pearls. These represent the invisible filters of belief that we each develop from childhood. They are formed by our upbringing, education and experiences.

As a listener, we perceive and assess situations and people through these filters. They are comprised of our personal values, biases, prejudices, views, expectations and so on. If the speaker doesn't measure up, if, for example, they appear nervous or disorganised or they're rambling, our tendency is to literally close our ears and revert to our own internal conversation. We listen on trust.

Again, beware paying too much attention to your carefully planned content. Rather, to get your listeners' buy-in, observe and react to their signals. By so doing, you will keep them coming with you and achieve your and their mutual purpose.

We regularly achieve the two objectives of leadership communication through natural, comfortable, person-to-person, conversational delivery. It's how we speak and listen successfully in all of our daily spoken communications. As I've also pointed out, it's how we build relationships.

When in a normal, meaningful conversation, we speak in short bursts, stopping and starting at random with regular pauses. We repeat ourselves. We constantly and naturally vary our pitch, intonation and inflection according to how we feel about what we're saying, why we're saying it and to whom. Like fingerprints, each of us the world over has a different, unique style. We all use eye contact and non-verbal communication, such as facial expressions and gestures, spontaneously and effectively every day.

The 6 Ps Drill

I have captured the conversation process in my 6 Ps Drill:

P 1: Think of your mind as your personal 'hard disc': full of data, experiences, thoughts and memories. Gather one piece of data at a time; Pause to bring it to life and make it your own (with deliberate 1:1 eye contact), then:

P 2–5: Punch your Point with Passion and Purpose

P 6: OK? Pause to reinforce and check (with meaningful 1:1 eye contact).

The 6 Ps Drill allows your listeners to see you thinking about what you intend to say; this builds **trust**. It enables you to encapsulate thoughts in distinct, easily digestible ideas and share them succinctly and with feeling; this is how they listen and it shows your **respect**. And it gives them time to think about what you're saying and relate it to their own personal knowledge and experience; this helps to achieve your and their **purpose**.

Importantly, the 6 Ps Drill also helps to remove the aforementioned 'ball and chain' phenomenon.

The overarching rule: Begin and end each point with silence, coupled with deliberate, meaningful, 1:1 eye contact. A useful analogy is a bow and arrow.

P 1: First, gather a thought (the 'arrow') from your mind or from your written notes. Having selected the 'arrow', pause with deliberate 1:1 eye contact as you focus on and engage with one of your listeners. This pause enables you to convert the thought into your point as you pull back on the 'bow' and the 'arrow' becomes a 'weapon'.

- P1 enables you, as speaker and leader of thought, to appear authentic, trustworthy, composed, competent, thoughtful, focused, natural and appropriate – and not nervous
- It builds the significance of the moment and creates listener anticipation
- It demonstrates your confidence and comfort

- It allows you to select your thought (fact) and covert it to your personal point (feeling) while connecting with the person with whom you want to share it
- It encourages you to 'read' the situation before you speak, ensuring that what you say and how you say it (i.e. your manner/demeanour) is appropriate and congruent
- It gives you the opportunity to think about what you really want to say before you say it
- It allows you to introduce real or genuine emphasis to your words, thereby creating natural 'theatre'. In other words, it helps you to express how you actually *feel* about the facts, naturally expressing them as your own ideas rather than merely delivering the facts
- In summary, it forces you to think and breathe before you speak: Open your eyes, open your brain, open your lungs and open your mouth in this order, every time!
- And your listeners will trust you

P 2, 3, 4, 5: Then, Punch your Point with Passion & Purpose. Here you share your points, one at a time (releasing each 'arrow' towards a listener) with natural and appropriate energy, feeling and meaning.

- You come across as articulate and neither slick nor glib
- Your points are easily heard and absorbed by your listeners
- And your listeners will buy into you.

P 6: Now, the 'OK?' Pause to reinforce each point and check in with your listeners, again with 1:1 deliberate eye contact. Here you stop to check that your 'arrow' has reached your 'target' (listener).

- P6 separates what you are saying into easily digestible thoughts and ideas
- It ensures you don't dismiss what you have just said; instead, you reinforce it
- It maintains trust with your listeners while letting them compare your ideas with theirs

- It reflects your normal conversational style so the listener feels comfortable and involved
- It allows you to observe and respond to listener 'signals' such as looking for the 'nod factor' – by listening with your eyes
- You gain a second or two to reflect on what you have just said – do you need to qualify or amplify?
- You are shown to be confident and committed, which ensures your credibility, sincerity and integrity in the eyes of your listeners
- This creates presence and impact, assists with long-term memory and helps to build a memorable emotional experience for your listeners
- And your listeners will come with you.

For a visual representation, please refer to the True Leader's 6 Ps Drill model overleaf.

I encourage you to observe yourself and others when in normal, meaningful everyday conversation. Note how you and they speak naturally in soundbites – short bursts of words connected by pauses. Again, meaningful conversation is how everyone around the world forms and maintains their important relationships. Why should you speak – and lead – any other way? It's the credible, respectful and purposeful thing to do.

Here are two more stories to bring this to life. Both show how 'public speaking' is nothing more than publicising one's thoughts. It is how we each share our ideas effectively with others every day.

The Power of the Pause

The topic was customer service and in the audience were 150 executives from a large industrial company. The speaker was nervous but things seemed to be going pretty well. Then she noticed the chief executive at the back of the conference room. His head was down and he was reading a newspaper. The speaker did not know the CEO but recalled the familiar look of the

The True Leader's 6 Ps Drill

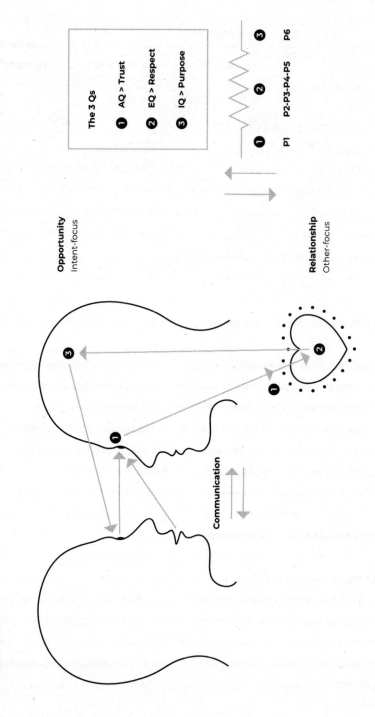

Opportunity
Intent-focus

Relationship
Other-focus

Communication

The 3 Qs

1 AQ > Trust

2 EQ > Respect

3 IQ > Purpose

P1   P2-P3-P4-P5   P6

Wall Street Journal, which she had noticed him holding as he entered the room.

The speaker's mind went blank. She could hear her voice quavering as she looked into the crowd. She began to panic, 'What was I saying? Help, I'm losing them!'

Her 'ball and chain' was pulling, driven by this unexpected situation. She had to do something to recover her poise and regain control of the room, but what? Then it came. She took a deep breath and said, 'Of course, communication is not only about making a noise, about speaking. Pausing is equally important. Let me show you how powerful silence can be.'

The speaker stood motionless with her eyes riveted to the woolly head of the chief executive at the back of the room. She could feel 150 pairs of eyes staring at her, perhaps waiting for some magic trick! She didn't dare look at them. Her gaze remained firmly on their boss. It felt like ages but after not more than six or seven seconds, the chief executive looked up and their eyes met.

The speaker continued looking directly at the CEO and, with a smile, said, 'Thank you, Mike.' The audience suddenly realised what had happened and began to laugh.

'I'm back in control,' she told herself. And she was. The chief executive appeared a little embarrassed as he pushed the newspaper aside. The speaker apologised to him after the session, explaining why she needed to get him to engage.

I urge you to practise my 6 Ps Drill when you speak in every situation, formal and informal. Listen for, use and enjoy your silence. When coupled with deliberate, meaningful one-to-one eye contact, you too will discover how silence can be the true leader's most powerful communication device.

The Constancy of Connection

In this second story, I'd been invited to speak at a human resources conference in London. There were almost one thousand attendees from around the world. The speakers ranged from academics and researchers from the leading business schools to experts from global consulting firms and senior executives from major international organisations. 'Why me?' I asked. Because you have some interesting and straightforward ideas on leadership, came the organisers' response.

Scotty, my brother-in-law, lives in London and, for the price of a good lunch, I persuaded him to attend my session. The previous evening, the organisers had put on a function for the speakers and those delegates who had bought premium tickets. There I bumped into a former CDP colleague, Tim, who was now group head of communications for a major institution in the City. Tim said he was looking forward to my talk. I confided that I was feeling rather nervous and asked him to sit where I could clearly see him among the crowd; his job was to give me an occasional nod and 'thumbs up'!

I was the first speaker on the second day. After being introduced, applying the 6 Ps Drill, I began, 'Good morning, everyone. It's great to be back in London.'

Then I paused and smiled at my brother-in-law just a few rows in front of me. 'Hi Scotty. Good to see you – thanks for coming.'

Pausing again, I now reached out to my former colleague seated further back, 'And great to see you after all these years, Tim. We have lots to catch up on!'

At that moment, I noticed a woman in the audience to my right. She was nodding as she looked at me.

'Good morning to you too. May I ask your name?' I asked.

'Barbara,' she replied with a broad smile.

'Where are you from, Barbara?'

'Birmingham,' she replied.

'Oh, so you're an out-of-towner like me, Barbara!' I laughed and so did she.

Turning to the centre of the auditorium, I continued, 'You see, the reason I'm always happy to be back in London is because I'm among friends.'

I could feel the crowd move. There were nods, smiles and even a few 'hear hears!' I knew then that they were with me and my nerves disappeared.

Every audience, large and small, is comprised of individuals. This story illustrates the point about not seeing groups of listeners as homogeneous. Audiences are comprised of men and women who all listen and think for themselves, just as you and I do in every situation every day.

To build a relationship with your listeners, you need to find something in common with them. Then reach out to individuals, connect and speak with them one to one with the 6 Ps Drill. Ideally, beforehand, ask a few attendees whom you know to give you some encouragement, as I did in London. Or simply arrive early and introduce yourself to some members of the audience and be sure to connect with any whom you recognise during your talk.

Use these people as your personal 'lighthouses' to encourage and give you energy as you speak. If neither option is possible, engage one to one with five or six people who are in different parts of the room and seem friendly! Seek and connect with more 'lighthouses' as you proceed and become more comfortable.

This way, the entire audience will listen to you because you are speaking in your normal, natural way. After all, this is how they each listen to everyone with whom they interact. As I have stressed, listening is voluntary. When speaking, you need to help your listeners choose to listen! Speak with them as individuals and make them feel special; give 100 per cent attitudinally, emotionally, rationally; open your mouth wide, articulate your words clearly and concisely. And, if like me, you often slur your words and run them together, deliberately enunciate your consonants and vowels.

Humanity in Summary

True leadership is relationship. Lasting relationships are only ever built and nurtured through meaningful conversation. This is why communication is the leader's most vital trait. Whatever the situation, even when fronting audiences of many hundreds of people, you need to connect with just a few individuals and share your thoughts with them one at a time, just as you and I do effectively every day.

In the new world of hybrid working, when communicating virtually, your listeners' needs do not change. Start by ensuring your eyes are at the same level as your camera lens. Lean in and speak with your listeners directly and conversationally through the lens, only glancing at their images on your screen occasionally.

Irrespective of the medium, with your intent clear, your content well prepared and the 6 Ps Drill, you will naturally engage your listeners in the language of leadership and in the manner of a true leader. When you achieve this, you will give your listeners an emotional as well as logical experience that they will enjoy, remember and want more of.

Speaking Content with Intent

The Hierarchy of Notes, Trampoline and Beanbag

Once you have formed your structure and content using the Larrymid, you need to convert them into speaking material that will enable you to share your ideas clearly, authentically and effectively using the 6 Ps Drill.

When preparing for formal situations, many speakers write out longhand what they want to say. This is what many in-house advisors recommend but it's not leadership communication. This is a 'paper' and is far better read by the audience later than by the speaker on the day! Preparing a full script is akin to writing an article or essay. It takes up too much time and results in words, grammar and syntax employed to be read but rarely to be heard. Worse, business writing tends to be dry, factual and jargon-rich, full of acronyms, nouns and verbs. This can work for the eye but rarely the ear.

We listen for expression and meaning from our leaders. We need adjectives, adverbs and images to add colour and movement to what's being said. This is dialogue. It's ephemeral and mostly made up of short sentences and phrases comprising just a handful of words each time. The words themselves are typically of just one or two syllables. Using a media term, if we want people to listen to us, we need to share our ideas with them in soundbites.

Put simply, prose is written for the eye and dialogue is spoken for the ear. Winston Churchill's writings and speeches exemplify the different styles – same author, often the same subject matter, and the same audiences who read with their eyes and listened with their ears.

However, when preparing for a meeting or talk, please resist the temptation to 'wing it'. Instead, whenever possible, speak from simple, short, bullet-point speaking notes/prompts. Why?

- Notes keep you on track and help you to recover quickly after interruptions
- Notes create confidence knowing that 'what comes next' is at your fingertips
- Notes ensure your focus while maintaining spontaneity
- Notes assist you to maintain both your physical and mental energy
- Using the 6 Ps Drill, notes enable you to speak naturally and help your listener listen!
- Notes demonstrate to your listener/audience that you're prepared and focused.

Think of notes as a pilot's flight plan to keep you on track and give you confidence, and as a trampoline to bounce on and give you energy rather than hold you down.

Using the Hierarchy of Notes below, ensure that speaking notes (or 'bullet points') are just one or two words (max five words per line) to remind you of your main points:

- Major bullet/point or idea
- Minor bullet/sub-point
- Mini bullet/supporting points

Write key words ('triggers'), with simple one- or two-word subheadings (as minor and mini bullets) to expand each point. And write phrases or ideas, *not* complete or incomplete sentences! So be comfortable with leaving words out. As always, less is more.

Using the 6 Ps Drill and with reference to my 'bow and arrow' analogy, gather the word or phrase from your notes. As you pause for thought (pull back on your 'bow'), your brain thinks about what you already know on that point. You then share it (with your 'target') spontaneously, thereby ensuring the natural and effective you.

You can simply handwrite your notes in a notebook; or you can type and print them on A4 paper and place them on the table (or lectern) in front of you. You could also use your mobile device to allow you freedom of movement. In less formal, more social situations, some handheld, postcard-sized cards will also do the job.

Stick to your structure and resist the temptation to go off at a tangent, especially when telling stories. If you have a flash of inspiration, make a brief note to yourself in the margin. Revert to it only when you've finished. Afterthoughts rarely enhance a well-planned talk.

Use the 6 Ps Drill to ensure you don't run your thoughts together. As I've advised, pause as we all do in normal conversation before and after each point or idea. If you don't, you are likely to swamp your listeners with information and ultimately lose their attention. Remember, you need to help them stay with you.

Speaking Naturally with a Formal Speech or Verbatim Script

As you may have gathered, I generally discourage formal speeches and verbatim scripts. If short notes are trampolines then longhand scripts could be thought of as beanbags! A script sucks you down and hinders your attempt to engage with your listeners naturally and effectively.

Nevertheless, scripts are sometimes required. This could be due to the lack of time for rehearsal or to a legal need to be precise about every word uttered on a particular occasion. It's important to recognise that putting across one's personality and ideas is much more difficult when reading from a script. Why?

· The language and style of written scripts are different to spoken dialogue
· You read scripts differently, and faster, than when speaking from notes
· Information is delivered more quickly than your listeners can absorb it
· Reading hinders you from expressing how you actually feel
· Your eye contact is both minimal and random, so has little impact
· It's an unnatural communication experience for both you and your listeners.

Using the notes on preparing speeches and scripts below, write in phrases instead of long sentences to reflect a conversational style. Write on one side of the page only and in enlarged text but not uppercase fonts. This will help you to employ the 6 Ps Drill more effectively. Place your material on the right-hand side of the table or lectern (not stapled or fastened) and slide each page across to the left as you complete it. Do not turn them over!

Be familiar with your material and put time aside for rehearsal with colleagues or family. Avoid talking to your mirror! What objective feedback can it give, seriously? Visualise what you're saying; this will help your audience to do so too. Remember, your listeners' imaginations are your most powerful visual aid.

The two aspects of speaking tempo are words pace (driven by the personality of the speaker) and ideas pace (driven by the comprehension of the recipient). Irrespective of your speaking material, your listeners' needs don't change. While ensuring that you do not overload your listeners with an avalanche of thoughts or ideas, you must also see that your words pace doesn't slow unnaturally. The 6 Ps Drill will help you to keep your energy level up, right through to the end.

So, when delivering a formal speech, use the 6 Ps Drill coupled with the *Grab & Sweep* technique I describe below. Together, they will help you to be more natural and engaging. Both *Grabs* and *Sweeps* start and end with pauses with meaningful eye contact.

Notes for Preparing Formal Speeches and Verbatim Scripts

- Prepare your structure using the Preparation Steps and Larrymid
- Type or handwrite your speech in 14 point size or larger
- Lay out the speech in *Grabs* (3–6 words on the same line) and *Sweeps* (6 or more words and can be more than one line)
- Insert double spaces between each *Grab* and *Sweep*
- Insert triple or quadruple spaces between each normal paragraph
- Type or write on one side of the page and don't use the bottom 20 per cent
- Consider putting in **bold** or <u>underlining</u> the main idea or focus of each phrase
- Number each page and don't pin or staple them together.

Again, reach out to and speak with one person at a time one to one – naturally, sincerely, warmly. Recognise that, as with any new physical technique, such as learning to play a sport or drive a car, it will take time and practice before the 6 Ps Drill and the *Grab & Sweep* techniques become second nature.

Impact

Please persevere! You will be astonished by the impact you can make even with a formal speech. I experienced this for real when attending a private event where former US president George W. Bush spoke. There were fewer than than 150 people in the audience and I sat immediately behind Condoleezza Rice, then US Secretary of State. The president delivered his speech using my 6 Ps Drill and my *Grabs & Sweeps*! While I sensed that few in the audience welcomed everything the president was saying, I could see that everyone was listening intently to his every word. The power of his delivery was compelling.

No, I didn't coach the US president! Although I did once travel with a US vice president in his Air Force Two plane. So, what was the president doing? One of the things I did when starting this business was to observe how various leaders communicated. Bill Clinton was then the US president and was recognised as a very good communicator. I studied him speaking in various situations and quickly understood that he was not presenting! He was simply conversing with his audiences one to one, irrespective of circumstance, location or size. This helped to confirm my own observations, and the 6 Ps Drill was born.

George W. Bush was exemplifying it perfectly that day. It seems he had been advised by his own 'Larry' or Burns! I've noticed that former US president Barack Obama employs a similar technique with his formal speeches.

Deep and Active Listening:

How we build and maintain meaningful relationships

Have you noticed how little many of us actually try to understand one another? I'm sure that appreciating others' perspectives better would save quite a few problems, heartaches and disagreements, and perhaps even wars. Listening is hard and requires conscious effort. Most of us overestimate our ability to listen. Few people with whom I have worked admit to being poor listeners. But is this failing all down to them?

As I've pointed out, the success of all spoken communication is governed by the recipient: the listener. When speaking we need to help listeners listen. If we don't, they won't! To understand the listening process, please reflect on the previous 'Humanity' section and then refer to the 3 Qs Listening Modes on the next page.

Listening Builds Trust and Shows Respect

The simplest way to build rapport with someone is to listen to them actively. Listening actively is fundamental to the art of conversation. It really helps to strengthen relationships. It demonstrates that you are interested in others, not only in yourself, and it's how you learn. Again, you must strive to be aware of any biases or prejudices, be less dogmatic and more encouraging, yielding and empathic. The golden rule here is that silence really is golden!

The 3 Qs Listening Modes

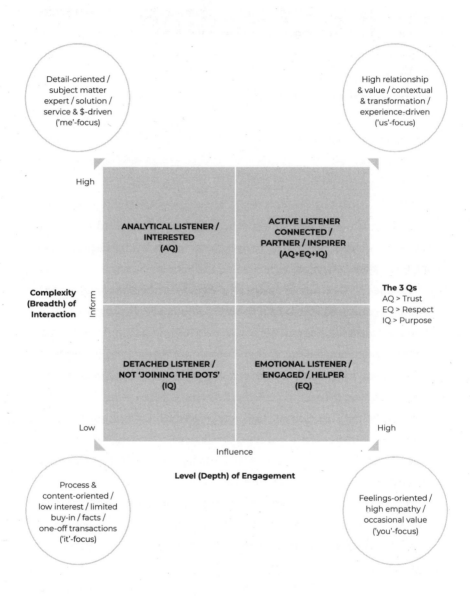

Detail-oriented / subject matter expert / solution / service & $-driven ('me'-focus)

High relationship & value / contextual & transformation / experience-driven ('us'-focus)

High

ANALYTICAL LISTENER / INTERESTED (AQ)

ACTIVE LISTENER CONNECTED / PARTNER / INSPIRER (AQ+EQ+IQ)

Complexity (Breadth) of Interaction

Inform

The 3 Qs
AQ > Trust
EQ > Respect
IQ > Purpose

DETACHED LISTENER / NOT 'JOINING THE DOTS' (IQ)

EMOTIONAL LISTENER / ENGAGED / HELPER (EQ)

Low

High

Influence

Level (Depth) of Engagement

Process & content-oriented / low interest / limited buy-in / facts / one-off transactions ('it'-focus)

Feelings-oriented / high empathy / occasional value ('you'-focus)

But we need to do more than stay silent. We need to listen deeply, as encapsulated in the Aboriginal word *Dadirri*, 'An almost spiritual skill based on respect' according to Dr Miriam Rose Ungunmerr-Baumann, 2021 Senior Australian of the Year. She describes it as 'inner, deep listening and quiet, still awareness and waiting'.*

Here are some thoughts on deep, active listening:

- Listening analytically alone isn't enough. Listen for feelings, not only facts – *how* things are being said as well as what is being said. And to help you identify what is not being said!
- Communication is reciprocal; you get what you give. Clients (and parents and children!) often say to me, 'They just don't seem to listen to me.' My response is always, 'Well, do you ever really listen to them? Try to listen more actively and deeply and so will they!'
- Understand the difference between empathy, which requires you to listen objectively, and sympathy, which you give by listening subjectively.
- Appreciate that, although it is always good to have a view, your own opinion is rarely the only one so don't dismiss those of others. Remain open-minded and treat every idea as of worth until it's overtaken, disproven or deemed impractical.
- Practise acknowledging others' points of view to avoid being perceived as judgemental or dismissive. 'I hear/understand what you say ...' does not have to mean you necessarily agree with what's being said but it does acknowledge others' perspectives.
- Give yourself 100 per cent. Again, try not to get frustrated – get fascinated! Active, effective listening is hard work. It requires that you give your full attention to the speaker and their actions, expressions, body language, tone and so forth.

---

* Dadirri is a reflection written by Dr Miriam-Rose Ungunmerr Baumann AM, and the word, the spiritual way of being and the concept that is Dadirri (da-did-ee) comes from the Ngan'gikurunggur and Ngen'giwumirri languages of the Aboriginal peoples of the Daly River region, Northern Territory, Australia.

- Make them feel special and display a sense of curiosity and genuine interest.
- Stay with them. Do not interrupt! Be courteous and be curious. Not so easy of course; it takes time! Try to hear them out and pause before responding.
- Beware tuning out or thinking about what you're going to say while someone is speaking – yes, we all do it! Instead, look them right in the eye and really focus on what they're saying, how they're saying it and why they're telling you.
- Listen constructively. By substituting 'and ...' where your immediate tendency would normally be to say 'but ...', you will show that you're actively thinking about what they are saying and want to build on it, as opposed to capping or dismissing it.
- If you are uncertain, try to build on what the other person has said. First pause and then, using their name, say, 'Rachel, perhaps I might build on that ...' or 'Tom, I'm just wondering if I might add to that ...' And use conditional language, such as 'perhaps', 'might', 'could', 'would', 'should'.
- Resist the temptation to fill the gap. Again, try to be comfortable with silence. Pausing for three, five even ten seconds can be very powerful, especially when discussions become heated.
- And beware providing solutions immediately, even if you have the answer. This is typically my biggest failing, as my daughters can attest! Instead, reflect on what you've heard and try to get a better understanding of their issue, problem or pain first. With care, ask some questions before responding. Occasionally respond to a comment with a question.
- A good way to ensure you really are listening (and demonstrate as such to the speaker) is to give feedback. Summarise or rephrase what you understand the other party to be saying.
- Another technique is to focus on a word, phrase or concept to which the speaker referred and build on it by asking a question, e.g. 'Oh, you live in Edinburgh. So, what are your favourite aspects of living in Edinburgh?'
- Repeating the last words someone says as a question, with an upward or downward inflection and then pausing, invites them to expand and reveal more of their thinking, e.g. 'Really? The Castle?'

- Insert a link to allow you time to think, e.g. 'That's really interesting ...' – pause – '... and then what happened?' This demonstrates that you are actively thinking about what has just been said.
- Ask open-ended, probing questions, e.g. 'Why do you believe/think ...?' or 'How do you ...?' or 'What specifically ...?', and really listen to the responses.
- Beware listening passively ... a failing of many of our clients! Listen with your body and your heart, as well as your mind. You need to be responsive and animated; with care, naturally 'mirror' the speaker's demeanour. For example, lean in, nod, smile, frown, maintain eye contact with hands open to demonstrate your appreciation of the feelings being expressed.
- To demonstrate you really are listening, focus on the speaker's eyes. What colour are they? But beware of staring, which can appear blank, motionless, dispassionate or cold. Try blinking, nodding, putting your head to one side to demonstrate empathy, interest and commitment.
- Ensure that you acknowledge and try to involve others in the room, even if they do not appear to be actively participating. Check they are with you and invite them to share their thoughts.
- Indicate that you're always willing to communicate, to exchange ideas with a view to reaching a common goal. Check with care that you're trying to achieve the same objective.

Here are some examples of open questions/comments to help build rapport:

Gaining understanding:

- How are you feeling?
- Where might it make best sense to begin?
- What are you focused on right now?
- What's your view on this?
- What are your main priorities?
- What are your concerns about this?
- Where do you see this initiative taking you?

- What are the likely challenges you'll face along the way?
- When do you feel it might be best to ...?
- What's working? What's not?
- What might you like to see more of?
- How do you see the current [e.g. economic] situation?

Exploring an issue:

- To help me better understand, perhaps you could ...?
- I would appreciate hearing more about your experience/views/concerns.
- Would you mind clarifying that please?
- That's really helpful/interesting; could you share more of your thinking on ...?
- What do you feel is holding you/the business back?
- What are your thoughts on this?
- Might it make sense to ...?
- Have you considered ...?
- I would love to hear your thoughts on ...
- Would you be open to different ideas on ...?
- Why do you feel that's the case?
- What do you feel could be the cause?
- What impact is this having on the business?
- How are you addressing this?
- Where do you see this headed?

Summarising what you have heard:

- I am getting the sense that ...
- So, what you are really saying is ...
- What you seem to be saying is ...
- What I am hearing is ...
- Perhaps I missed something – what I've understood so far is ...

Active Listening in Summary

Listening is not so much a skill but an attitude with a single focus: the more I am known by those I want to follow me, and the more I can know them, the greater will be our ability to do great things together.

DAVID S. POTTRUCK, FORMER PRESIDENT AND CEO, CHARLES SCHWAB INC. (1948–)

We need to be sensitive to those around us; everyone has a story to tell. Like you and me, they also have needs, wants and feelings. We have to be seen and felt to be listening, really listening; don't just say you are! Respect the individual by focusing on their overriding issues and objectives and inviting them to elaborate. You cannot assume you already know what matters to them.

Recognise that another person's opinion may not meet with your own but acknowledge it all the same, however irritating. Their view may not be right in your mind but they do have the right to express it. Try to avoid arguments and maintain your sense of calm, humility and humour. Not always easy, I accept, but worth a try!

In a heated discussion, strive to maintain perspective. Pause, think objectively and focus on the issue not the person. If necessary, suggest leaving the matter to rest for a while. Take time out to reflect, consider any new information and reconvene later. Ask yourself: Given this relationship, is it more important for me to win this argument or for us to win-win it?

As the old adage goes, we are born with two eyes, two ears and one mouth. We should aim to use them in that proportion! Practise, practise, practise listening actively every day, everywhere.

The bottom line is that listening deeply and actively is plain good manners. As in every other facet of having a successful and fulfilling life, as true leaders, we must constantly strike a balance between self/task and others/feeling. Look beyond the short-term transaction (push) to the longer-term transformation (pull).

Handling Questions:

Questions are opportunities

Many people with whom I work feel they do not need to prepare for questions. Others, not unlike most politicians, seemingly, regard being questioned as an affront and become defensive or, worse, aggressive. As a result, leaders often discredit themselves and what they have been speaking about by obfuscating, being long-winded and even dismissive when responding to questions.

Treat questions not as challenges but as opportunities. Being questioned means someone is listening and interested in what you have to say. It also provides the opportunity to put across or reinforce your ideas and point of view. It's an opportunity for you to lead your questioner's thinking and, perhaps, that of their audience, and to inform, influence and even inspire them.

The core true leadership principle of mutuality still applies and preparation is important whenever possible. Many of the points covered in the previous leadership communication sections underpin the effective handling of questions. You need to be appropriately authentic, treat the questioner with respect, and respond clearly and succinctly.

Below are some pointers when preparing for and answering questions. Please also refer back to the Larrymid (page 219) to help with structure.

- Again, think context and intent before content: Who is the questioner and what's their role? Why you? Why are they asking you this question and what are they really seeking? Be aware of their and your wider audience.

- As a general rule, identify their likely issues and acknowledge a legitimate concern. Then bridge by putting each issue in context, and have a clear headline answer, ideally reinforcing one of your earlier key points. Next, support it with certainty by giving two or three reasons. Then pause to offer some content and colour (e.g. facts, details or examples to illustrate your reasons). Conclude with the consequence, repeating your headline answer and what it means for your listener.
- To help with handling tough questions, I suggest you prepare a short aide-memoire with three columns. At the top of the left column, write Issue/Context. Above the middle column, write Clarity/Certainty/Content/Colour. And write Consequence/Impact at the top of the right column, as follows:

  - Let's assume one of the issues that's likely to be raised is your organisation's poor customer service. Write *Service levels* in the Issue column.
  - Frame the issue acknowledging any concerns (Context): e.g. *Of course, attracting and retaining customers is critical if we are to succeed long term. We must consistently give our customers the level of service they expect.*
  - Next, decide on your headline answer/assertion (Clarity) and write it in the middle column: e.g. *Service levels are much improved.*
  - Support your answer by writing one or, maximum, two points (Certainty): e.g. *Service levels: Much improved + Confirmed by quality of service report.*
  - In the third column, write some detail (Content) to prove one or both points and perhaps illustrate with examples or anecdotes (Colour): e.g. *Service levels: Much improved + Confirmed by quality of service report + Evidence shows 10 per cent increase in customer satisfaction each month for past six months + Customer feedback confirms they feel more valued; conversations with call centre operatives affirm happier customers; seeing reduced churn.*
  - Conclude with a brief summary by repeating your headline and adding the 'So what?' (Consequence/Impact): e.g. *Service levels: Much improved + Confirmed by quality of service report + Heading in right direction + More to*

do + Not just about raw numbers but improving customer-focused culture and experience and building sustainable business for long term.

- Over-answering and circumlocution are the easiest and most dangerous pitfalls when answering questions. Always structure your answers and keep them short. I well remember a chief executive who, following an excellent briefing, undid his previous good work with loose and verbose answers to questions and lost his audience.
- Check you have answered their question and addressed their concern: e.g. *'Does that answer your question? Can I explain anything else?'*
- If you do not know or have the answer, say so and offer to provide it later.
- Bridge from an issue you cannot fully address then to what you can say: e.g. *'I'm sorry, I cannot recall the detail'* or *'I don't have all the information to hand. I'll get back to you (when). However, what I can say now is ...'* or *'I think the real question here is ...'.* And make sure you do get back to them!
- Treat leading questions, for example questions or statements that infer a blatant untruth, respectfully but assertively and then bridge from them: e.g. *'That's just not true. We always ...'*
- Using the 6 Ps Drill helps to maintain composure and control. Be sure to pause as you answer, to listen to and check in with yourself: With whom am I speaking and why? What have I just said and where am I going with this?

How you handle questions can either underpin or undermine your leadership. As with every aspect of communication, questions provide opportunities to engage and move your listeners. They can also present risks, so don't leave them to chance. Whenever possible, prepare.

Speaking Impromptu:

What we all do every day

Thinking on your feet and speaking with little or no notice requires mental agility. Expressing your thoughts spontaneously also requires structure. You need to be taking your listeners 'somewhere'. Let me use the example of taking your colleagues or other stakeholders for a drive in a car. I imagine few would agree just to go for a drive; they're busy people. They need to know where you are taking them, why, and what the journey will look and feel like.

So always try to prepare a plan in your head. Be aware of your audience and why you are speaking with them; identify your topic; and decide your overarching message or opinion. The main preparation headings included in the Clarity section and Handling Questions chapter above will give you a good sense of how to structure and unpack your ideas.

Visualise an image of the Larrymid. If you are in a room, using the walls to your right, facing you and to your left will provide a structural device to represent the three points that support your message. Of course, if you have time, jot down a few 'dot' points. A scrap of paper, the back of your business card if you have one, a menu or even your cuff will suffice.

Talking unscripted is similar to answering questions. So, study the flow and example covered in the previous chapter. As in every communication situation, to speak impromptu effectively, you must also employ the 6 Ps Drill.

Crisis Communication:

Be prepared

I include a brief mention of this topic here because it's possible that, as a leader, you will be faced with unexpected situations which may negatively affect your organisation's brand, stock price or viability, or indeed your people, your customers and yourself.

As you have seen, some of the stories I include in the book have a mix of these. In several, personal reputations and careers were also at stake. In such situations, maintaining confidence – your own and that of your stakeholders – is critical. As I write, cyber-attacks, data breaches, greenwashing exposures and behaviour-related scandals are on the increase.

Unplanned and unwanted events can occur at any time and from any source. Of course, you cannot control a crisis but you can decide how you respond. And how you do so will have a major impact on how your organisation and its brand emerge from it. Remaining true to your organisation's values and purpose must always be the foundation upon which to form and execute your response.

The first thing is to recognise that the words in the heading above are equal. Every crisis requires instant, deliberate and constant communication. Second, view every crisis through the twin lenses of clarity and humanity as described earlier.

Much has been written about how oil and gas giant BP handled its crisis communications following the disastrous 2010 Deepwater Horizon oil spill in the Gulf of Mexico. Unfortunately, it is an example of how not to do it.

Here is a simple crisis communication checklist. It's not exhaustive and the precise cause and components of each crisis will be different. I therefore encourage you to seek professional advice relevant to your particular circumstance, especially when needing to communicate with the media.

- As a true leader, you are also 'crisis communications officer'. Prepare a crisis communication plan with your colleagues and review it regularly. Be clear about who is responsible for what.
- During a crisis, do not delegate the communication of crisis management. As I have pointed out, leaders must be audible, visible and accessible. Step up, get on the ground, take charge and be seen and felt to do so.
- Move quickly, keep it simple, tell the truth and acknowledge what has occurred.
- Do not apportion blame but do accept responsibility to put things right and, where applicable, admit mistakes and apologise.
- Despite any uncertainty, remain calm and composed while demonstrating your personal distress and resolve.
- If lives have been lost or are at risk, they and the associated family members must be your first priority.
- Be present and show your personal concern and care for all those affected. Give them comfort and all your stakeholders hope.
- Explain what action is being taken to ameliorate the situation and when.

Strategic Narrative:

Creating clarity and alignment

This six-step process will help you and your team put together and tell your organisation's story. It will provide the pathway to its success and yours. I refer to it indirectly in some of the stories in the book. Depending on your individual circumstance and that of your team or organisation, not everything here will be needed to form your narrative. Just answer the six key questions in the order I have set them out. Again, please refer to the Larrymid (page 219).

1. Who is your team/organisation/how are you different/what do you stand for?
- Brand: identity/reputation/what you're known for
- Values: standards/what matters to you
- Operational environment: stakeholders, market, challenges
- Organisation: strengths, weaknesses, opportunities, threats (SWOT)

2. Why does your team/organisation exist/what difference does it make and for whom?
- Mission: purpose, and higher, mutual intent
- Brand promise: commitment and relevance to your stakeholders

3. Where is your team/organisation headed? What is its destiny/what will success look like/what do you want it to be known or famous for?
- Vision: ambition/the 'light on the hill'
- Recognised by whom and how: rational/emotional

4. How will your team/organisation achieve this?
- Strategy: core strategic priorities/drivers/principles
- Context: environment/geography
- Structure: model/capabilities/skills
- Resources: finance/alliances/intermediaries
- Market: customers/competition/products/services/cost structure
- Culture: values-led, performance-driven ('the glue')

5. What actions/operations/initiatives/changes/behaviours are required?
- What are you already doing right, or could do better or differently?
- Priorities/sequence/timelines
- Tactics/innovation/efficiencies/performance improvement/customer service
- Delegation/coordination
- Responsibilities and accountabilities
- Values-driven behaviours to deliver the desired culture
- Open, true leadership and cohesive, high-performance teamwork
- Collective and individual operational and behavioural team commitments
- Engaging, communicating with and empowering your colleagues/people/ stakeholders
- Sense of urgency to act

6. When will you know you are succeeding?
- Regularly review, measure performance against goals and refresh as necessary
- Base your own and your team's KPIs on measures such as: benchmarks/ revenue/profit/enterprise valuation/budgets/targets/milestones/deadlines/ customer and investor feedback/market and community sentiment/ employee attraction, satisfaction and retention

Your answers to the six questions, supported by as much or as little detail as you need, can form your personal, organisation or team charter. As an example of the first of these, please refer to my own on page 283.

Delegation:

How you and your people grow

As leader, you determine and are accountable for the participation and development of your team members. Delegation provides opportunities for each of your team to contribute. In doing so, the feeling of joint ownership of the task will have a positive impact on their individual commitment and personal growth. It will also free you up for other tasks and more strategic thinking.

Your main roles here are those of coach, empowerer, supporter, encourager, advisor, guide, facilitator and listener. I know myself that it's never easy to let go and to trust other people with tasks – but you can't do it all on your own! And one of your most important roles as a true leader is to identify and develop future leaders. Here are some basic steps for successful delegation.

- Assess the task. Identify the duties and assignments to be delegated. Echoing author Stephen Covey, start with the end in mind. What is to be accomplished? Why? By when? What are the procedures and standards? How much authority should be delegated? Accountability must match responsibility but always remember that, ultimately the buck stops with you! What resources and budget are required? Do you need to be involved? If so, how and when?
- Select the right person (no favourites!). Are they the most suitable, skilled and interested? Are they available? Get them to buy into the project: will they find it challenging? Are they the most reliable and will they do the best job? Will it help with their development? If so, get them excited by its purpose and the opportunity to make a wider impact.

- Communicate. Be clear that you are sharing work around and why, and are not just offloading it. Describe the task and the expected results and put these in the context of the overall business plan or goal. Don't just expect people to pull their weight without explaining the load! Share any information sources; and make suggestions, don't give directions. Explain if anyone else is involved.
- Agree guidelines and timings. Determine if your people need any support. Define parameters, including budget and resources. Be clear about how much authority is being delegated. Let others know who is in charge of the task.
- Maintain momentum. Stay abreast of progress through regular communication. Agree the reporting and review schedule at the outset and stick to it. Express your confidence in the individual; respect the authority you have delegated to them. Encourage, guide and support them by reinforcing their abilities and strengths. Avoid micromanaging and intervene only if really necessary.
- Give feedback. On completion, thank people and, where due, offer praise. Of course, few of us get it right every time. As I've mentioned, mistakes, even failures, are OK: how else do we learn? In such instances, start by asking how they feel the project is going or how it went; then, tell them what you observed went well, point out what didn't, and seek their feedback as to why. Perhaps you didn't explain your expectations with sufficient clarity or urgency at the outset. As a general rule, give feedback spontaneously and regularly.

The True Leader's Communication Toolkit in Summary

This section covers many situations where leaders need to communicate. It is not intended to be comprehensive and you may well think of others.

Irrespective of the circumstance, as a true leader, communicating effectively with those around you is your primary task. You need to maintain your self-awareness and that of the prevailing situation. Sometimes this will require you to be comfortable with the uncomfortable.

You also need to understand your listeners' needs and expectations. Strive to listen better, every time! And listen without judgement, then give them your most and be your best – the appropriately authentic you that will gain their trust, earn their respect and bring them with you every time.

And remember, no one has to listen to you! In every situation, you must help people to do so. Structure your thoughts clearly and share them, don't just say or present them. Business language, as I've pointed out, tends to be dry and factual, so be sure to include adjectives for colour and adverbs for movement. As they say in Australia, engage and speak with others as if at a barbecue: clearly, simply, warmly, sincerely and to the point. And, employing the 6 Ps Drill, strive to give 100 per cent of yourself, just as we do naturally and effectively in everyday situations. When you do so people will reciprocate.

Research by Vanessa Van Edwards, lead investigator at human behaviour research lab Science of People, found that the top TED talks receive similar ratings on intelligence, charisma and credibility whether someone watches the entire talk or just the first seven seconds. And, contrary to the long-held view that smiling is a low-power behaviour, their research also shows that a speaker who smiles is rated as more intelligent and trustworthy than those who don't.

Using the tools included in this section and regarding every situation through the twin lenses of clarity and humanity, you will be able to achieve the right balance of head and heart. Always place context and intent before content: your message is not just the facts, but how you *feel* about those facts and why. Only you can confidently and effectively convey your personal conviction, emotion and, ultimately, persuade.

Part 4: Pitching to Win

Nothing in the world can take the place of persistence. Talent will not; nothing is more common than unsuccessful men with talent. Genius will not; unrewarded genius is almost a proverb. Education will not; the world is full of educated derelicts. Persistence and determination alone are omnipotent. The slogan 'Press On!' has solved and always will solve the problems of the human race.

CALVIN COOLIDGE (1872-1933)

People Choose People

'Why didn't we win the "Megastore" account?'

My assistant, Pat Rogers, and I faced this type of question many times when running my first Australian business. Much of what I learned then has contributed to my thinking during the ensuing years as a leadership and communication advisor. While the scenarios described in this section focus largely on the advertising industry, the underlying learning and principles are applicable to every sector and in any situation where you need to pitch ideas to others. Examples could include competing for business or investment or some other form of backing, when proposing an initiative to your boss, or even when pursuing a new job.

With barely enough time to catch an Aussie suntan, I started the Agency Register and it took off. The idea was not entirely new. I had come across the concept as an advertising account director working in London and New York and had then set up the Australian version. John Cunningham, a former CDP colleague then living in Sydney, generously put up some of the seed capital. The overseas founders of the original register also made a contribution and I held the majority stake courtesy of my trusting local bank manager.

The concept was straightforward. We acted as facilitator. Focusing on the advertising and public relations market, we took the heat out of the search and assessment process for both agencies and advertisers (prospective clients).

Before the arrival of the internet, it was very hard for advertisers to get close to agencies without the entire industry getting wind of it. Once it was known that a major brand was looking around, perhaps to test the market, change their advertising or PR account or appoint an additional supplier, every agency in town and beyond would flood the client's switchboard and mail room with offers. This resulted in a very unsatisfactory and unproductive situation for all parties. It brought unwanted attention for the advertisers and was wasteful and time-consuming for the agencies.

The Agency Register offered a simple, discreet and inexpensive alternative. We invited ad and PR agencies from all around the country to join. Annual fees were modest and related to size. Our promise was that we would save them time and money, and that any prospective clients (advertisers) we introduced to them would have already undertaken a rigorous assessment and would be serious about making an appointment. We also guaranteed to limit those agencies to a maximum of four, preferably three: a real shortlist!

We attracted advertisers to use the service through direct marketing, advertising and articles in the national business and trade media. We promised to save them time and enable better agency selections. They ranged from major multinationals and government departments to not-for-profits and smaller local businesses.

Advertisers loved the idea of 'peeking behind the curtain' to get a good look inside the agencies, discovering which was doing what and for whom. And they could do so while preserving their current agency relationship since the incumbent would be none the wiser.

Advertising and PR agencies also welcomed the Register. As we promised, it saved them both time and money. It indicated that the prospective clients whom they met through our service were serious and that they had a one in three, or perhaps four, chance of winning.

As facilitator, we neither advised advertisers nor broke their confidence. All sides respected this and it helped to build a strong bond of trust between the parties.

There were three phases. In the first, advertisers would approach us seeking an overview of the almost 100 agencies we held on our books. We were a unique depository of this information and received a weekly update from each agency.

If they wished to proceed to the next stage, advertisers would self-select their longlist of up to eight agencies. Occasionally, they might add an agency that was not on our books. If so, we would contact the agency and invite it to participate in this next phase for a small fee.

Each chosen agency was invited to submit their response to a brief that we had co-written with the advertiser. These briefs described that particular advertiser's business and industry sector, the need, the budget and so forth. Again, their identity was not disclosed.

About ten days later, the advertiser would return to our office to go through the longlisted agencies' responses. These included how each agency would address the prospective client's particular requirements, information about key personnel, and examples of work for similar advertisers.

At the end of the advertiser's evaluation of the longlist, now with three piles of agency materials in front of them, we would ask them what they thought. They always pointed to the pile on the right saying: 'These are the Probables, our shortlist. In the middle are the Possibles; those on the left, the Unlikelies.'

Pat and I would sometimes tease them and say: 'Why don't you save yourselves more time by closing your eyes and sticking a pin at random into one of those three or four agencies' documents on the right?' Of course, while they may have been leaning towards a particular agency, they never did. Instead, they would want to meet their three or four 'Probable' agencies and, in almost every case, put them through a formal tender and pitch process.

Following the pitches, the advertiser either selected their new agency or perhaps they decided to retain their incumbent. The losing agencies would then call us and ask the inevitable question: 'Why did we not win the "Megastore" account? We flew in our top industry expert.'

Each time, we would go back to the advertiser and ask: 'Why did you choose Goodfellows and not Creative Market, Bluestreak or Rabbit?' After all, as was usually the case, each was well regarded in the market.

The answers always fell into three distinct camps. You have come across them throughout this book. As I've reminded you, mutual trust, mutual respect and mutual purpose are the basic tenets of effective communication and of strong relationships. And they are the fundamental qualities of true, successful leadership.

So, back to the advertisers' answers, which typically went as follows:

Limited Credibility: Low AQ

'We had been impressed by what we read in Rabbit's submission. We were keen to meet their director, Paul, who seemed to have what we were seeking. But frankly, we were surprised – even disappointed – by their pitch. There was a distinct lack of congruence between what we were expecting from what they had sent us and what they delivered on the day.

'Furthermore, Paul seemed uncomfortable, not on top of his game as we had expected. Overall, it did not feel right. We are going to spend a lot of money on this campaign. We were not confident that we could rely on this agency. We felt we couldn't *trust* them.'

No Meaningful Engagement: Low EQ

'Yes, the Creative Market people came across as very confident, even slick. We imagined this was their "A Team". They were impressive and appeared to know their stuff. But, when I compared notes with my colleagues afterwards, we all expressed the same feeling. While the agency's team was clearly keen to include "Megastore" in their client list and doubtless looked forward to spending our budget on some fancy ads, they didn't appear to be very interested in us.

'Ultimately, every business is about people; people do business with people. These people did not seem to *respect* us as their potential clients. They made little attempt to engage us, so we chose not to engage them!'

Unclear or Irrelevant Proposition: Low IQ

'It was a fascinating meeting. Bluestreak put up a strong team. From what they had sent us, they also seemed to understand our culture and how we might work together. Disappointingly, they overwhelmed us with content. They had lots of research and analysis, key messages and solutions, cool technology and endless visuals but didn't seem to have a clear proposition.

'Perhaps they hadn't really understood us or our brief. They certainly didn't articulate our market positioning or differentiators well. As engaging as they were and as entertaining as their pitch was, we came away scratching our heads. What was their *purpose* and would they be able to help us achieve ours?

The Right Approach and Solution: High AQ, EQ and IQ

'In contrast, Goodfellows met all our requirements. They clearly understand what we're seeking and want to work with us; their enthusiasm for our business was palpable; and they gave us total confidence that they will deliver as promised'.

Pitching: The Basics

As you can see, all the elements of the 3 Qs come into play here. How else will anyone be persuaded to choose you? Just as you need to lead the thinking of your colleagues and other stakeholders, winning mandates of every type requires you to lead the thinking of your prospective customers, clients, investors or backers.

Start by asking yourself: 'Who are they and what's it like to be them? What do they really want, not only what do I think they need? What does success look like for them and what could stop them achieving it? What's the feeling I want to leave behind, to be remembered for, as well as the facts?'

We are often too busy convincing ourselves that we should win a particular account or project. We fail to ask ourselves the most important question of all: Why will we not? Consider not only how you, your team and your offer will measure up but how your competitors will too. After all, they will also believe they have the best team with the best idea or solution!

The True Leader's 'Win-Win' 3 Qs Trivium

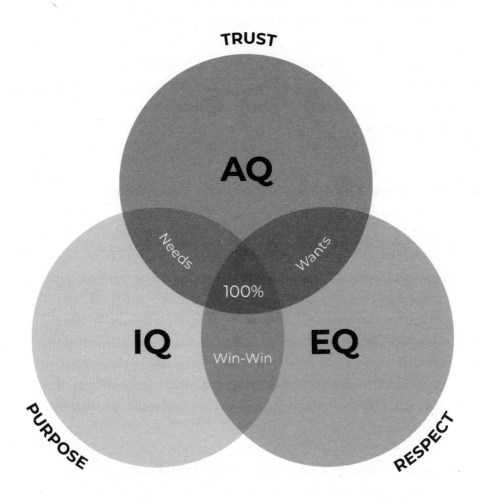

The 6 Vs for Victory

You will note that I have adjusted the True Leader's 3 Qs Trivium for this section. And here is another useful framework to help you prepare your pitches and win. Of course, it's not foolproof – there's no magic cure!

Vs 1–4: Applying your AQ & EQ

1. Identify their Veracity. Get in their shoes: Who/what is the prospective client, customer or investor? What's interesting, fascinating, even exciting about them and their organisation? Their brand and purpose? Their history and current circumstance? Their market and competitors? What's going on in their world and what's important to them? Why are they considering potential new suppliers, products, services or investments? What are their selection criteria and evaluation process? Who are the decision-makers and influencers?

2. Identify their Values. Understand what each of these people and their organisation stands for and the culture that drives them: What are their principles, standards, beliefs?

3. Identify their Vision. Ascertain what success looks like for their organisation and the individual decision-makers: What are their opportunities, ambitions, goals, aspirations and their higher intent?

4. Identify their Vulnerabilities. Discover what may hinder their progress: What clouds are on their horizon (or closer)? What could be stopping this organisation from achieving its ambition and/or may be keeping these people awake at night: What are their challenges, concerns, frustrations, problems, issues, etc.?

Now apply these 4 Vs to your team and your product or service: Who and why us? Do we have what it takes and are we likely to be a good fit for this prospect?

Vs 5–6: Applying your IQ

5. Identify the real Value you and your team will give them: Your offer. This becomes your overarching pitch theme. Discover what they really want: Which of their issues will you address/overcome and what's the real benefit or difference you will deliver for them, e.g. improved culture, risk mitigation, security, efficiencies, quality, best price, additional services or products, knowledge, insights, reputation, business growth, financial return etc.? How will you do so and by when? And how can you give them the confidence that you will achieve this?

6. Visualise your pitch. Imagine and reveal how you and your team will bring it all together: avoid a formal presentation. Instead, plan for an insightful and uplifting conversation, perhaps supported with a placemat, a flipchart, a few slides or a short video. Employ the tools I've covered in the True Leader's Communication Toolkit and be sure to rehearse several times, preferably in front of colleagues, family or friends who can give objective, valuable feedback. Give 100 per cent, and you will give your prospect the winning emotional experience that they will enjoy and want more of.

Whether writing proposals or actually pitching, always think 'them' first! Whenever you are inclined to write or say 'I' or 'we', try to replace these pronouns with 'you'! As I mentioned at the start, achieving this hasn't been easy when writing this book!

And, as I've also advised, don't forget to challenge yourselves – why will you *not* win? Put yourselves in your competitors' shoes. In particular, how are they likely to address the 6 Vs?

The Who and the Wow

Over the past 30 years, we have had the opportunity to help many people, as true leaders of thought, to influence and inspire their prospective clients, customers, investors and employers in order to be selected. For example, we've supported more than 300 team pitches and tenders across 30 countries. Some have earned fees for our clients of less than US $50,000; some more than a billion. They do not win every time, of course. When they do, we celebrate with them. When they don't, we rally round and, together, lick our wounds. Then we seek the prospect's feedback, learn from it and resolve to do better.

Feedback following many successful pitches tells the story, for example:

'We (a competitor) were amazed we lost. We heard later that ABC was so compelling in the morning that the directors were still thinking about them during our pitch five hours later.'

'We had already decided not to change from our incumbent provider but, within minutes of DEF leaving our boardroom, we unanimously voted to change to them.'

'After a process lasting over 12 months, both finalists were still equal. GHI finally nailed it with their pitch – energy, passion, teamwork, clarity, insights ... and fun.'

'JKL, well done! That was an outstanding display of professionalism and humanity.'

'We had intended to change (from MNO), but, following their pitch, I looked at my colleagues and said, "We would be mad to change!" They agreed and we didn't.'

'If we'd seen that passion and energy from PQR over the past three or so years, we wouldn't have decided on the review. However, they admitted their shortcomings, pulled up their socks, asked good questions and really listened. They put themselves in our shoes and articulated precisely what we were seeking – More!'

Note: Again, throughout this section, each organisation's name has been changed. Those referred to alphabetically above were our clients.

Pitching in Summary

The constant challenge for every pitcher is differentiation. Winning is about the who and the wow, rarely just the what and the how. It's the emotional experience as well as the rational solution. As with every aspect of leadership communication, it's less about the content and more about the intent.

Be sure to follow the 6 Vs and also apply the lessons and tools in the True Leader's Communication Toolkit, especially keeping your proposals and pitches short and simple. Based on our experience, some formal pitches might involve a dozen or more participants and last from several hours to several days. More often, they comprise teams of between four and six people and typically last around 60 to 90 minutes. With fewer participants, perhaps one or two, they can run from, say, 30 minutes to just three!

'More' in the example above was the single-word proposition that we had encouraged our client, despite their initial scepticism, to adopt in this instance. Their client loved it and the account was saved. As Sir Richard Branson puts it: 'If something can't be explained on the back of an envelope, it's rubbish.'

Experience tells me that the concept of 'more' should be applied in every supplier/client engagement. Like me, you are in the help business. When it comes to serving your backers, clients, customers and even your boss, never lose sight that you are pitching to them every day, however informally.

It starts with being in awe of them, fascinated by who they are and the journey they're on. It manifests on the phone, in an email, at the front gate, in the lift or at the reception desk. It requires maintaining their confidence, showing you care and helping them to address their challenges and to succeed. Ultimately, it means being your best and giving them your most. It's what true leaders at every level do.

Bringing It Together

Thank you for reading this far. I hope you have enjoyed the book and found it useful. No, it's not a leadership blueprint. There is no magic model of leadership excellence, no single or perfect way to be a leader. True leadership is not new; nor is it a concept or a position. True leadership is real, practical and has purpose. It's about informing, influencing and inspiring others. It's about helping others choose what to think, feel and do and then having them decide to act with you.

Manage with the Head and Lead with both the Head and the Heart

The skill of good management is about getting things done and done right. The science of effective leadership is about setting the vision and direction and joining up the dots to move forward. The art of true leadership is about determining and consistently exemplifying your desired standards, and then reaching out to others, engaging them and bringing them with you to achieve the goal, while always remembering that they have a choice! And they will make that choice on the basis of mutual trust, respect and purpose.

Mutuality

True leadership is relationship. I have attempted to show this as the foundation stone on which to build your own personal model of leadership excellence. Deploying the twin lenses of clarity and humanity, I have set out the three qualities of trust, respect and purpose with mutuality at their heart. In bringing them to life through stories and examples, I have highlighted communication as the most critical requirement for the true leader. Also included are some common-sense but not so commonly practised ideas to help you lift your own leadership and communication proficiency.

I have also introduced several models, tools, checklists, the 3 Qs Trivium and, on page 282, the True Leader's 3 Qs Compendium. I hope you now feel inspired to study them and give them a go. Strive to apply the qualities, strengths and traits in your own unique way so that you yourself are seen and felt to be a true leader in every aspect of your life.

In Part 2, I refer to the end of the 104-year relationship between Firestone and Ford. The Firestone president articulated the reasons for this very clearly: a breakdown of mutual trust and respect. This forced him to conclude that Firestone could no longer supply Ford with tyres, meaning these two great corporations' mutual purpose was also lost. Their long-standing collaboration was ended, as was the successful business they had built over many years.

Mutual Trust – Revealing your AQ

This starts with your personal brand, your character. Who you really are and what you stand for: your self-worth, beliefs and values. The building blocks are your mindset, your attitude, your awareness and how you behave: which version of you turns up each time and what you offer. It is about measuring up to what those around you expect of you: your authenticity, credibility, competence, consistency and vulnerability – your truth. And it's having the confidence to believe what's right and the courage to say and do it, whatever the pressure. As I once heard it said so well: 'Without trust we're dust.'

Mutual Respect – Awakening your EQ

This is recognising that you cannot achieve much on your own. Whatever your background, discipline, profession or qualifications, you will never truly lead, let alone succeed, by yourself. It requires being genuinely interested in those around you: reaching out, connecting, listening, influencing, teaming, empowering and partnering with them. People want true leaders who share their humanity and their passion and who genuinely appreciate others. Leaders who are keen to engage, understand and respond to what makes those around them tick and who want to support their aspirations. Leaders who are accountable and recognise that their people's performance starts with them.

Mutual Purpose – Activating your IQ

This is about understanding context and seeking opportunities, about having an eye to the future while maintaining perspective: identifying where you're headed and why. It's also understanding what success looks like for those around you and helping them achieve it. It's about aligning your interests with theirs and forming a clear sense of direction. It's determining the goals along the way in order to measure progress and about forging the path to reach them. Committed to the vision, you must then inspire your people to come with you, move forward and attain it together, while having the awareness, humility and willingness to adapt and flex your plan when necessary.

True Leadership Starts with You Knowing and Being You

True, successful leaders are self-aware. They reveal their uniqueness, their beliefs, their character. Charisma and character are linked; the former is dependent on how much they reveal of the latter. At their heart is a generosity of spirit that encourages kindness of word and deed. Both really count and neither are hard.

Whatever the circumstance, true leaders are at ease with themselves. They manage tension, behave ethically, and have the confidence to let go, reach out and engage with others and bring them along on the journey. They begin each day with a sense of purpose and end it with a feeling of accomplishment. Whatever it looks like, making a difference is their ultimate goal and they are quick to celebrate with those who enable it.

True leaders are comfortable enough not to be right every time but they consistently strive to do the right thing. They look deeply in the mirror each night, not to admire themselves or to rehearse their pitch but to check that they gave their most and did their best. And to reflect on what they might have done better or differently.

No, it's not easy, especially when the stakes are high and uncertainty abounds. True leadership requires constant application. Stepping up to the challenges I have set and forming the necessary habits to uphold them will help you on your journey.

Occasionally, you will doubt yourself; you will feel fear; and you will sometimes let yourself and others down. Like every journey, your leadership will have unforeseen twists and turns along the way.

What happens to you is not as important as how you respond. How quickly you embrace your humanity, share your vulnerability, pick yourself up, dust yourself off, apply the lessons, seek help if necessary and – empowered by your resilience – press on as a true leader with those around you. This is your ultimate Daily, Habit-forming Challenge.

'Come to the Edge' (1968)

Come to the edge.
We might fall.
Come to the edge.
It's too high!
COME TO THE EDGE!
And they came,
And he pushed,
And they flew.

© CHRISTOPHER LOGUE (1926–2011), FOR GUILLAUME APOLLINAIRE

This poem is a favourite of mine. It reminds me of a chief executive with whom I worked when he was under a lot of pressure. Following a particularly challenging session, I sent him a note to which he replied: 'You pushed me to the very edge, Larry. Be careful.' My reply: 'Yes, Guy. I want you to jump off ... and fly!'

Final Thoughts

'I am not what happened to me; I am what I choose to become.'
ATTRIBUTED TO CARL GUSTAV JUNG (1875–1961)

Both this quotation and 'The Dash', a poem written by Linda Ellis in 1996, have encouraged me to think about my life and my legacy. When I die, perhaps a tombstone will be placed over my grave or a plaque on a memorial wall. It will show the dates when I was born and when I died. In between those dates will be a dash, like this –. I ask myself: What will the dash represent and what will I have done with my life? What did I choose to become?

I invite you to do the same.

As I have stressed, however smart or experienced, true leaders know they will not achieve much on their own. Attracting and retaining good people around them is critical for their own, their team's and their organisation's success.

It is the same for each of us in our personal lives. We need to attract and surround ourselves with people who want to support us, nurture us and be there for us. Practising the 3 Qs will help you achieve this.

Loyalty

Despite being an old-fashioned concept, the need for loyalty is relevant today. Loyalty is something which I'm fortunate to have both given and received throughout my personal and professional life. Unfortunately, as a result of management and investor-driven short-termism, self-obsessed political games and a focus on personal success above all else that is often fuelled by social media, loyalty is ignored by too many people and organisations to their detriment.

The power of loyalty should not be underestimated, as the entrepreneurial true leaders of the current range of start-ups are demonstrating. Unlike many more traditional businesses that attempt to buy engagement and loyalty through titles, higher salaries and bonuses, start-up founders attract and retain employees by wholeheartedly applying their passion, energy and skills to what they are doing.

They trust and encourage those around them to step up, perform and contribute autonomously. They cut through bureaucratic blockages. They replace complexity with clarity and simplicity. As I experienced at CDP all those years ago, they create open and collaborative environments where everyone is empowered to speak up, grow and succeed as, together, they uphold their purpose and pursue their vision. These are workplaces where mutual trust, respect and purpose are constant, palpable and thriving. Then the rewards flow.

As I have also pointed out, we humans look to be recognised and appreciated. We are excited about belonging and want to feel encouraged as we contribute with others to something meaningful and worthwhile beyond ourselves. This forms the kernel of loyalty.

Politics

The arch-enemy of loyalty is politics. Politics in organisations is inexcusable and insidious. Yet I can think of few places where I have worked in this job that did not suffer from this cancer in some form. As you've learned, I have witnessed appalling behaviour by some small-minded, insecure, selfish, greedy and childish men. Perhaps you have too.

Yes, they are almost always men. Men who are focused on themselves and what's in it for them. From the outset of their careers, these people's mindsets appear to be rooted in the locker room whence they played student sport.

They become adept at kissing up and kicking down. Even when they reach senior positions, their personal 'boys' club' continues. As you have also seen, they can misuse their power to influence, block and even destroy the careers of well-intentioned, hard-working and often naive, trusting colleagues. All too often, the good ones become disillusioned and move on.

These workplace 'politicians' are takers, driven by their personal agendas, by how their own efforts are measured and rewarded. Such behaviours are entirely contrary to the purpose and values of truly successful organisations yet they still occur and must change. These self-absorbed people ignore the qualities of true leadership. They can shame, blame, bully, play games, build fiefdoms, fight turf wars and support and promote favourites, often way above capabilities.

There is no place for favouritism, gossip, backstabbing or bullying in any organisation. Is this really how the perpetrators behave at home or with friends? Despite their positions of authority, these people are not true leaders and standard rules are rarely enough to control them. They must be called out for what they are, sanctioned and, if they will not change, removed.

To survive and flourish in such organisations, you need to be organisationally savvy while avoiding the temptation to be partisan. Resist the bullies and have the tough conversations when needed. Transcend traditional boundaries and avoid adopting favourites. Focus selflessly and relentlessly on the 'true north' – your organisation and its culture, its common purpose and its aspiration – and on how you and your team colleagues can best contribute to the united whole and the task in hand.

I have noticed that some parliamentarians also appear to forget this. They display a woeful lack of self-awareness and awareness of others' expectations of them, both while in office and later when they jump aboard the lobbyist or sponsor gravy train. To maintain their trustworthiness, show respect for their fellow citizens and protect their own legacy, they just need to answer one question: 'Given who I am, is this really the right thing to say or do now?'

It's about living as a true leader and being a better person. Like all of us who aspire to lead, current and former parliamentarians need to uphold true leadership tenets such as openness, integrity, propriety, selflessness, respect, service and mutuality. Answering questions truthfully, admitting mistakes, accepting responsibility and being accountable when in office would be a good start.

Humility

Humility is not thinking less of yourself; it is thinking of yourself less.
RICK WARREN (1954–)

We are rightly taught that pride is a sin. Pride as conceit, arrogance, haughtiness, pomposity, vanity or self-centredness is distasteful and always unwarranted. However, pride as self-respect, when balanced with humility, honour, a belief in ourself, a quiet acknowledgement of our achievements, the difference we make with and for others and the desire to be a better person, is proper.

So, at the end of each day, simply ask yourself: What difference did I make and for whom today? What have I done to make me feel proud, while also humbled?

I have deliberately emphasised humility throughout the book. Nothing truly great can be achieved without humility. There is no weakness in being humble, nor shame in being vulnerable. It takes courage to be both. Humility is not about focusing on how successful you can be but how useful you can be. By adopting and promoting a culture of service, you will be a truly successful and impactful leader at every stage of your life.

You are more than your technical skill, your social label and your organisational role. Your true identity is your individuality. And your real strength is how you apply it for the benefit of others. True leaders are givers and enablers. They take what they do and with whom they do it seriously, but not themselves. Their sense of humour and sense of proportion remain with them, whatever the pressure.

As I have also stressed, true leadership is not about perfection. Nor is it precious. In every aspect of life, as a true leader of both thought and action, you have the opportunity to make your mark and to leave people and places better than you find them. Doing so starts with understanding yourself and a genuine desire to lift your own game while helping those around you do the same. Only that way will you do so too. Whatever the uncertainty, be bold, aim high and give your best. No, it's not easy, but believe in you and so will they.

So, Why Choose You?

Why should others want to listen to you, work with you, support you, buy from you, follow you? I hope I have helped you discover the answers.

Mutual trust, respect and purpose have never been more important. As I reminded you at the start, the world is facing significant challenges. Disruption and uncertainty are constant. Addressing the growing adverse impacts on the natural environment, confronting rising geopolitical tensions, harnessing the ever-increasing power of technology and meeting society's changing expectations are all critical leadership challenges that are not going away.

I add what I refer to as the three rights: standing up for what's right; upholding the basic human right to think for oneself and share one's thoughts freely and respectfully without arbitrary censure; and doing the right thing.

Better, Relevant and Relational Leadership

In this new world, leaders who fail to respond will fail to lead. The industrial approach to leadership will not cut it. We need to get back to basics. Communities everywhere crave for leaders who uphold the ethical and moral standards they demand. True leaders who understand their role is to engage, listen, serve and deliver meaningful outcomes for their stakeholders as best they can.

As I mentioned at the start, despite the plethora of leadership programmes on offer, too few true leaders are in evidence today. For the most part, I believe this is because these programmes focus on the wrong things. Writer Adrian Wooldridge puts it well: 'Business schools should throw out grappling hooks to humanities departments ... studying (and performing) Shakespeare is a better preparation for the practical demands of business leadership than studying accountancy, as well as an infinitely greater source of wisdom.'[*]

---

[*] Adrian Wooldridge, 'If execs studied more humanities, it might be good for business', Bloomberg Opinion, 17 March 2023

Right around the world, we must seek out and support courageous and empathic leaders who are curious to learn, who see things holistically, make sense, give hope and guide us. Leaders who recognise that change is inevitable and whose optimism provides the confidence to embrace and fashion it. Leaders who dare to step up, speak out, communicate their individuality and challenge when necessary.

We need leaders who provide clarity and rekindle humanity for their followers. Leaders whose vision, selfless energy and commitment excite, empower and inspire us. Leaders who see and pursue things that are more significant than themselves. Leaders who accept the possibility of failure and are willing to learn from it. And leaders who are dependable and constantly striving to make a valuable and sustainable difference, however small, for the world around them.

Put simply, true leaders who, as I've heard said, 'can capture hearts, challenge minds and change lives by helping others think, feel and achieve more'. This is true leadership communication in practice.

The World Economic Forum declares that eight of the ten skills required for future leaders are 'soft'. Applying many of these so-called, yet misnamed, 'soft skills' requires dedication. This is what true leaders display, not as champions of one but as leaders of many. You can, too, if you so choose. Real, true leadership is relationship. If you want 100 per cent from others, you need to give 100 per cent of yourself. So, reveal your AQ, awaken your EQ and activate your IQ.

We each of us have a better version of ourselves within. Whoever and wherever you are, I encourage you to seek that better self out every day and enjoy becoming the true leader in life you really can be.

I end with the words of scholar Warren Bennis: 'Becoming a leader is synonymous with becoming yourself. It is precisely that simple, and it's also that difficult.'

I wish you all the very best on your journey. Just be sure to give your most and be your best every time. When you do, you will be a true leader and others will choose to come with you.

You will be enough.

The True Leader's 3 Qs Compendium

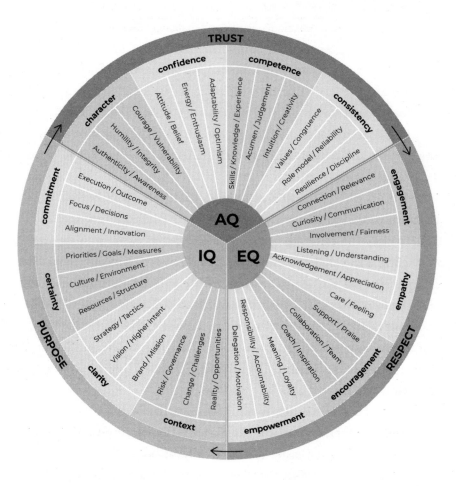

Larry's Charter

My brand promise that fulfils me:
I enjoy being in the help business.

My purpose that drives me:
I dare people to truly lead and help them succeed by making a worthwhile difference for others and themselves.

My core principles that underpin my work:
I believe real leadership is relational, founded on mutual trust, mutual respect and mutual purpose.

My values that I do my best to uphold:

Aim true: *Give my most and be my best, and help others do the same.*
Strength of character with the highest intent is paramount. Being true to myself and balancing the needs of the head with the wants of the heart is how I try to bring this to life.

Show up: *Make a real, lasting and worthwhile difference, and show others how.* I must be generous of spirit if I am to influence and inspire others. Be there for them before myself, maintaining a positive mindset and doing what I say I will do.

Live with conviction: *Give 100 per cent to others and everything I do, every time.* I am committed to my beliefs and must have the courage to say and do what's right. Through my sincerity, clarity and confidence, I strive to empower those whom I am privileged to serve.

Engage, excite, enthuse: *Remind myself and others no one succeeds on their own.* Humility and humour are attractive. The passion to deliver, with curiosity, compassion and creativity, is infectious. Getting on with it and achieving together is teamwork.

My vision that I strive for:
I want to see more engaged, enthusiastic and energised true leaders at every level, inspiring others and enabling change to a better world in its every corner.

My twin lenses approach that guides me:

Clarity: *Thinking and Doing*
Identifying and maintaining a rigorous focus on the desired outcome.

balanced with

Humanity: *Feeling and Being*
Bringing out the most and best of ourselves and of those around us, and acknowledging that no one, including me, is perfect and never will be.

Dream. Believe. Dare. Do. *

* These words are sometimes incorrectly attributed to a quotation by Walt Disney.

References and Sources

Warren Bennis, *On Becoming a Leader* (1989)

Clare Boothe Luce, *Stuffed Shirts* (1931)

Lee Bowman and Andrew Crofts, *High Impact Business Presentations: How to Speak Like an Expert and Sound Like a Statesman* (1991)

Stephen Covey, *The 7 Habits of Highly Effective People: Powerful Lessons in Personal Change* (1989)

Peter F. Drucker, *The Effective Executive: The Definitive Guide to Getting the Right Things Done* (2006)

Grant Duncan, *Looking Beyond the Car in Front: A Guide to Making the Right Career Choices at the Right Time* (2021)

Linda Ellis, 'The Dash' (1996): Copyright © Inspire Kindness Productions, Canada

Forbes, various employee surveys

Harvard Business Review, various employee surveys

SEEK, various employee surveys

Workstars, various employee surveys

Viktor E. Frankl, *In Search for Meaning* (1946)

Harvard Business Review, 'Listening to People' (1957)

James Kerr, *Legacy: What the All Blacks Can Teach Us About the Business of Life: 15 Lessons in Leadership* (2013)

Rudyard Kipling, 'If' (1910)

Patrick Lencioni, *The Five Temptations of a CEO: A Leadership Fable* (1998)

Christopher Logue, 'Come to the Edge' (1968)

Ministry of Defence, *The Army Leadership Doctrine* (2021)

PwC, 'Megatrends: Five Deep and Profound Shifts Reshaping the World We Live In' (2023)

Michelle Ray, *Leading in Real Time: How to Drive Success in a Radically Changing World* (2021)

Dr Miriam Rose Ungunmerr-Baumann AM and The Miriam Rose Foundation, 'Dadirri – Inner Deep Listening and Quiet Still Awareness' (*c.* 1988)

Vanessa Van Edwards, www.scienceofpeople.com, '5 Secrets of a Successful TED Talk' (2015)

Rick Warren, *The Purpose Driven Life: What on Earth Am I Here For?* (2002)

Marianne Williamson, *A Return to Love: Reflections on the Principles of A Course in Miracles* (1992)

The World Economic Forum, *The Future of Jobs Report 2020*

Acknowledgements

I acknowledge the many people who have influenced my thinking. At various stages in my life, each has generously encouraged, helped and, on occasions, sponsored me. They include: Abel Hadden, Alexander Zaininger, Allan Parker, Andrew Griffiths, Andrew Barnes, Professor Blair Sheppard, David Said, Dieter Kahsnitz, Dion Shango, Dom Edward Corbould, Emma Davis, Grant Duncan, James Harding, Jan Muysken, John Cunningham, Jon Yeo, Mages Ruiz Diaz, Mark Bouris, Matthew Playfair, Mickey Bruntisfield, Nigel Hadden-Paton, Nils Vesk, Pat Rogers, Patrick Hungerford, Patty Di Biase-Dyson, Paul Calthrop, Philip Chronican, Rahoul Chowdry, Richard Oldfield, Roly Grimshaw, Ross Geddes, Tim Wilkinson, Tony Harrington and Warwick Hunt as well as several who have sadly passed on, including Marshal of the Royal Air Force Sir Andrew Humphrey, Christopher Tennant, Admiral of the Fleet Sir Edward Ashmore, Georges Castel, Colonel Giles Allan, Sir Iain Moncreiffe of Moncreiffe of that Ilk, Sir James Cayzer, The Hon. John Dawson-Damer, The Dowager Lady Hesketh, Field-Marshal Lord Carver and Nigel Clark.

I also acknowledge colleagues of my former regiment The Irish Guards, my former employer Collett Dickenson Pearce, and the Professional Speakers Association.

And, finally, I thank Peter Jones and his colleagues at Profile Books for their patience, encouragement and, most importantly, good humour!